How the New Education
Establishment Betrayed the World's
Poorest Children

Also Available from Bloomsbury

Conflict, Education and Peace in Nepal, Tejendra Pherali
Peace Education, edited by Monisha Bajaj and Maria Hantzopoulos
Education and International Development, edited by Tristan McCowan and Elaine Unterhalter
Education and Reconciliation, edited by Julia Paulson
Educational Transitions in Post-Revolutionary Spaces, Tavis D. Jules and Teresa Barton
Teaching for Peace and Social Justice in Myanmar, edited by Mary Shepard Wong
Educating for Peace and Human Rights, Maria Hantzopoulos and Monisha Bajaj
Education for Social Change, Douglas Bourn
Borderless Higher Education for Refugees, edited by Wenona Giles and Lorrie Miller
Education in Radical Uncertainty, Stephen Carney and Ulla Ambrosius Madsen

How the New Education Establishment Betrayed the World's Poorest Children

Broken Promises, Broken Schools

Joanna Härmä

BLOOMSBURY ACADEMIC
LONDON • NEW YORK • OXFORD • NEW DELHI • SYDNEY

BLOOMSBURY ACADEMIC
Bloomsbury Publishing Plc
50 Bedford Square, London, WC1B 3DP, UK
1385 Broadway, New York, NY 10018, USA
29 Earlsfort Terrace, Dublin 2, Ireland

BLOOMSBURY, BLOOMSBURY ACADEMIC and the Diana logo are
trademarks of Bloomsbury Publishing Plc

First published in Great Britain 2025

Copyright © Joanna Härmä, 2025

Joanna Härmä has asserted her right under the Copyright, Designs and
Patents Act, 1988, to be identified as Author of this work.

For legal purposes the Acknowledgements on p. xv constitute
an extension of this copyright page.

Cover design by Grace Ridge
Cover image © Jasmin Merdan via Getty Images

All rights reserved. No part of this publication may be reproduced or transmitted
in any form or by any means, electronic or mechanical, including photocopying,
recording, or any information storage or retrieval system, without
prior permission in writing from the publishers.

Bloomsbury Publishing Plc does not have any control over, or responsibility for,
any third-party websites referred to or in this book. All internet addresses
given in this book were correct at the time of going to press. The author and
publisher regret any inconvenience caused if addresses have changed or sites
have ceased to exist, but can accept no responsibility for any such changes.

A catalogue record for this book is available from the British Library.

A catalog record for this book is available from the Library of Congress.

ISBN: HB: 978-1-3504-6922-8
PB: 978-1-3504-6921-1
ePDF: 978-1-3504-6924-2
eBook: 978-1-3504-6923-5

Typeset by Integra Software Services Pvt. Ltd.
Printed and bound in Great Britain

To find out more about our authors and books visit www.bloomsbury.com
and sign up for our newsletters.

The real story of education in poor countries and why ordinary people make extreme sacrifices to reject free government schools in favour of shoddy private ones.

Contents

Foreword *Ben Phillips*	viii
Preface and Note on Sources	x
Acknowledgements	xv
1 Introduction	1
2 School's in but No-one Is Learning	11
3 Mushrooms from Shit: How UN Efforts Meant Education Quality Would Die and Private Schools Would Explode	25
4 The Real Issue: Neglected Child Development	45
5 The Crisis Response from the Community: Cheap Private Schools	61
6 Damage and Loss: What Empire Did to Education in India	75
7 Well-intentioned (?) Blundering in 'Advising' National Governments	89
8 Bad Advice Regarding the Regulation of Cheap Private Schools	103
9 Thinking about Education the Way Starbucks Thinks about Coffee	119
10 Seeking Billions from the Bottom Billions: Capitalizing on Aid Spending through Northern 'Partnership' Policies	139
11 Searching for Solutions That Don't Exist	163
12 Thousands of Tiny Lights in the Darkness: In Defence of Small Endeavours	179
Notes	187
References	202
Index	213

Foreword

Ben Phillips, author of *How to Fight to Inequality*

Millions of children are being let down by broken promises – children who are as precious as our own. Joanna Härmä's book will make a lot of people angry. This is good. Who are the people it will make angry? Here are some:

- The predatory tycoons running the global school chains, who claim to be innovators but who clamp down on innovation from teachers and learners, and whose profits are rooted not in mythical free markets but in shady 'public–private partnerships' secured by influence peddling and maintained by the fiddling of numbers and the covering up of abuse.
- The development consulting industry complex, who claim to be providers of tailored technical evidence-based guidance, but who too often focus on delivering expensive reports that are designed to reaffirm donors' preexisting assumptions and which provide little of use for the practitioners expected to implement them.
- Donor governments, who claim to be devoted to helping developing countries to strengthen their economic and social development, but who hold back meaningful progress through rigged economic relationships and impose wholesale and harmful experiments on schools.

Reading those, many activists in the West will find themselves cheering. But Härmä's challenge to the arrogance of Western interventionism is deeper, for she also confronts the purism of human rights activists and the liberal mantra that education drives development. And here some progressive readers may find themselves feeling discomforted, even affronted, at Härmä's words. But this is also good.

Because, as devotees of education, we should remember that one does not need to agree with everything a writer writes to learn from reading them. Because a refusal to be challenged on the shortcomings of our arguments and of our record will not ensure that our efforts will succeed but will only block us from seeing where we may need to correct course. Because ultimately our commitment should not be to any set of nostrums but to the messier but vital task of supporting the real flourishing of people.

Härmä records how much damage has been done not only by profiteers but by prophets, not only by charlatans but by do-gooders. Härmä's challenge to do-gooding interventionism is reminiscent of Henry David Thoreau's remark that 'if I knew for a certainty that a man was coming to my house with the conscious design of doing me good, I should run for my life'. Just as we now reject the saviourism of the colonialists and missionaries of old, we need to be conscious of the danger of modern-day saviourism. Walk humbly, urges Härmä, and do no harm.

Härmä's argument is that theory needs to be remade from practice. Härmä's own life story exemplifies why this is necessary. Her education, training and professional experience equipped her to be an ideal member of the international educational policy expert elite. But her empathy, her humility and her humanity, enabled her to keep her eyes, her mind and her heart open wide enough to observe how much of what she had been trained to proselytize was incorrect and harmful. Having started with the intention to learn what was needed from the elite centres of formation in the West and to bring this insight to the residents of slums in Asia and Africa, she found herself learning what was needed from the residents of those slums and seeking to bring back that wisdom to the global elites who dominate policy. Those elites did not want to hear. Through this book, Härmä takes her case beyond them.

Härmä's book is not in the jargon-filled style of the international reports that she was once commissioned to write and has come to repudiate. Neither is it in the style of imaginary distanced objectivity that holds back too much of academia. Hers is a deeply personal book, a journal of a journey. You can hear in her writing what has made *her* angry – the injustice of unequal life chances, the vultures who come after the victims, the self-appointed saviours who do more harm than good. Above all, her anger is at the refusal of the powerful and privileged to listen to those who have the wisdom of the periphery. She does not claim innocence. Indeed, Härmä is explicit that her knowledge of the inner workings of a broken system comes from having been part of that system. This is a confessional. The vulnerability of this is what makes it so powerful.

At the core of all injustice is the imbalance of power and status. Some folks never get heard; other folks never get challenged. Härmä, seeking to challenge that, exalts the humble and humbles the exalted. This is why you should read this book.

Preface and Note on Sources

In this book, I have tried to cram in as much of my learning as possible from twenty years of working in this field, with experience at the level of the school and the home gained across many sub-Saharan African countries. But much deeper than these experiences, I have had an ongoing relationship with India, specifically with one tiny corner of remote, rural Western Uttar Pradesh, in my husband Gaurav's ancestral village. He was never meant to end up there – education was meant to prevent that. His father was educated to become an engineer, and he got out, leaving the village behind, ultimately raising his children in various provincial cities in Uttar Pradesh. Gaurav would go on to complete his undergraduate studies at Delhi University and his Master's at the prestigious Delhi School of Economics.

We naively decided in September 2002 to start a school in the village, and it came to fruition, opening in July 2004. But we didn't intend to be there and become involved on a day-to-day basis. We left it in the hands of hired staff to get on with things for fourteen years, but then we realized this had gone on for far too long, and Gaurav took it on full time in January 2018. Gaurav has therefore been spending nearly the whole year there ever since, while I spend all of the months that I can survive there – the coolest six months of the year – and I wrote the first draft of this preface and half of this book in Chakarsi. I am not a teacher and would be ill-suited to the role, feeling more care and sympathy towards animals, while Gaurav, not a 'trained teacher', is a natural. Yet I do put my hand in here and there also. I was still doing paid research consultancy work until late 2019 when I decided I could no longer stomach the futility and the sham of that career in the international education and development industry, so I went on to write two books – this being the second, and to become more and more involved with Sea Shepherd (marine conservation) and my Indian cows.

This preface aims to explain why there will be much in this text that would usually have an associated endnote to explain the source but doesn't. So, I will explain my somewhat unusual career trajectory and the unusual background knowledge that much of this book is informed by. For most of my colleagues, the normal trajectory was to do field work in one place for a doctoral study, not really re-visiting that work or that place much thereafter. After that, those who go into international education consultancy will spend chunks of time in the countries where their projects are; in the case of the big Nigeria programme I cut my teeth on, many of us lived there for a period of some years. Most academics will be able to spend only relatively short periods 'in the field' once gainfully employed at some university. When these people get frustrated with one institution, they cycle through into another and then to another; university to UN body to consultancy – although some just stay put.

My path has been different, having found myself in demand to study the phenomenon of cheap private schooling in a pretty long list of countries. I have pounded the pavements (where there was pavement – earth and sand where there wasn't) with my research teams, hunting out all cheap private schools existing in target low-income areas in Abidjan, Ivory Coast; Accra, Ghana; Lagos, Abuja and urban and rural Kwara State, Nigeria; Kampala, Uganda; Dar es Salaam, Tanzania; Maputo, Mozambique; and Lusaka, Zambia (although I was unable to take part in the fieldwork for Lusaka). I have done further research in and around Monrovia, Liberia; rural Malawi; participated in another evaluation project in Uganda; and done some training with civil servants in urban and rural Bangladesh. My final job before I quit my research consultancy career in December 2019 was an extensive piece of background research, both school and household-based, to provide context and some explanatory information around the Government of Ghana's 2018 National Education Assessment survey, in rural Central Region, just along the coast from Accra. It is with mixed feelings that I write this catalogue of assignments as there is only one that I can point to that apparently made a difference to someone other than myself. The comprehensive private school census in Lagos State that I designed, oversaw and participated in, in 2010–11 made the state authorities sit up and take notice, and treat cheap private schools with a bit more respect, or so I was told in 2016 by the formidable Mrs Dada, President of the Association for Formidable Educational Development in Makoko, Lagos.

My research assignments entailed designing the study from the ground up, around the research needs of the clients. I designed the questionnaires and the fieldwork strategy, which always entailed combing specific low-income areas, usually urban informal settlements that most people would call slums, to find each and every cheap private school that existed. This included the tiniest kernel of a school, right up to large, successful schools. I trained research teams on how to hunt these often-hidden schools out, and how to approach schools to ask them to take part in a survey and school visit. First came the school listing phase, and then would come the random sampling from the resulting school list.

Because these schools are often hidden and illegal, no government lists exist that could be relied on for research purposes.

For the duration of the fieldwork, I would walk through heat, rain, dust, mud and whatever else, along with my researchers, spending each day with a different member of the team. I was there ostensibly to support and monitor what they were doing, and how, so that I could give feedback to the entire team at the start of every day based on what I witnessed the day before. I learned an incalculable amount during the weeks and weeks I spent in the field, more than could ever have been taught as part of any degree or through any book, or through the finished, cleaned dataset landing in my inbox. People were very often generous with their time, although sometimes because of the expectations we raised as part of these research visits – in order to get people to take part, we had to tell them what our intentions were. The intention was always to end up with a programme or project that would ultimately be able to help these schools somehow, but determining that was always up to the client after the research report was submitted and I usually had a nagging feeling that nothing would materialize for these people.

In any case, it was sometimes difficult and sometimes easy but ultimately all of the school owners and managers who agreed to take part in the research shared of their time and knowledge. I have done fewer household surveys, but I have done this in Kwara and Lagos in Nigeria; in India for my doctoral research; and in rural Central Region, Ghana for my last ever job, and of course in Uttar Pradesh for my doctoral work. Again, these families opened up to me and my researchers, welcoming us into their homes and telling us about their lives. Having carried out this much fieldwork, I believe, has kept me connected to reality, with my feet firmly on the ground, and given me some slight understanding of the difficulties so many families face. In addition to this, I have spent countless nights in hotels, eating dinner with colleagues from the same programme and from other projects and undertakings, swapping stories and sharing insights. I also learned a tremendous amount through this means.

But by far, the most I have learned has been through my half-residence in Uttar Pradesh, through being part of a rural household, through our school and the handful of boarding girls that call our household home for years at a time, and through the myriad challenges that face Gaurav every day in running a school and a farm in this remote place. He also has to put up with my constant requests for upgrading the living conditions of our cows. Supporting and leading ill-prepared teachers, children coming from all sorts of family and household situations, and confronting parents from the most contrarian and unreasonable to the supremely supportive and the staunchest of allies are daily challenges.

I've seen first hand what I write about in this book, and I hope it will shine through in the pages that follow. So, there is not always a source to attach to a particular statement or observation that I make, and of course, some of the things I say are my own opinion based on these experiences and rooted in my own individual world view. I am not pro-private, but at the same time, I have felt great anger and frustration at the apathy, indifference and sometimes disingenuousness of many government teachers and civil servants I have met. Many would fight tooth and nail to prevent themselves from being held to any sort of professional standard or expectation that the children they are meant to teach should perhaps come before their own comfort. But look closely, and you get to understand how they got the way they are; how anyone who is really dedicated to the work of providing government education of good quality is fighting a losing battle in the circumstances; how crushingly difficult it would be to keep up the side in the remotest, most forgotten villages of any country I have worked in. I have seen too many of these failings to be pro-government either. Rather, I consider that I am fighting for the underdog in the pages that follow, setting out the challenges facing normal people as far as I have been able, outsider as I am, to scratch the surface of their reality, and how they have chosen to address these challenges – through setting up and using cheap private schools from within their own community.

I think education is important, and I am enormously grateful for the fourteen years of Steiner/Waldorf education that I received as a young person. I was then privileged to attend St Andrews University to study modern history at a time when student numbers were relatively small, and the experience of learning from wonderful lecturers was second to none. I subsequently studied English law, then international human rights law at Essex, and then completed my doctorate at Sussex. These experiences were extremely important to the life I would end up leading. Few of us globally are as lucky as I have been, and when it comes to education in name only, where children are being failed and no one has any solutions to offer, I feel less sanguine about education. Of much more pressing importance for the world is to address how we are degrading the global environment and callously torturing animals for our own wants (not needs) in genocidal numbers (although we breed ever more so we can kill at that level on a daily basis and never run out). And the worst is done to other people, animals and the planet by the most educated and advanced countries and the very richest people on the planet – so where has education got us in that sense? At the same time, the dream of education is as impossible to grasp as a puff of smoke for the hundreds of millions (maybe even billions) who have mentally latched onto its promise but have no way to access anything like a real mind-freeing education, worthy of the name.

In any case, my personal views on education and the model of schooling that prevails across the world are not terribly important. I have stronger opinions about trying to push education on everyone, even when there are no true teachers to provide it, making people want what they can never really have. They sit in offices in Washington, New York, London, Paris and elsewhere, writing about education and the challenges of education at quite some far remove. In this book, I am hoping to impart some information of interest to those curious about the plight of people in poor countries, those who believe in the power of education to transform lives. I think everyone who has ever donated to an educational cause deserves to understand what is really going on and the scale of the challenges we face. I hope I am able to do justice to the stories of people and schools as shared with me, and any errors of interpretation or fact are solely my own.

Edinburgh, 10 June 2024

Acknowledgements

I would like to thank Bloomsbury and specifically Mark Richardson for being my conduit into the book publishing world, and all of the anonymous reviewers of my book proposal. I don't have a long list of people to thank for reading chapters and giving comments, as this has never happened. For me then, more than for most authors whose acknowledgement sections I have read, I can take full responsibility for any mistakes, but I certainly owe good copy editors for help with the minutiae. The exceptions: sincere thanks go to Ben Phillips for writing a stirring and provocative foreword for my provocative book. I am grateful to Dr Poonam Sharma at the Tata Institute for Social Sciences in Mumbai for providing insightful comments and feedback on the full manuscript, and for being sincerely interested in my work for many years now. I was so happy to meet her in Mumbai in December 2023, having been invited to have the privilege of speaking to her students about my work.

Most of all, I am grateful every day to and for Gaurav Siddhu. I am constantly in awe of what he does for the girls at our school in Uttar Pradesh, showing a level of patience and generosity for his fellow humans that I struggle to share. We work closely entwined with my mother, Rosemary, in Edinburgh and Gaurav's parents, Rajveer and Saroj, in Uttar Pradesh, whose support has made what we do possible. Lastly, I thank all of the people in Africa and India who have welcomed me across the threshold of home and school, and the wonderful field researchers with whom I worked, as I followed them around in their assigned interviewing and school-hunting duties. They both taught me and facilitated my learning of much of what was actually worth understanding. The generosity of spirit with which I was received has never ceased to amaze me, especially in Nigeria where I was open about my long family history with the country. My grandfather was a colonial officer there from 1929 to 1961, my mum even attending St Mary's, a private school on Lagos Island that was still in operation until recently. Because of, and in spite of this, to be told 'ah, you are a Nigerian!' touched me more than I could ever say.

1

Introduction

'Guess what folks, you need to be talking about food insecurity among children … they're not learning because they're fuckin' hungry. That's what we need you focussed on.' This is what Scott Galloway, NYU professor and *Pivot* podcast host, had to say on a day back in March 2022. He was talking specifically about Florida and the red herrings that were slipping through nets at the time, but the implication was much broader than that for the United States as a whole, where nearly a fifth of children live in poverty.[1] In fact, the implications are much wider, for millions of children in the countries of the Global South, especially in sub-Saharan Africa, and in parts or just pockets of many, many countries. Indeed, if children are failing to reach their potential while studying at government schools in the United States, then imagine how bad the problem is in poor countries. Children's development from their earliest days is under assault from an enormous number of forces, and yet probably most of what is written about children and education is all coming from people whose children suffer to the least possible extent. People like me can only imagine (and do research about) what it's like to grow up and try to learn at school when there are no resources in the home, your parents are illiterate or barely literate, and the community is poor. Government schools in the Global South are packed to the rafters with children like this, so those whose parents have any money to scrape together *try to buy a way out – and into a cheap private school.*

Inexplicably, the challenges facing children and their parents are put aside by those examining education systems: a great deal is expected of teachers and schools in rich and poor countries alike, and the demands and expectations are just not fair. Teachers are blamed for what is happening, or not happening, in the classroom. Probably most who engage in this blame game think they are right to, but it allows our attention to be diverted from the much more important problems facing societies; it is sleight of hand to deflect us from the much worse ways in which children are being failed.

I got into education because of some girls I met; girls sewing footballs for a living, who told me and my colleagues that they worked because they couldn't go to school. This is not the way people usually think about child labour – the more usual mental image conjured up is a situation where children are kept out of school because they need to earn money for the family. These two girls told us that their parents could have sent them to school if it was really free of cost to do so. The problem was that the parents couldn't support their children and pay for things like materials and uniforms. And so, they spent their days stitching footballs instead of going to school. Because if you can't go to school, then you might as well work.

At the time that I had this interaction with these girls, back in late summer 2002, along with Gaurav, who would become my husband the following year, I was new to India and new to anywhere outside of Britain, Finland and the United States. I was twenty four years old and things looked rather black and white – it was crazy to me that girls would be prevented from getting an education because their parents couldn't afford whatever out-of-pocket costs were associated with going to a free government school. How much could pencils, papers and a few books cost? How could the government or charities let this become a barrier? I wasn't an education person at the time, and I had no idea about all of the 'hidden' costs that come with supposedly free government education. Later, I would learn that in some countries there are even illegal fees charged by teachers at schools, against government policy (and indeed, against the law), although it is usually because teacher salaries haven't been paid (sometimes for months at a time) or paid in full, chipped away at by corrupt officials up the food chain. Illegal fees are levied just to keep the school afloat.

I don't remember where we went on this day twenty years ago for this mini field trip for anti-child labour workers[2] (it was close enough to Delhi to make it there and back in a day), but what I wouldn't learn until a while later was that in some places in India, the authorities had already gone to the extent of making everything free; even giving school lunches and a cash stipend on top that really made it free of any cost at all to go to the village (government) school. They were even giving bundles of cloth from which to get a uniform stitched to the parents of enrolled girls. Taking the stipend into account, even eroded as it was through corruption, what parents got in-hand *put them in profit* if they enrolled their child in the village school. What I would further learn is that still, people would do anything they could to get their children away from these practically non-functioning schools. *They would choose cheap private schools instead*, and they would describe how they had to 'cut their bellies' to afford the costs.

***

This interaction that we had with these girls played on our minds, and on a night not long after, Gaurav and I were talking about it when I asked him, 'How much would it cost to build a school?' He did a rough calculation based on the per-square-foot costs of the house his parents were, at that time, building for their retirement. I think the sum he came up with was something like £6,000. I said, 'I can find that much money.' And so our plan was hatched that night, a date I would not forget because it was the first anniversary of the 11 September attacks in the United States. The next day, I got to work on a project proposal – something that I had never done before – that we would send to everyone we knew to elicit donations. We decided that our school would be funded out of charitable giving that I would somehow arrange because we wanted children to attend our school free of any cost whatsoever, including all learning materials. At the time, I thought it was all about money. *The problem was not enough money*. I didn't apply my mind to the question of what happens once children are in school. That would come later, for me in my naïve state but also for many, many older and more experienced people, and over and over again over the course of decades.

One of these experienced people was Jeffrey Sachs (whom I had never heard of at the time), friend to U2's Bono and benefactor to many a newly minted Russian oligarch. It was much later in my career, while I was working at UNESCO in Paris, that I would be shocked to hear him say earnestly that the name of the game was needing to find more aid money. While speaking to the board of the education report that I was working on, he suggested that everyone just hit up their friendly neighbourhood billionaire to solve the world's education problems. I had already figured out my mistake in interpreting certain situations in the way I had done, like the message I took from that one tiny experience on my first-ever visit to a village in the Global South, combined with all of the charity appeals I had seen on TV since my earliest memories – the message that the problem was people just not being given enough money. Once we gave enough in donations and once a child got to school, then everything would be fine, and let's just keep our eyes closed to how we keep poor countries poor, despite the real problems that are now finding their way into mainstream newspaper editorials.[3]

In a way, it is really all about money, but I had no idea then how complicated the picture actually was. Like someone watching the performance of a convincing magic trick – the sleight of hand – I was looking in entirely the wrong place to find where the money problem actually lay. The development and philanthropy industry had diverted my attention from the source of the real problem, as they have for the average person living in a rich country, and I have been on a two-decade-long journey to find the real source. I finally found it (it was no discovery of my own), and it's not in the villages of India, but rather at the very top, with the trade and financial relationships between countries doing so much to keep poor countries poor.[4] Weirdly, the brash and loud Professor Galloway on a tech podcast summed up the ultimate end result we witness now in schools by saying *the kids are fuckin' hungry*,[5] and so, unsurprisingly, they struggle to learn.

***

When people in rich countries see rural villages and urban communities in India and in sub-Saharan African countries, whether in person or through photographs or film, they tend to see poverty. I've felt the same way because, in rich countries, the middle classes[6] grow up with *so much stuff* that it is hard to see a no-frills home environment as 'middle class' or even 'lower-middle class'. I've recalibrated my perceptions, learning through countless conversations with people as part of my research career that what it is to be middle class varies drastically from place to place. Furthermore, when working in low-income communities, there is every shade of grey between those who consider themselves to be living in poverty and those who feel financially alright, and it might be difficult sometimes to tell the difference as an outsider. So, during fieldwork, I would always find people too poor to send their children to school at all; those who send them to government school; and then those who wouldn't even consider sending their children anywhere but a private school. There is also a great middle ground between these poles, and it is many of these who would say that they were desperate to send their children to private school to get the best chance of a decent education and would do anything to afford such a thing (but can't).

But it will likely be a novel idea to most readers that I am writing about what most people will call 'slums'[7] and villages, and 'private schools' together. Yet most who pick up this book will have read or seen in the media something about Malala Yousafzai, the girl shot by the Taliban in Pakistan for voicing her views in support of girls' education. The school she attended was a private school run by her father, not a government school[8]; had she attended a government school, there's a reasonable chance she would have remained functionally illiterate. Other more recent media reports about schools in the Global South include many on Uganda and its record for having the longest COVID-related school closures. Newspaper stories discussed how parents did not continue to pay school fees, meaning that many schools have disappeared and their buildings have been repurposed during the pandemic.[9] But the articles never went into how it was that fees were an issue in a context of free, universal primary education (as is Ugandan government policy). The schools that most people in urban areas, and the vast majority of people in Kampala, use are cheap private schools, the likes of which I have been studying my whole career. These are slum schools and village schools, and people use them where government schools are not enough and so too far from home, or over-crowded and under-performing. When parents could not or would not pay fees any longer due to the pandemic, schools could no longer afford to keep their premises and gave up. These were all private schools – because government schools cannot go out of business, as such.

This book is about how children are failed every day – this is happening even in rich countries, as Scott Galloway has pointed out – but it is happening to a much greater extent in the poor countries of the Global South. Government systems the world over are meant to provide education as a human right and as a public good. There are differences in opinion as to exactly when *free* government education should start (at primary grade 1 or earlier?) and at what point it should end, and what types of education should be included. But what seems now to be the received wisdom is that families can't be expected to foot the bill and provide the schooling their children need, and it is long settled that all children, irrespective of their families' means, should be able to access a government education of acceptable quality.

So far, so good – but as government education has been rolled out in the Global South, this has been done in such a shoddy and haphazard way as to embody almost an insult to the children of the middle and poorer classes. The rich do not enter in here – they have always been able to avail themselves of something better. As access was extended through the abolition of primary school fees and then later secondary school fees too, nothing was done to make provision for the influx into classrooms that resulted. At the same time, new schools were not being built to cater to the children of ever-expanding urban informal settlements, and governments chose not to extend services (and therefore, legitimacy) to communities that they viewed as illegally occupying land on which they built their 'slum' communities. Where schools did exist, classrooms became thronged spaces with no resources, where teachers had to engage in crowd control instead of teaching. Whatever standards there might have been before, then collapsed, and families found themselves with a paradoxical situation where school's in but no-one's learning. Urged on to land themselves in this situation by the many international organizations that make up the United Nations system, government education has provided the substrate, or the shit and rotten matter out of which millions of tiny, cheap private schools would 'mushroom', unplanned and unencouraged by anyone beyond the immediate community, and seemingly in the dark (that mushrooms need) as far as government oversight or regulation was concerned. These are the schools that get only obliquely referred to in media reports about Malala's education struggles; those of children in Afghanistan whose schools were closed when the Taliban retook the country[10]; and those schools serving most of the children in Kampala that *The Guardian* has written about repeatedly since the outbreak of the pandemic.

What has been ignored all along, as I indicated in my opening paragraph, is that the elephant in the room is and will continue for many years to be the utterly neglected area of child development, particularly the first 1,000 days of the child's life. Projects, reports and entire organizations are aimed at understanding why government school systems are failing, and nearly all of them at least drop a passing mention of the importance of the socioeconomic status of the child – that is, whether the child comes from a household that provides for all her needs (or, whether or not the child is *fuckin' hungry*). The enormous importance of this gets mentioned, but the writing of education specialists just moves on to focusing almost exclusively on the school and discussing how it and the teachers who work there are utterly failing.

Especially when Northern writers address this, there is never any comparison with how schools in rich countries cope with extremely challenged and challenging students, such as the children of refugees who come to the classroom not speaking English and probably suffering serious post-traumatic stress. For such children, there is sometimes a separate class set up with a small number of students for each teacher, and the work is intensive until the child can be transitioned into the right mainstream class – Diane Ravitch writes about this in the United States.[11] In the literature, there just isn't the acknowledgement of the glaring truth that any Northern school would crumble under the formidable odds of classrooms filled overnight to far beyond their intended capacity with terribly needy children, requiring much extra support. Yet this is what classrooms in the Global South are like, and we act surprised that they are failing. I won't even go into the issue of the vastly unprepared teachers here, or the fact that teachers and children are expected to cope with teaching and learning in foreign languages, as these issues will be dealt with in depth later (as will all of the other issues mentioned here).

Enter the cheap private school that I've been studying for nearly two decades – the spontaneous crisis response to the dysfunctional classroom situation that families found themselves confronted with. As strange as it may seem, the establishment of private schools for the not-so-well-off was a very natural response, and these schools took off in many parts of the world – a self-help crisis response to unmet needs. It's less surprising when you spend time in these countries and realize that much crucial infrastructure is privately provided. Communities are built, and it takes ages for the government to figure out that people might need roads, so people build them themselves. No electricity? They buy generators. No water and sanitation? They pay for water deliveries or drill tube wells and bury septic tanks or dig pit latrines. Many more privileged people seem to think of education as some sort of sacred cow that deserves and needs to be treated entirely differently from the rest of these essentials. Yet, coming from this context, it's just another thing that terrible public services make it a necessity for people to seek out on their own – it is not some shock to the system, but rather just another thing to stretch a family's resources. I hope that what I write here does not sound as if I approve of any part of this situation. Rather, I am just describing what happens in the here and now.

The well-off and motivated were sending their children to Christian mission schools already in the 1980s and well before that, many such schools dating from the colonial era. Then, as it started to become clear that poor governments would not come up with the educational goods, firstly in the 1990s and early 2000s, the more financially comfortable started to create their own small, local private schools. As the trend grew into the 2010s, it became more and more something that some less well-off families would also use. These initiatives are invariably far from what one would imagine a private school to be. The infrastructure is usually very poor and often temporary and downright makeshift. Yet these schools still managed to attract parents because they look good in comparison to the dire government alternative, and it seems worth their while to pay for such schools. It has been hard for me to come to see these schools as anything other than a crisis response to a perceived need that no one else is fulfilling, and they will only be around for as long as government schools remain unconscionably bad or otherwise inaccessible.

***

As I've already mentioned, education has come to be seen as a human right and is widely promoted in the UN's international human rights treaty regime. Those in the North who are privileged enough to rely on public services find outrage in the fact that relatively poor people must pay for school. They are outraged that these schools very often operate outside of the law and flout government regulations in all manner of areas, including teacher qualifications. So they recommend impossible-to-meet regulations that no school affordable to the non-wealthy would be able to deliver, paid for out of parents' fees. They want these schools regulated to death, and they advise this to national governments. It is only recently that UNESCO wrote a report (the 2022 instalment of the report series that I used to work on myself) stating that private schools should do all sorts of fantastical things and that endemically corrupt governments that can't manage their own schools should be overseeing and quality-assuring them. Yet these thousands of private schools operate within national borders due to the government's own failings. In short, UNESCO and their ilk speak from on high, preaching to their brethren in the dust,[12] and they have no idea what they are talking about, about the reality on the ground.

This egregious meddling can only be described as paternalistic and neo-colonial, and it's not the first time northern people have decided to meddle in the education systems of people in the south, telling them they are not good enough, not acceptable (for the country's own children), and then proceeding to ruin them (or try to, in the current situation). In the eighteenth and nineteenth centuries, the British in India did far worse than what is being tried today by northern people wielding opinions like swords. When they arrived, the British found a village school system so effective and of such high quality that they copied and exported the methodology. Others – East India Company men effectively administering the country – then took it into their heads to stamp the system out, only to bring in a foreign and far-too-costly model of education.[13] What India lost through this cultural demolition is incalculable, and today's cultural confusion and sad continuation of the local copies of all systems British is painful to contemplate. I will skip over the glaring issue that this whole model of education is a colonial import that has done untold damage to local cultures and languages and their perceived worth – that is a subject that could fill an entire volume on its own.

The meddlers have pivoted somewhat, or the nay-sayers and over-regulators have found themselves to be on the losing side, and others have come in with diametrically opposed plans to run with the crisis response model, and even to capitalize on it and profit from it – from the bottom billion. This next approach is no better in seeking to concretize, formalize, package and ship the rigged-up crisis response to children everywhere. Some groups think it natural to 'think about education the way Starbucks thinks about coffee', for poor people in the Global South, that is. They created a product that is standardized and de-skilled so it can allegedly be delivered at scale to thousands via scripts downloaded to e-reader devices, and now they are selling this model to governments. Other groups are on the bandwagon and push governments to embrace the private sector to make up for their own failings – yet they (the governments) are meant to engage constructively with their private partners, regulate them and make sure they are doing all the right things as per the terms laid down in a contract. The private players hope the government will sleep-walk through their part in the public-private partnership so they can keep invoicing with minimal scrutiny.

This is all just as much pie in the sky as everything else, as much as throwing the school doors open and assuming that that would be enough. Children would flock to school, learn like middle-class children at well-equipped schools, and go on to live more productive, growth-enabling lives as *Homo Economicus*. But these mostly Northern groups all just want to see what they want to see, and they don't seem to take into account that there is no enabling environment right now for education to succeed in the poorest countries. They are looking for solutions to *education* problems that just don't exist – because the problems are much, much wider than education itself. Global economic and political relationships are dramatically skewed to favour the rich and powerful gang of nations, meaning that poor countries are disadvantaged at every turn and, for multiple reasons, fail to advance their own development and progress. Countries stay poor, kids stay 'fuckin' hungry' and their teachers don't stand a chance unless superhuman. Education systems are not the answers that people often like to claim because there is a truly devastating lack of the skilled personnel needed by functional national education systems. Education does not lead to all other positive national developments, but sadly it is a necessary ingredient for these other positive changes. It is difficult to see how things improve when every year whatever skilled teachers there were leave the profession or are ever more diluted in expanding seas of supposedly qualified but woefully inadequate new teachers.

In the meantime, all there is to give us hope are the thousands of tiny lights in the darkness, the valiant individual endeavours of hundreds of thousands of small schools that are working every day. Some are good, some are shockingly bad, and most are somewhere in between. But for many, there simply is no other hope, and the rest of us had better deliver some miracle solution or shut up, step aside and stay out of the way of local people delivering for themselves and each other. This book explores all of these issues from the vantage point of my two decades in this field, and I hope it helps drive home the need for humility amongst Northern commentators, 'experts', and even those just seeking to do good. Every time we sign petitions or send donations for education in the Global South, we need to know what it is that is actually happening down there.

2

School's in but No-one Is Learning

No matter where you live, the quality of education is a topic of debate and often concern. UK news outlets provide frequent stories of the latest cycle of education reform, often highly politicized (both the policies and the media coverage). I have had colleagues who were once teachers in the English school system who left that world because of the endless reforms, and there seems to be a constant feeling that things need to improve, even when the numbers of A and A* grades on A-level and GCSE secondary school exams seem to keep on rising. In Edinburgh, where I live and where half of this book was written, teacher friends of mine talk about Scotland's dropping ranking in the OECD's Programme for International Student Assessment (better known as PISA) that takes place every three years. For just about as long as I can remember, in the UK there has been a feeling of malaise about the government education system, and of course, there is an inordinate number of private schools catering to the disaffected better-off. Indeed, I live in the private schooling capital of the UK, where a quarter of all school children attend private schools.[1]

On what do we base our ideas that education quality is not what we wish it was, particularly when there are so many more A-grade senior secondary school completers every year in the UK? In rich countries this is a far greyer area, while some of the same issues affect what goes on in schools globally: the degree of poverty/wealth level of the children attending schools affects how the schools appear to be performing. In the most disadvantaged parts of poor countries, the state of schools is evident, a simple test able to show loud and clear what is going on. In rich countries, teachers are literate and usually have to possess certain qualifications which are unlikely to be fake or essentially meaningless. Not so in the Global South, in particular in sub-Saharan Africa and South Asia that I know to some limited extent.

In writing this, I have cast my own mind back to the time when I first found out that children can actually attend school, more or less, for an entire primary cycle and still come out hardly able to write their own or their parents' names. More surprising still was finding out that children in private, fully fee-dependent schools also learn precious little. Yet another shock comes from learning that children are expected to go to school and study in a second language – something very rarely expected of children in rich countries – a language that they do not hear spoken at home and that their parents might not be very proficient in. In 2019 the World Bank came up with an estimate, beloved of communications people, proclaiming that globally 53 per cent of children aged ten years cannot read or comprehend a simple text.[2] Yet children go to school in good faith, hoping to pick up at least reading and writing. Their parents are only too happy to have a child's name inscribed on the official register as a school-going student. And in the development industry world, it has been a tradition to celebrate increasing enrolment numbers reported by national governments to the United Nations and publicized widely. The proud and happy child attending school for the first time is included in numbers passed up through the ranks from school to local government; from there to the national ministry of education, and from there up to the UNESCO Institute for Statistics. A child from remote, rural India – from villages right around me now as I write this – is reflected in reports published online by UNESCO. And for a while it was broadly supposed that growing shares of children enrolled in schools meant we were winning in our efforts to get the world's children educated. But to illustrate just how bad the reality is in quite a few countries, this chapter takes a journey through the data we have on learning from many countries in the Global South. I draw most on data from countries where I have personally worked, so that I am writing mostly (but not exclusively) about places for which I have at least some feel for the lie of the land.

In trying to establish whether children are learning at all, there is an attraction in putting a test in front of children and considering a score to be a definite, objective reflection of learning. The more test scores available, the better, and even better is when the tests and the scores are comparable across countries and across points in time – at least, according to the international education-development industry. Yet designing such tests is immensely difficult, with some pitched at a particular grade level, so the results show how many children are performing at the level expected of them by the set curriculum. Such tests are necessarily context-specific, although even if curricula differ between one country and another, it can still be considered a valid comparison to report how good a country's schools are at making sure children can manage the curriculum (while recognizing that country A might have a more challenging curriculum at primary 3 than country B).

Tests or assessments can be high-stakes for the schools and students, or they can be aimed purely at diagnosing the system, used only by policy makers. The directly high-stakes examinations are those that determine the future trajectories of the students taking them, such as the examinations at the end of the primary school cycle in Kenya and Uganda (their cycle being longer than many countries', at eight years), or examinations at the end of the lower- and upper-secondary cycles. Low- or rather no-stakes examinations include assessments carried out by the governments of the United States, Finland, Ghana and others on just some of each country's students, usually a 'nationally representative sample' of children. The results are used by education authorities to monitor the progress of learning and to try to identify weak spots that appropriate policies would then ideally be geared towards addressing. These countries may or may not choose to publish the results but will probably not do so in a way that names and shames (or glorifies) particular schools.

***

Not all tests nor types of tests are born equal, as already pointed out, but it is test scores that we have in relative abundance, and it is test scores that have become the key proxy for the notion of what a quality education is. In a marketized context, the results from examinations such as the Kenya Certificate of Primary Education (KCPE) or Uganda's Certificate of Primary Education (CPE) are serious business for the schools involved, particularly the private schools, because these exam results help to establish the reputation of the schools. Schools use good results to attract other 'good students'. They are, of course, also important for the students involved because they help to determine their future prospects. These examination results are less useful for properly judging the quality of schools and the teaching happening there because they are more manipulable by the school – weaker students can be made to repeat a year or otherwise be put off from sitting the exams. School management can also organize special 'cram school' sessions in order to get their students all set to pass. I visited a small chain of schools in Lagos that used just this sort of approach.[3] Lastly, and quite significantly, national exams assess children who have been lucky and successful enough to reach the final year of a particular level of school, while assessments such as Ghana's National Educational Assessment show how children are doing along the way through primary schooling, testing children in grades 3 and 6 rather than grade 8 in the case of the KCPE or CPE. It may be surprising to read that making it to the completion of your primary schooling is an achievement and a marker of relative privilege, but it is so, and the more disadvantaged the child, the more likely she is to drop out well before ever sitting an exam at the end of a schooling cycle. Many drop out before getting to the halfway point.[4]

Some of the most interesting learning assessments are run by NGOs such as Pratham in India, conducted using large teams of volunteers that visit thousands of households within villages to administer tests of learning, on the spot, to children aged ten to nineteen years. These 'citizen-led assessments', conducted in quite a few sub-Saharan African and South Asian countries, test children's (and young adults') skills in numeracy, reading and writing at home in the community,[5] and they report the results according to the share of children who can read a whole short passage; those who can read a paragraph; those who can only manage a sentence; and lastly, those who could decipher no more than single words. They also show whether the child could understand what they read, demonstrating this by answering questions about whatever they were able to read. A similar scale of number tasks is also used to assess children's numeracy. It does not matter if the child is out of school for whatever reason (such children can be those who never went to school, or those who went but dropped out), or if they attend private or government schools. Because children are found in their households, rather than through their school, it means even children attending unregistered or illegal private schools (more on that in Chapter 5) are included. It also includes children who are getting extra tutorial support for their learning, something that has become quite the craze, common in poor countries and now increasingly so in rich ones, meaning that within a given community, all can be included from the richest to the poorest, both educationally and materially.[6]

The original one of these home-based learning surveys is Pratham's Annual Status of Education Report, which has documented every year how much children in India's villages are learning in terms of the very basics. Worryingly, at the same time as it has been getting harder for illiterate or otherwise impossibly ill-equipped teachers to get into the teaching profession in India, thanks to the Teacher Eligibility Test (to be discussed later), learning levels amongst their pupils have actually been declining. The situation in government schools is dire, where only 42 per cent of school children in grade 5 are able to read a grade 2 level text. While much higher, it is still crushingly bad that only 63 per cent of private school grade 5 children could do the same.[7] This is while the share of children in rural parts of India attending private school has been rising, although this participation varies enormously from state to state. The message from these large datasets is that schools serving the bulk of India's rural children are failing, and failing badly, with the share of children actually at grade level being *extremely low*.[8] The story of decline from this same annual assessment exercise for Uttar Pradesh, from where I am writing, shows that in 2006, 24 per cent of grade 3 pupils could read a grade 1 level text, but by 2014 this had fallen to 13 per cent.[9] But India is far from alone in this terrible situation.

The situation is echoed across the water in Africa. A similar citizen-led assessment called Uwezo (basically the local equivalent of Pratham India's ASER) in Kenya, Tanzania and Uganda found similarly depressing learning levels in both government and private schools. The opening summary for Uganda is that 'learning outcomes in literacy and numeracy have remained low, with little, if any, signs of improvement'.[10] This provides a gentle slide into the terrible meat of the matter, which is that only a few children reached primary 2 level reading competence at the right age – seven to eight years old. But if left behind, the odds are that children stay that way. Less than one-third of all children tested from primary 3 to primary 7 were able to cope with primary 2-level language and mathematics. And over time, things are not changing: the share of children in primary grades 3–7 able to read a primary 2-level story dropped from 39 per cent in 2015, to 33 per cent in 2018 and then somehow went up again to 40 per cent in 2021. Considering only primary 3 students' ability to read in their local language, those who could *not* read at all *increased* from 41 per cent in 2018 to 55 per cent in 2021.[11] It seems that some children have lost out while others have fared better during the pandemic, which is of course a global tale. In Uganda, as in so many other places, there is a significant differential in test scores between government and private schools, with 55 per cent of private school children from primary 3 to primary 7 mastering primary 2 numeracy and 50 per cent mastering primary 2 language. The shares for government schools are 45 per cent and 34 per cent, respectively.[12] This shows that private school children score considerably better than their government school peers, but it is still astonishingly poor when considering that parents are paying school fees and children in higher grades still can't reliably cope with primary 2 level material.

Overall in Kenya, somewhat well regarded as the relatively high achiever it is, 43 per cent of girls and 38 per cent of boys in primary class 4 were able to meet expectations in reading a class 3 text. Nearly half of these children were able to solve grade 3 maths problems. As ever, major urban–rural, and government–private school divides are catalogued in detail, with the added challenges stemming from the COVID-19 pandemic also proving more deleterious to rural and government schools and the surrounding communities.[13] Things are similarly bad in Tanzania, with just 45 per cent of children aged nine to thirteen years able to pass tests of primary grade 2 level material in Kiswahili, English and maths, with the usual urban–rural disparity.[14] At least, children do way better in their national language, Kiswahili, than in English. There isn't much in the way of government–private disparity in Tanzania, other than at the pre-primary level, because there is not any really significant cheap private schooling sector in Tanzania.[15]

In the same suite of countries, plus six more,[16] the World Bank has conducted its Service Delivery Indicator (SDI) surveys, which gather rich data on how schools (and also health centres) seem to be performing. This includes schools' basic facilities, information on teachers, and an assessment of their own subject content and pedagogical knowledge, as well as how reliable they are in actually teaching. Additionally, the surveys assess children's learning. Nationally representative samples of primary grade 4 children are tested in mathematics and language (both local vernacular and language of instruction), drawn from across urban and rural areas and government and private schools. This means that the SDI learning assessment work done by the World Bank professes to be representative (which has a particular meaning in statistics) of 39 per cent of the school-aged population in sub-Saharan Africa.[17] For the nine African countries included in a 2021 summary of findings from the previous decade, the headline figure is that fewer than half of students are able to read a simple sentence correctly by primary 4, when children should be about nine or ten years old, but are often a year or more older. Fewer than two-fifths could manage single-digit multiplication successfully, and less than 15 per cent managed to multiply triple digits. This is the headline finding, but there are massive differences between countries and also within countries by sub-national region, urban–rural divides, and whether children attend government school or not.[18]

Looking specifically at Uganda again, primary 4 students, tested on material up to grade 3 level, were pretty likely to be able to recognize letters of the alphabet when shown them randomly, but only 76 per cent could read single words in English. Just over half could read all ten words in a sentence and 10 per cent could read all fifty-eight words in a simple paragraph. Nearly one in ten students could then answer a single question about the text to see if they had understood it. Of course you have to be able to read a text before you can understand it and answer questions on it. Only 24 per cent could correctly answer 7 x 8, while 1.5 per cent could do multiplication with double digit numbers. Only 37 per cent of primary 4 children were able to divide 6 by 3.[19] This is a truly parlous situation when a child aged at least nine and in primary school for well over three years cannot divide 6 by 3 or read and comprehend a short, simple paragraph. The later Uwezo assessment found similarly that only 29 per cent of primary 4 children could read and comprehend a primary 2 level text, while fully 43 per cent were entirely non-numerate in primary 4 (up from 37 per cent in 2018).[20]

The World Bank researchers found that children in private schools answered 28 per cent more English questions correctly and 16 per cent more maths questions, also outperforming government school children by 6 percentage points in verbal reasoning. Private school children also managed 7 x 8 correctly twice as often as government school children. Private school children were roughly three times more likely to do more complex operations correctly. This sounds great comparatively, but still, *standards in all schools are shockingly bad*. For two-digit division, 29 per cent of private school children did this correctly, versus 11 per cent at government schools; while for two-digit multiplication, less than 4 per cent of private school students and just over 1 per cent of government school students could do this.[21] Within Uganda, there is not just massive score variation with regard to school type, but also between rural and urban areas, and richer and more disadvantaged areas. Kampala comes out on top, while students from northern and eastern areas of the country learn much less.

A similar picture emerges in Kenya, although achievement is somewhat higher, yet only 42 per cent of children could read all fifty-eight words in a simple paragraph. Only half of the children could answer a factual question from the text, while many fewer could answer a question about the meaning of what they had read. On the numeracy side, children were mostly comfortable with single digits, but when it came to double and triple-digit operations, things fell apart. Private school children were able to score 17 per cent higher in English and 11 per cent higher in mathematics than their government school peers.[22] These findings are corroborated by an extremely detailed and careful study of learning in schools in six low-income urban centres in Kenya in 2013[23] – and things change slowly in education so the intervening decade may not mean much. They found that students in better private schools (which are called 'formal' private schools there) were learning the most in comparison with 'informal' or cheap private schools in Nairobi and also government schools in all six locations. However, as soon as it came to demonstrating the ability to apply concepts and knowledge in new and novel situations, then results dropped. It showed that even in probably the best-performing country in sub-Saharan Africa, school education teaches the memorization of material rather than a deeper version of learning that can be applied to solve problems. This begs the question: if students' education, government or private, is not teaching them anything that they can *actually use*, then what is the point?

While things look quite uniformly bad, there is always nuance, as I have indicated through urban–rural gaps, for example. What the World Bank's research found in Tanzania was interesting.[24] While the central government's policy on language has some downsides for very young children who don't speak Kiswahili at home, it would appear that at the national level, the relatively large number of Kiswahili speakers find learning, and therefore the language assessment, in this, the official language of instruction, much easier. The overall average score on the English assessment was 37 per cent, but 81 per cent on the Kiswahili test. Three-quarters of children could read a fifty-word paragraph, with nearly two-thirds able to answer a factual question about the paragraph. Forty-three per cent could manage to answer a question requiring higher analytical skills, which of course compares favourably with Kenya's 30 per cent. But, turning to English, things look much worse, with less than 3 per cent able to read the fifty-eight-word paragraph. There are the usual disparities between urban and rural areas, with children in the capital doing best – better than those in other urban areas while all urban areas came out better than their rural peers. However, the private-government school distinction is not really applicable in the country. There are virtually no private schools, even in Dar es Salaam.[25] I was sent there to hunt for unregistered and therefore undocumented cheap private schools, and almost all that the research team and I found were pre-primary schools and a handful running primary sections (virtually all of the primary schools were registered and documented, while the stand-alone pre-primaries were mostly unregistered, falling in the crack between two government ministries). There were so few private schools that nationally only 2 per cent of children were documented as attending private primary school, according to the 2012/13 National Panel Survey.[26]

Mozambique is another interesting case and another country whose capital I explored, hunting for an unregistered private school sector that does not exist. My Maputo study[27] had very similar results to my Dar es Salaam study – the few private schools found were registered with the government, while most pre-primary schools we found were unregistered private ones. Indeed, the World Bank, in conducting their research there, stated that private school students accounted for just 1 per cent of all primary 4 students in the country.[28] The two countries share some historical parallels, and in both countries, quite severe poverty and a strongly socialist past were offered up by locals as at least partial explanations for the lack of a spontaneous budding of cheap private schools as found in other countries. The government schooling seemed particularly terrible in Maputo from my relatively brief time there, with double-shift schools (and even triple shifts mentioned in places), and yet cheap private schools did not develop because people were reportedly just too poor to pay fees.

The World Bank's assessment results from Mozambique are pitiable, with just 7 per cent of children able to read a whole paragraph, while 5 per cent could show some understanding. In mathematics, students had real trouble beyond single-digit addition and subtraction. Nearly 9 per cent could do division with single-digit numbers, and only 4 per cent could do single digit multiplication.[29] Another departure from most other countries was that there was overall not a major difference between urban and rural areas, but there was by region. The south, where Maputo is, did best, followed by the central region, while the worst outcomes were found in the north.

Moving west to Nigeria, the World Bank's research was carried out and was representative of four states: Anambra and Ekiti in the southern half of the country, and Bauchi in the north and Niger in the middle-to-north-west, right outside of the capital. The key story in Nigeria is the government–private school split, with just 6 per cent of government school students able to read a paragraph, while nearly six times as many (35 per cent – still terrible) private school students were able to do so. Over twice as many private pupils were able to do the dreaded single-digit multiplication at 38 per cent, while 18 per cent of government students were able to do so.[30]

The government–private divide is nowhere starker than in Lagos, where I spent a great deal of time working with the state government and conducting research on the private school sector, of which the unregistered and undocumented share is exceptionally large.[31] An entirely new type of education programme funded by the UK government came out of the research I led during my time in Lagos. The programme was designed to stimulate market mechanisms in Lagos to work better for schools and families, and part of this work entailed finding out how well private schools were doing. In one study comparing learning in the usual array of schools, as well as schools from an international chain of private schools (more on them in Chapter 9), the difference between government and private schools was astonishing, with only 34 per cent of government school children able to read the majority of words in a primary 2-level text correctly, while this was 86 per cent for private schools (and 97 per cent for the international chain with heavy investment and research and development behind it).[32] At least for this assessment, the children tested were actually in primary 2. In another evaluation for the same UK-funded programme in Lagos, assessing learning only in private schools in four local government areas, only half of the grade 3 children were performing at the level expected for their grade in English literature, but in numeracy this was only 6 per cent. Some children were lagging far, far behind the learning levels expected in grade 3.[33] Despite the clear advantage that all this varied research finds for private schools, even their scores are abysmally low. Their considerable advantage over catastrophically poor government schools should be read as an equity problem of extreme proportions.

For the last study of my consultancy career, I worked with the Ghanaian government's no-stakes system-monitoring learning assessment data from 2018, designing a study around the results from one part of the country, Central Region, just west along the coast from Greater Accra. The results were abysmal,[34] but there was a clear gap between government schools and private schools; rural schools and urban schools – the extent of the abysmalness was not equally distributed, highlighting the great disparity that exists in most poor countries (and many rich ones, too). Taking the national view, the northern half of the country was in much worse shape than the south, as is also the case with Nigeria, Kenya, Uganda, Mozambique, and the list could go on.[35] In my Ghana study, it turned out that while most schools are government schools, overall, the students at urban schools scored much more highly (although still badly) than rural students. Most private schools were urban, and all but one (in my sample of fifty-five schools) were cheap private schools; they had much higher scores than government students, urban and rural. Overall, the results at urban private schools were middling – so, still shockingly poor, and much of the gap between the average scores of government and private schools was explained by the considerably more privileged family background of the children enrolled at private schools.[36] Simply put, most of the children were living in circumstances in their particular houses or in their immediate communities, whether urban or rural, that were not conducive to their focusing well and succeeding in their studies. I walked seemingly endless kilometres through urban streets and back-alleys, and along dusty village paths, to be part of research interviews with parents to understand the challenges both from the views of these parents and in terms of their immediate physical circumstances. In all types of settings where poor or lower-middle-class children live, it is remarkable that children are ever able to concentrate properly on academic learning after the model set up by Europeans, just due to the way homes are set up and what is going on around them.

***

The OECD's PISA assesses fifteen-year-olds in a way meant to be applicable across national contexts and curricula. It is touted as a high-quality assessment that is able to reflect students' ability to apply material they have learned in school to novel problems, rather than simply regurgitating material they have memorized. It is meant to avoid problems of specificity to any given country's curriculum. Because the Global North and South are just too different to be directly compared using the same assessment, for many years they had been working on a version of PISA to be used in poor countries in the south, and in 2018 they released results for the seven countries in the first round of PISA for Development. This made grim reading, showing that only 23 per cent of young people in Cambodia, Ecuador, Guatemala, Honduras, Paraguay, Senegal and Zambia attained at least the minimum level of proficiency in reading. For comparison, four-fifths of students in OECD countries reach this benchmark.[37] But in Cambodia, Senegal and Zambia, more than half scored at the lowest levels, meaning that they could, 'at best, solve the easiest text-comprehension tasks … such as retrieving a single piece of explicitly stated information, e.g. from the title of a simple, familiar text or from a straightforward list. In these three countries, more than 10% of students scored below this level'.[38] This means that the time these teenagers have spent in school has been little better than wasted because they have gained hardly anything useable in terms of skills or competencies.

Going back into what now seems the distant past, a seminal report was published in 1999 on Indian education called the Public Report on Basic Education, or PROBE for short.[39] This early and very easily digestible report on the failings of education at that time focused primarily on government schools but did also address the rise of cheap private schools as a response to government failures. Researchers listened in on lessons taking place in government schools and then asked children questions about what they had learned in a friendly and conversational way, not in the manner of a test or a formal interview. What has always stuck in my memory was the example of a lesson on air, during which children recited what (gasses) air is made up of, what air is essential for (life!), and the fact that it is all around us, everywhere. When asked if there was air in their school bags, the students were emphatic in denying the possibility. This type of thing is repeated endlessly across the Global South, and all of the examinations and monitoring tests and even eligibility tests to enter the teaching profession only serve to reinforce memorization and regurgitation in preference to true learning. Indeed, out of necessity, the entire style of education in so many classrooms emphasizes memorization and repetition of material in the form of sentences. Where there are few textbooks and no opportunity for learning-by-doing, indeed much of the time in classrooms is taken up with teachers calling out sentences and having the class repeat them back in unison, usually in a particular sing-song manner. The rest of class time tends to be taken up with teachers writing material on the blackboard for children to copy down into their aptly named 'copy books'. Some question–answer sessions do happen, but the nature of the questioning often leaves much to be desired.

The reasons for the truly dire situation I have outlined here will be given in the following chapter. What researchers and enormous national teams of community volunteers have found – and there is much more where these findings came from, including for countries in Southern Africa, in Francophone Africa, and in Pakistan[40] – is that the less-well-off are very unlikely to be able to find good-quality education for their children no matter what they do and whether or not they pay every penny that they can afford (and more). Many children are consigned to a fate of school days far worse than we could ever contemplate for our own children. It's hard to imagine the boredom and frustration of the would-be learners who either nominally attend school – that is, those who are just names on a school register and who rarely sit in a classroom being taught by a teacher – or who attend but just do not get what the teacher is saying (not infrequently because the teacher is having to use a language that is not theirs or the children's own) and don't get the extra help to enable them to grasp the material or actually learn the language they are meant to be learning in.

During my time in the field, I have watched children visibly putting on a show of participating in class, moving their fingers across the page as another child reads aloud, but that finger is at entirely the wrong part of the text. Depending on what exactly is going on, it can be easier or harder to spot when children are going through the motions, there in the classroom in body but not really in spirit or in mind, and simply skimming over the surface of the deep body of material they are meant to learn but whose substance they will probably never truly even come to grapple with. It is relatively little in terms of early grades learning that has to be missed out on, little in the way of foundations being only part-built, to make sure that the edifice of learning shoddily constructed on top is completely unstable. Indeed, parallels can be drawn between the flimsy make-shift structures housing schools and the shaky, partial learning going on inside. To understand the situation with some few decades' worth of historical background, one could do worse than consult the work of Philip Coombs, who was early in documenting the 'world educational crisis' in the mid-1960s, and revisiting it once again in the 1980s.[41] It is unlikely that he would be very shocked about the state of learning today.

One last detail to add to the bleak picture I am just starting to lay out through this second of many chapters: many of the children shown through these datasets to be hardly learning anything not only attend school of whatever sort, but also 'benefit' from extra tutoring on the side. Now, in the south, many, many parents pay for what is meant to be extra support, but in some places, such as Egypt, Mozambique and Tanzania, it has come to supplant at least some of the teaching that is meant to take place in school. There is the incentive that teaching less in school will lead parents to think they have no choice but to pay for tuition to make sure their children learn. In places such as Egypt, this has become an epidemic.[42] The datasets cited above include children who attend only government or private school, as well as many that attend either school type along with extra tutoring. *And yet the children do not learn.*

Well then, what now? Returning to where we started, I grew up thinking that if we just give more money, then most of the problems of education (and health, and food scarcity, and other ills) in the Global South will be sorted out. As far as I can remember from my younger life as an outsider, the problem always seemed to have been mostly one of money, but then this money problem is exacerbated by corruption and, well, just not knowing how to do things better – meaning, *the way northerners do things*. If we pump more money into education systems and give good advice, then teachers will be able to teach more effectively, and it's clear that more effective teaching is badly needed. These naïve, simplistic assumptions are, of course, all wrong. The secret is that maybe in looking just to school systems, we are not looking in all of the right places for the causes of the problems we wish could be remedied. More on these 'right places' to look, in Chapter 4.

3

Mushrooms from Shit: How UN Efforts Meant Education Quality Would Die and Private Schools Would Explode

Within living memory, many countries have newly burst onto the international scene of the community of nations as independent states in their own right, starting most prominently with India in 1947. The new states emerged from the trauma of extreme exploitation and human-exacerbated famine, being messed around and asset-stripped; their people taught to self-loathe (sub-consciously) to the point where they want their children to learn in the language of their old oppressors; tribes randomly cobbled together into 'nation-states' that really didn't make sense. Some departing colonials took their enforced exit from their former dominions in the worst spirit possible, like spoilt children who break things so that no one else can enjoy them. My research partners in Maputo told me how, when the Portuguese realized the writing was on the wall, they poured concrete down lift shafts in buildings, vandalizing and destroying as much as they could that they had to leave behind. Other colonial powers just cut and ran, leaving a growing, rumbling chaos and strife in their wake, like the British leaving Nigeria. Others didn't really leave at all but changed from overt to less visible means, such as the French in Mali and elsewhere in the Sahel. And of course, they are not done with such conduct, as evidenced by the chaos of the recent British and American withdrawal from Afghanistan. The heavy legacy and burden of the damage done under colonialism will be explored in Chapter 6, but this chapter looks at more recent history, but history nonetheless, of more up-to-date efforts of rich countries through the United Nations to push the education agenda that is rooted in the colonial period.

Coming into the writing of this book, I had initially believed that the bulk of the blame for today's terrible schooling situation in the Global South was the fault of presumably well-intentioned people working under the auspices of the UN's

Education for All (EFA) agenda, which began in the build up to the international education gathering in Jomtien, Thailand. It was at that jamboree in 1990 that the first round of Education for All ideas was formalized, and the world was meant to achieve universal primary education and so many other things by the turn of the millennium. Well, the goals were not achieved, and neither was the subsequent set of Education for All goals that ran in parallel with their more famous siblings, the Millennium Development Goals (MDGs). Unabashed, the global 'we' are now on Sustainable Development Goal 4 in all its mind-bending complexity, because apparently the first two sets of goals we failed to achieve were not challenging enough.

In any case, in looking for the roots of today's problems, I first went back to fee abolition at the primary level, thinking particularly about the regions I am most familiar with now – pockets of sub-Saharan Africa and South Asia. In terms of the timeframe, this was well within the Education for All era – 1990 onwards. Even at the Centre for International Education, where I did my doctoral studies at the University of Sussex, they didn't send us far enough back in time. I had interpreted, based on limited information, that African country governments had decided to abolish school fees at the contemporaneous urging of the international donor community. But once you scratch the surface, you find that the roots extend far below the surface and far back in time, to the initial hooking in of colonized people into the drug that is the idea of advancement above one's fellows based on one's formal educational achievements.[1] This drug was pushed in small quantities and really happened through a demonstration effect; a heavy and imposing door to an elite world was left tantalizingly just a tiny bit ajar to allow the masses to have their appetites whetted.

But whatever came before, the cajoling of countries into engaging with the Education for All agenda did push them to abolish school fees in a headlong rush without any of the necessary planning, allocation of funds, and hiring of teachers to cope with the change. The result was a catastrophe and the burgeoning of a cheap private school sector that appeared like a boil developing on the skin – a very visible symptom of the plague raging under the surface; the canary in the coalmine. It should be noted that the 1990s and 2000s fee abolitions were often not first attempts. Many countries tried soon after independence to universalise access but failed because it was unsustainable, reintroducing the rationing mechanism that was the user fee, which also funded school-level costs. This happened in countries I know to an extent: Nigeria, Ghana, Kenya and Tanzania. Naturally, those excluded by the school fee would be the poor, and living in poverty often goes along with coming from remote, rural communities. This was just the way it was for a long run of years. The measure took the extreme pressure off the finances of the government and off the shoulders of teachers, but it certainly did not contribute to fairness or opportunity. Yet even without having to cope with unmanageable numbers in the classroom, schooling was still not great in so many cases.[2]

Before Jomtien and the birth of EFA in 1990, education was not treated as a terribly high priority in the international development field, which was dominated by economists much more focused on industrial, agricultural and infrastructural development. In addition, the first major Debt Crisis in the post-independence era took place in the 1980s, which, along with famine in Ethiopia, spurred a new era of celebrity-pushed 'development' and debt-relief advocacy work with Bono, Bob Geldoff and friends. But 1990 would see education at last recognized on the international stage. Enrolments did expand over the course of the 1990s, but the decade was a bit of a practice run for later. The aim of universalizing primary education was in 2000 adopted in the Millennium Development Goals, while the EFA goals were much broader. There was really not much thought directed at the question of whether children can actually learn when packed like sardines in classrooms with no resources and too few teachers, in the absence of the planning needed to avoid this situation and to cope with the complex needs of first-generation learners *en masse*. The narrative pushed out relentlessly was one-part pure fantasy about what amazing things education in such schools as existed would do for children (and this continues today). But it was two-parts economic/social theory not based on much evidence, that education contributes so much to national development and that skilled workers would be needed to allow industrial and formal sector growth.

One anecdote that regularly gets trotted out is the case of South Korea juxtaposed with Ghana. The countries were at about the same wealth level in the 1960s, or rather, Ghana was slightly ahead. Korea was still recovering from war, while Ghana was recovering from colonialism, having recently gained its independence in 1957. Korea poured money into developing its school system right up through the secondary school level, while Ghana did not. In comparison to the sharp upward trajectory of Korea's economy in the decades that followed, Ghana's just about flatlined. This correlation is sold to students as verging on causation – a quantitative analysis sin of interpretation (or spin) that should never be committed – while a full picture of all of the other areas of society and economy that Korea spent money on makes it clear that getting education 'right' was just a piece of a much bigger puzzle. Educational and industrial developments were happening at the same time, and Korea even had its own second-rate private schooling sector.[3] However, things in Korea look somewhat less successful today when another form of measure is used. There is extreme pressure on students, and parents pray frantically for their children before the infamous Suneung university entrance exam that takes place every November, determining much of the rest of the student's life. The exam is associated with mental health problems and even suicide[4] resulting from all the pressure involved. If some degree of balance in life is valued, Korea's 'success' begins to look somewhat questionable.

***

The role that poverty plays in the current state of global education is frequently invoked but only selectively allowed to enter in (this is discussed in detail in the next chapter). At the time that the push for Education for All was being formally adopted by the international community of nations, it was evident that having to pay fees was an insurmountable obstacle for many families. For other excluded children, it was distance and the insufficient geographical coverage of government education systems. The education goals called for universal primary school free of cost to parents, so the single biggest barrier, user fees, would have to be abolished. It should have been equally clear that not only would the need for funds at the school level continue after fee abolition, but they would drastically increase due to the rise in enrolments that would result. The government would also need to provide much more in the way of resourcing from the central level, most importantly building new rooms and deploying teachers to staff them. All of this was abundantly clear from the failed attempts at universalization of primary schooling that took place in so many countries during the last few decades of the twentieth century.

India was an early adopter of free primary schooling, abolishing primary school fees in the 1990s. In the MDGs period after 2000, to give just a few examples, Malawi and Uganda led the fee abolition trend in Africa. Kenya followed suit in 2003. The predictable (and intended) happened: children flocked to schools, no longer denied them based on their parents' poverty, with Malawi's enrolment growing 51 per cent in a year and Uganda's rising 68 per cent.[5] Fees were abolished even when many rural village and urban slum settings had no school within their reach. Villages are difficult places to reach and to extend services to, while governments have failed on purpose to bring services of just about any kind to slums that spring up to house migrants congregating around cities from rural areas, seeking opportunities for work. The fear is that if the government provides in these areas what they provide for their better-off citizens elsewhere, then a sort of legitimacy will be bestowed on them, and the feeling of having a right to remain will set in. When the city would expand over time, as seems almost inevitable these days, then any perceived rights asserted will only get in the way of more upmarket developments. The less-than-universal coverage of government school systems meant that children were piling into the few government schools that existed at the time, and which had until then just been rumbling along, serving the children of the somewhat better off who could afford to pay fees. It's worth restating that none of the impending disaster could credibly be described as unforeseeable, because of the previous fee abolition attempts of so many countries.

While there was real demand for education that was inculcated under colonialism, the growing international community pressure from 1990 onwards led to a massive increase in the number of names on enrolment registers. It's been lauded as a major achievement in and of itself by the ringleaders: the World Bank,[6] UNESCO[7] and others. Admittedly, getting children into school is usually the first step to academic learning, or even just numeracy and literacy, especially where these children have no one literate in their households to teach them. But going to a terrible school does not mean getting an actual education, and the numbers of enrolled students reported does not provide an accurate picture of the situation in schools. The official rolls would not reflect the enormous numbers of children dropping out in frustration and bewilderment every year, as well as how the numbers are inflated somewhere along the way from the school level to the Ministry.[8] In the circumstances of the unfolding catastrophe, local people with some disposable income had little other option than to seek a private alternative, which started to appear in these slums and, to a lesser extent and much later, in the small towns and then villages.

****

How did things play out in the real world, away from Washington and Paris, where it was just taken as a given that bums on seats through fee abolition was a great thing? The donors were jollying national governments along, and the 'beneficiaries' of donor largesse started to make rather rash decisions, perhaps due to the fact that they did not have to find the necessary resources from within their own national budgeting and planning processes. Even where development 'assistance' comes in the form of a loan that must be repaid, it might still not feel like spending 'real' money, especially when the spending is urged on by influential outside forces.[9] Kenya's fee abolition provides a prime example of planning-free madness in a country that is a bit ahead of its peers and really could have done things better. In the run-up to an election in December 2002, the soon-to-be NARC government was campaigning at least partly with the promise of fee abolition. They won, and rather than this promise being broken or delayed as so many campaign promises are, the powers that be swiftly declared that families should come forward from 4 January 2003 onwards to start registering their children in school. A crisis meeting of Ministry of Education officials took place on 3 January, with key staff trying to figure out how to handle this, but of course there was nothing that could be done in time, and the full weight of this promise came crashing down on schools with great force. This took place halfway through the financial year which meant that there wasn't even any way to allocate any extra funds. School started 6 January 2003.[10]

Malawi did little better with a four-month planning period. The implications for staffing – for the need to find more teachers, and to find them fast – were immediately obvious, and 20,000 people were hired. I say 'people' to distinguish these hires from professional teachers because nine out of ten of them were just secondary school graduates. They were given a two-and-a-half-week crash course and then sent in to battle the throngs in the classroom. These ill-equipped young people were like cannon-fodder, completely unprepared to handle the complex and myriad needs of the masses of first-generation learners who turned up for their free education. For any development 'partner' to encourage such an approach to addressing education demand shows a complete lack of respect for the teaching profession and what it takes to become a teacher, and to the children who would be fooled into thinking they were going to school to learn. No rich country parent would consider such a situation to be in any way acceptable, and yet the outcomes were inevitable. Where were the teachers meant to come from? Most countries in a similar position fell back on hiring totally untrained people, volunteers and trying to get retired teachers back in action.[11] As UNESCO's Task Force on Teachers writes in a 2024 report, this continues even today.[12] Ethiopia planned for a whole year towards the abolition of fees, and yet they fared little better, while some other countries chose to phase fees out. It shouldn't be surprising that a year did not help – you can't expand training capacity as well as train enormous numbers of additional teachers at the same time, in one year.

Not long ago in Lagos, I experienced classrooms with 150 to 200 children in them. Teachers didn't know the children's names and struggled hopelessly with crowd control, pointing and shouting at particular students to get their attention to discipline them. This was while I was living in the country, from early 2009 to late 2011. A teacher could not realistically hope to achieve any sort of mission at all under these conditions, where there are few to no textbooks and writing materials, and hardly a surface for any student to write on. A very common complaint of parents within communities around government schools while I was researching these issues was that teachers 'do not take good care of the children' [their pupils]; that children can 'roam around' and wander out of the school compound any time they like without anyone doing anything about it or noting their absence, let alone contacting the parents. I have observed this to be true over the course of years, and I could entirely understand the concern of the parents, particularly relating to adolescent or even younger girls wandering freely in risky urban environments. Teachers in Nigeria remain in short supply[13] in many government schools despite the colleges of education, of which there are three in just the small state where I lived, Kwara State, turning out enormous numbers of on-paper 'qualified' teachers. As late as 2022, there were states in Nigeria where a significant share of teachers in secondary schools had only primary-level education themselves.[14] A barely retired senior government official told me only recently that what teachers learn is not relevant – they learn about the history of education and other interesting things, but not about how to actually teach children in often-packed classroom.[15] It is very difficult to understand what the point is of making young people think they are transitioning to a higher level of education when, in some cases, their teachers have less education than the students themselves.

At the same time as it was being discovered that countries did not have cohorts of prepared and ready teachers just waiting around in the wings, it was already well known that the existing salary bill took up most of the education budget in any lower-income country. In the 'before times', schools used the fee income from parents for school-level expenses and to tide teachers over when their salaries were paid late or were eaten into by the central or local government (or both). What would head teachers now use to fill this gap? So now, not only did the ministry have to find teachers from somewhere and find some budget with which to pay them, but they also had to find money to send to schools to cover expenses. The chosen solution was the 'capitation grant', meaning that for every child enrolled, the school would receive a fixed sum. These payments were meant to go to paying for teaching and learning materials and anything else that came up at the school-level, but they mostly fell far short, at between $1 and $3 per child. Only in Kenya did they manage a slightly less pitiful $14, which was still not enough to make really decent provision to support children's learning.[16] Incidentally, it was also these payments that set the scene for extreme distortion of enrolment data reported from schools through the relevant organs of government and finally to the national ministry before winding their way to

UNESCO's Institute for Statistics. I have direct experience of the mess that this sort of administrative data gets into, from my time working with state ministries in Nigeria. It was in the school head's interests to report more students in order to get more funds, especially when they expected that they would never receive the officially set amount per child. So, if your school has 200 students, you know corruption and insufficient budgets will mean your school might receive funds for maybe 120 students. It makes sense then to report 290 enrolled children so that you might get capitation grants for 200; one corrupt practice to compensate for another.

Another artefact of this period that has returned in pockets (and possibly whole countries) during recessions and the pandemic is that teacher salaries are often not paid fully and/or on time. In Nigeria, irregularity was the norm for decades, with teachers not seeing their salaries arrive for months on end, and this became the case again during the global recession of the 2010s. Liberia was re-gripped by the same problem in Autumn-Winter 2019, even before the pandemic had struck. It is an extremely difficult thing to expect that teachers might be motivated to work hard when they don't know when their next pay might come, and whether it will be the full amount. Partly as a result of such serious blows to morale, an overall atmosphere of lack of care and decay becomes a self-feeding thing. Both students and teachers started to attend erratically, with no one empowered or motivated to take an interest, let alone effectively monitor the situation and apply sanctions where needed.[17] Into gloomy, neglected school environments, bright-eyed fresh recruits enter, if and when they do end up entering, and quickly have their eagerness and any idealism squashed.[18] Schools as buildings and the scene of collective human efforts became fixed on a downward trajectory, and bad-quality schooling led directly to the growth of cheap, shoddy private schools.

The end results of the terrible under-supply of real, professional teachers and any teaching and learning materials, furniture, proper school rooms and toilets with hand-washing facilities was a disaster that unfolded first quickly, and then slowly and continuously in schools. Malawi was one of the worst-affected countries, and still faces enormous challenges. When I went to Malawi in 2008, some fourteen years after their primary school fees were abolished, the schools I visited were some of the worst I have ever seen, especially in light of the relatively calm and peaceful history of the country. The buildings were simply empty shells, with no furniture or learning materials at all. Even the doors to the rooms and what were meant to be storage cupboards were gone, as were the wooden shutters on the windows. They had just been stripped out by thieves; my local research host also told me that it was useless to get a landline phone installed at home because thieves would steal the cable connecting your house to the phone lines. Even if there had been any classroom materials, there would have been nowhere safe to keep them, and what seats there ever were in the classrooms were because parents provided them (just each for their own child, not as some sort of collective arrangement). My experiences in Maputo in 2015 and Liberia in 2017 were nearly as dismal. Everything that makes a school capable of providing an educational experience was missing, and the state of knowledge of the actual teachers was similarly lacking.

While Liberia, Malawi and Mozambique topped the list for having the most depressing possible schools, the situation was not much better in the countries where I spent most of my time between 2002 and 2012; Nigeria (parts of the southern half of the country) and India (Uttar Pradesh and just tangentially in Delhi). In my part of western Uttar Pradesh, there were fewer children than in the utterly packed schools I saw in Nigeria, but this made no real difference to children's learning because the teachers felt no pressure or inner compulsion to do anything. They were just kicking back, relaxing and chatting when they should have been teaching, as I observed during my doctoral study visits. A few teachers expressed slight concern that a government representative might come by unexpectedly, so they felt the need to turn up at least part of the time. They would wait until the end of the day to mark all their students present in case a hypothetical government officer checked the register against the number of children actually present. Some sixteen years later, just before the COVID-19 pandemic, I returned to a few of my doctoral fieldwork schools and the situation had reached such an extreme that in one school there were several teachers but only two students present. The cost to the government in salaries for such a school with no attending students is an unconscionable, condemnable waste. In another school, there were about ten or fifteen children playing while the teacher was there but not doing anything; he was just hanging out and happy to chat with Gaurav and me. No explanation is needed for why they are not actually holding a class, because they have no compunction about doing no work.[19] Different village, slightly different situation at the school, same outcome: government money wasted on no learning under a regime of ludicrously high teacher salaries (for this area) – the salaries resulting from significant input from teachers' unions at the state legislature level.

Nigerian schools ranged from moderately attended rural schools to massive urban compounds often housing several government schools and accommodating, somehow, utter throngs of students, as I have already mentioned. I never encountered a well-equipped school during my time there, but at least when I visited the very worst one, which was actually physically dangerous (being multi-storey but lacking the railings and window coverings that had once existed), the large compound was actually a construction site with an entirely new building being built to replace it. There were countless other dangerous schools, such as those with roofs in just about every stage of slow collapse. It was commonplace to see sections of corrugated iron hanging by just a few strands of metal, flapping in the breeze over the heads of children. When I asked why they did not just remove these precarious pieces, they explained to me that when the structure gets to that stage, trying to remove one piece brings the rest down with it. Still, there were usually teachers present and doing something, and sometimes there were a great many teachers. I will never forget finding a few boys behind one classroom block one day, trying to hammer one of the plethora of broken desks that live at schools, usually stacked in one classroom in a massive pile, easily repairable but with no one to do the work. The boys were using a single nail and a rock to hammer it with, eager to have something other than the damp ground or a stone to sit on. I always wondered why head teachers couldn't organize parents to come in one weekend per year to repair desks and benches and do other basic maintenance. But this sort of thing just doesn't happen, and the government maintenance logs were full (I had the chance to examine them in the government offices) and the waiting lists were very long with almost no funds to pay for repairs. Added to rooms full of broken furniture, there are now also rooms, locked and abandoned, full of documents carefully printed out by the UK-funded programme I was working on fifteen years ago.[20]

The bottom line from my time across West Africa and East Africa down to Mozambique and in India was that schools could be found in all sorts of states, from tiny and with hardly any students, to massive and severely overstrained, to having maybe one staff member at best to having loads. From having severely under-educated and basically illiterate teachers to having those with degrees as well as teaching qualifications. In India, the government was brilliant at providing textbooks, free of cost, as compared to all of the African settings where I worked, where it was commonplace that hardly a complete, non-torn textbook would be found in a classroom. But varying levels of nearly no learning, or vastly insufficient learning, in the face of significant money being spent[21] has been the result of all this effort to universalize primary schooling, moving up to universalizing even secondary schooling, against all of the indications to the contrary from the experience with primary schooling. As is the point of this book and what has already been made clear in brief, all of this failure has pushed anyone who could afford to pay fees to do so, to avoid the soul-crushing failure of these schools. Having shown how an enormous mess was created at the macro level, the rest of this chapter will explain how a national education system being utterly swamped and overwhelmed, lacking in the right people, and expanded and allowed to run with little to no planning plays out in reality, by explaining what challenges there are within schools that we in rich countries are not really accustomed to having to confront.

* * *

The bedrock of each individual school is the teaching staff.[22] The macro picture that I have tried to outline above is overwhelming when you get your teeth into it and really digest and understand it. It is so big and so bad that it can seem disconnected from the workaday reality for the people who come to school and interact there. While more teachers are almost eternally needed for a country's education system to work well in a context of population expansion, drilling down to the school level reveals widely varying pictures. There's no single generalization that can be made – as I have mentioned, terrible schools in Lagos could have well over a hundred children in a classroom while my local schools here in India have a handful in the whole school. The overall ratio of the total students in a country's primary school system to the total teaching staff can give a very misleading pupil–teacher ratio, with conditions at individual schools often varying wildly. No one wants to be posted to the remotest rural schools where there are no local amenities, no housing to rent and access roads that are so bad that relatively short distances nevertheless entail inordinately long journey times.

Some of these schools are like intellectual wastelands for an educated person, as unkind as it may sound to say so; the feeling of such forgotten rural pockets stays with me after years away from the field. One Ghanaian school research visit stays with me in particular, but this sort of situation is commonplace. To reach such schools, one turns off a main road to start what feels like the endless jolting down long-ago paved or totally unpaved roads, doing a slalom course zig-zagging across the whole width of the road to avoid truly massive potholes, the speed achievable being just about a relaxed sort of cycling speed. The eventual arrival at an extremely remote school and the feeling of stepping out; the heat, the dust, the school being the only evidence that the government or wider society even exists. Visiting classrooms to see what's happening, with what you find being anywhere from a reasonable sort of lesson in progress, to chaos, to nothing at all. Sometimes it feels like these schools are just somewhere to hang out. The smell in coastal West Africa of cocoa beans being turned in the sun, the fermentation giving off a distinct, pungent odour. The locals for whom this visit is a big event come by to watch what happens and to listen in, despite any researcher's best research ethics-inspired intentions for privacy and confidentiality. It was a lucky school visit in Ghana where a coconut vendor was present, meaning that at least there was endless thirst-quenching coconut water to drink.

Teachers are keen to talk about their travails – the children who don't attend regularly and who are often to be found in the fields or just hanging about the village; the lack of decent housing and the landlords renting rooms who then expect the lodging teacher to accept their family guests into the room for which the teacher is paying full rent! The complaints about parents who do not understand how to support their children in their education. Teachers want to run away from this sort of living and working environment and petition the administration to transfer them to where their family members are, or to any urban centre where a more modern standard of living can be found. It is easy to sink into apathy in such environments, and teachers complain that no one from the administration visits or provides any support or assistance. Teachers are expected to get on with things despite feeling totally cut off and forgotten, trying to do something with children who often do not have the parentally enforced discipline and regularity needed to properly pursue conventional educational goals. On the parents' end, they tend to complain about teachers who do not do much at school or don't even turn up, and it becomes clear there is a chicken-and-egg question to be answered as to which end of the teacher community see-saw the apathy was born on.

Because of teachers' desire to get away from such life- and morale-sucking environments, some teachers either live far from their school and show up erratically or show up and give minimal effort, while others succeed in wheedling their way to being transferred to an urban posting. There are obvious reasons why rural teachers might require extra support to cope with the remoteness of their postings, while urban teachers might argue that their cost of living is much higher. However this issue is viewed, teacher deployment is a serious problem to this day, and in many countries there simply are not enough people educated well enough to become teachers. Added to this, I don't think there's a realistic incentive in existence that will attract teachers to remote villages with no infrastructure and services, and no wider educated community. Incentives like 'hardship posting' bonuses and housing might work for a little while, but such places will only ever be good enough for a short while. I don't believe there's a solution that means such remote schools will ever function well – or at least not in my lifetime or until technology reaches a state nearly unimaginable now. In such schools, there will never be an in-school authority who is fully invested and takes charge to ensure the school functions well. Those who might scoff and suggest the rate of technological change is so great that soon there will be teacher robots – they need to remember the challenges facing the children living here (described in the next chapter) and the difficulties in providing tech support in these remote places.

At the same time, there are not enough people with the right skills and education to even *train* new teachers. So, when training colleges have 'mushroomed' as they have in India, or drastically expanded their output as in Nigeria, the result is only on paper, and does not reflect a properly educated and developed teacher. In India, private teacher training colleges have popped up everywhere, just as cheap private schools have, and no one is monitoring the quality of the training provided, or even whether or not there is any actual training given. Many of these colleges are just diploma mills.[23] Paradoxically, UNESCO's Task Force on Teachers hints that there may be issues with teacher training regimes without explicitly addressing the mismatch between what teacher training institutions provide, and what real-world teachers actually need. They go on emphasizing the pupil-to-trained-teacher ratio as a meaningful thing.[24] Teacher training is more helpful in some places than in others of course, but many qualifications are essentially useless to a young person stepping into the real-world of government schools today.

Early on during the Education for All era of expanding need for teachers, the inevitable decision was taken to waive the requirement for full teacher preparation, which took considerable time, and crash courses were introduced, as in Ghana, Malawi and Kenya. None of today's lack of well-educated and prepared teachers should come as a surprise, as the shortage was already being felt and documented in the immediate post-colonial period. Concern was greatest for the extension to the secondary level, when there simply weren't enough educated people to support expansion, and it's noteworthy that these concerns well predate any fee abolition. This was under just the usual force of numbers before equitable access was even a worry.[25] Reports from the time can now be read as the writing on the wall for dreams of rapidly scaled-up, high-quality and equitable, inclusive access to education. Sixty years later, UNESCO has issued a report[26] that states the exact same thing; the teachers needed for secondary school expansion are simply not there. In the intervening six decades, the quality of those original teachers facing much smaller numbers has been diluted with every year that passes and with every new teacher given basic training and sent to the front line. No degree of pessimism in the reading of this situation should be considered too extreme.

So, teachers, the most important people in any school, are in short supply overall; they are desperately needed in the areas where life and morale are the hardest to sustain; and many teachers are just not well enough educated to ever be able to do the job properly. Add to this, classrooms with no equipment or furniture, which also has a negative impact on children's and teachers' morale. Add to this the difficulty of teaching children who have few to no textbooks (and often textbooks are torn and missing parts) and few writing materials. Teachers then have to spend much of their time writing on the blackboard (something that most school systems seem able to supply, thankfully) for children to copy down (for those children with writing material). In the poor planning and management that sees teachers unevenly deployed and materials lacking in schools, corruption often plays a starring role, with contracting for infrastructure building (when repairing existing buildings might have sufficed) a favourite way of sucking money out of the system and into private hands. Another form of dishonesty is many civil service teachers' idleness even when physically at school – the World Bank Service Delivery Indicators survey data, used extensively in the last chapter, show that this is a much more significant drain on the system than teachers actually absent from school premises. Again, the magnitude of this problem is enormous.

Contracts to supply textbooks and other materials are rich with possibilities for the corrupt. Opportunities abound to poke holes in the public finance bucket, letting the money leak out at any and all angles. There are 'ghost schools', 'ghost teachers' and 'ghost students' which exist only on government records, and money flows out because of them but doesn't add to the sum total of learning. School grants are misused, diverted and chipped away at the district level and the school level. The reality at the school level is often that there is simply no cash to meet needs that arise from regional or national government's failure and parents' inability to provide all that is needed for a school to run properly. So, the final layer of corruption at the school level then impacts directly on children and their parents, as teachers feel they have no choice but to charge unofficial (illegal) fees just to allow the school to run. This runs contrary to the equity motivations for fee abolitions, and parents come to view schools as being corrupt and unfair when it is likely the fault of a higher level of government – yet in other cases, it might just be that teachers do this because they can get away with it.

Problems of apathy, inertia and corruption tend to snowball, and there is very little that community members can do about it because of the lack of any mechanism through which schools are accountable to the families that they serve. There is (officially) no fee relationship between schools and families, with a school's mandate handed down from on high at the local, regional or central government level. When I've asked parents if they ever go to government schools to complain or to ask for more seriousness and commitment, the often poor and unempowered parents generally tell negative stories. In Lagos, one parent said that the reply she got was, 'You can't complain here, this is a government service, and it's just like that'. In another quite astonishing teacher interview in Uttar Pradesh, my respondent, the village government school teacher, made his contempt for the families of his erratically attending pupils clear. In Uganda, parents reported the inability to prevent their children from being beaten at government schools, corroborated by other researchers who documented the same.[27] In the face of such a brick wall as many parents find in their local government school, there is little that they can do but withdraw their children from the school to send them to a cheap private school instead, but this avenue is not available for many.

***

I have asked countless parents from India to West Africa if they would ever consider sending their child to a government school under the prevailing conditions. An embarrassed and incredulous, almost disgusted look passed across the faces of the Liberian parents I spoke to in a small focus group. Their expressions said it all, and when they finally spoke up, it was to say no, that was not something to be countenanced. Parents in places where cheap private schools have sprung up and who are highly motivated regarding their children's education tend to do everything they can to send their children to private school, making at times quite severe sacrifices – *cutting their bellies*. They scrimp and save and swerve other 'essential' expenditures for the household in order to pay school fees, and many never manage to pay in full. Saving is difficult because someone gets ill or some unforeseeable expense comes up and gobbles up the education pot. While within the same community some children go to government school and some to private, the line of segregation is along socioeconomic lines, and it is a clear fault line.

There is much discussion in the education literature about what happens when all of those even somewhat better off than the bulk of the population get an off-ramp to exit public services into a private territory where children are insulated from those of other backgrounds and those less fortunate economically. Less voice is exercised in favour and defence of the government school. Less pressure is piled onto politicians to make sure that schools get the attention and support they need and deserve. Fewer protests take place when cuts or closures happen. There is less widespread feeling for making sure that enough is spent on the education system that serves everyone because it no longer serves everyone. The least well-off are left behind and are least likely to be able to bring these kinds of pressures to bear on the government, if for no other reason than that they are working so many hours that there is no time or energy left over to fight such fights. Really, when we allow people to live and toil in poverty, the least we can do as a society is make sure that government schools are sorted to take one burden off them. This goes for health services too, of course.

A parent living in the informal settlement of Makoko in Lagos told me clearly, 'no one is willing to send their child to government school. The only parents who do are the very poorest in our community, or drunks and others who have no interest in education'. This type of view I have come across again and again in my research, and when such views become entrenched, government school attendance becomes stigmatized – the mark of a bad family with parents who don't care. The children in government schools are the left-behind, highly likely to come to school unprepared to learn, and to attend sporadically. Their parents might not even know how to support their children in an effort to learn, even if they had the time and the resources, and there are no school peers to push things in the right direction for the poorer ones. These children are the hardest to reach, and already unaccountable civil service teachers become jaded and disdainful of their own students, perceiving no need to strive for their welfare and learning when no pressure is coming from any direction at all, including from parents. This 'middle-class flight' is similar to the hollowing out of urban areas in the United States when white, middle-class families fled to the burgeoning suburbs. With government schools in poor countries, ghettoization or 'pauperization' ensues, further eroding quality and community confidence.[28]

***

Yet, as sad as this story is, and as difficult as things might be in a particular government school, it's possible for the government to – again – make things still worse. Policies like free, universal primary education and the banning of school fees might sound like a great idea. But what happens when the government is not keeping up their end of the bargain? What used to come to schools through user fees has to be replaced from some source if the fee ban is to hold. When I went on a research trip to a rural area outside of Monrovia in Liberia, I was interviewing the local education officer in her small government office when she told an illuminating story about how a community pitched in to support its school, one of the schools in her jurisdiction. It's the type of story that, in other circumstances, is rolled out as a heart warming example of community cooperation and mutual support.

In the face of a lack of funds for anything at all at the school level, the school's parent–teacher association came together to do something about this. The group would meet regularly, and parents at the school paid into a communal pot that went to support the school and supply its needs. Necessities were provided, and teachers felt supported and that the community was taking an interest and wanted them to really do something at school – a really positive form of pressure was brought to bear, coupled with vital financial and moral support. But someone at the Ministry of Education got wind of this, and from on high came word that the arrangement must be stopped. There are no fees at government primary schools in Liberia, and so parents must be prevented from providing this regular support through the PTA. This local education officer was rueful in telling how, without being able to render this sort of support to the school, the point of the PTA seemed to shrivel up. Presumably, without being able to make sure that the school received things that were needed for education to work, teachers no longer felt supported, and parents felt they had no leverage or means of helping. The PTA died, and the school was left in the same sad, unsupported state as all the rest. But at least the UN's vision of fee-free schooling was upheld.

***

I've concentrated more on classrooms than other aspects of the physical environment that confront children when they come to school every day. For the nuts-and-bolts of learning the material in the curriculum, it is the environment of the classroom and the existence, or not, of materials for learning, and somewhere to sit and write that are the most important. I've had conversations with people – donors to the school that Gaurav and I started over two decades ago – who think that there is no real need to invest in buildings for schools because a good teacher can teach under a tree. This particular man, quite a forceful but very kind character, wanted his monthly contribution to go to teacher salaries instead. I think I understand where he was coming from. He had probably heard stories about school buildings being built and then nothing happening in those buildings. At the same time, no one would have expected his children or grandchildren to sit under a tree to learn, without an all-weather classroom and a decent seat and writing space. So, unwittingly and unintentionally, the attitude was something like, 'well, *they* are used to *that*'. These days, in my part of India, that would never fly. Children sit on mats on the floor in government schools, which doesn't feel so bad because the buildings are quite light and airy, and there is good outdoor space. In these government schools, it is certainly the failure of teachers to do something about children's attendance that is the main event. Most of them have so few students that they could easily visit the households and try to get support from parents in return for taking their employment seriously, but the teachers are not interested in making such allowances for the poverty of their pupils. They feel that their responsibility starts and finishes at the school gate (if they feel any real responsibility at all).

But there are things other than classrooms and teacher effort that matter. Looking at these issues from the outside, we have to consider things in context, balancing what children are indisputably used to from the circumstances of their home lives and what looks like basic decency in terms of facilities when children are spending their days at school. Toilets are a major issue, although the linking of them to learning outcomes in the research literature is, in my view, almost insulting. Children should have basic sanitation simply because they are human beings and deserve it, irrespective of whether or not their scores on some test increase as a result (which is the usual rationale deployed by donors for justifying such investment). Indeed, having decent toilets can be an issue of actual safety. A head teacher that Gaurav met while working in India reported that she just happened to be outside of the school building at a time when a very young child was going out to the bush to pee. The teacher happened to be in the right place at just the right moment to stop the child from being snatched by someone hiding in the undergrowth for just this purpose. She was barely able to grab hold of the child just as she was being grabbed from the other side in something resembling a scene from a film. Had the school had toilets on the premises, such a risk during the school day would be avoided. At the other extreme, in urban Lagos, Nigeria, there is no bush to squat in as just about every inch of land is built up. I remember distinctly the smell emanating from one block of classrooms that was next to the boundary wall in one corner of the school compound. The classrooms were rendered unusable because of the smell from children using the slightly secluded space between the boundary wall and those classrooms to defecate. Teachers refused, understandably, to use that classroom block, and after the children were done with what they had no choice but to do, they had nowhere to wash their hands. And if the old reasons were not enough, as we all know too well in the post-pandemic and post-Ebola era, hand washing is more important than ever. For girls, once they start to menstruate, the toilet issue becomes that much more important.

No one can credibly expect or justifiably urge children to attend schools all day with tens or hundreds of others if they are not provided with the basic necessities that any of the people doing the expecting and urging would demand for themselves and for their own children. At the same time, there are crazy tussles over the type of toilet – a western flush toilet preferred over a pit latrine – but without a regular source of water, the flush toilet quickly becomes unusable. To enable that flush to happen, usually a pump will be required to get some water from below the ground up to a rooftop water tank. To get that water pumped up there requires a source of electricity, either from a generator (that in turn requires a regular supply of diesel) or from mains or solar electricity. If national governments and the wider international community push children to attend schools, then they owe it to children to make damned sure that the teachers are willing to do what they can to fulfil the duties of a teacher. They also have the obligation to provide decent and safe facilities, and children should be looked after in a way commensurate with their age, while the parents have entrusted their children to the school's care. It should be considered only intuitive that children might learn better under better physical conditions. But if toilets are installed and test scores don't go up? This should be neither here nor there, because children deserve decent toilets.

This chapter has sought to set out all of the myriad reasons at the level of the school and the classroom that children are not learning, as I showed in the preceding chapter. Yet I have not even covered the other major, baked-in problems to do with over-ambitious curricula and the expectation that poor children, first-generation learners, be able to learn in a language that is not their own. Countries have so many languages and usually one or more official languages that it is quite impossible to implement the current schooling model in all children's mother tongues, and the resulting mess has been clearly set out in the work of Nadia Naviwala.[29] The next chapter looks to the home to find the main reasons why children are not learning, mostly to do with where and how they grow up. But to wrap up here, if we demand that children go to school, then the school should be worthy of the name.

4

The Real Issue: Neglected Child Development

I started the book with the rather bluntly expressed, non-expert view of Scott Galloway that the reason children (in that case, in Florida in the United States) were not learning was that they were 'fuckin hungry'. To put this another way (the academic way), 'countries, regions, or school districts can expect to continue to have difficulty achieving high levels of student learning in school if the children live in a sociopolitical context outside school that does not provide the safety, health, and moral support needed to function well in a classroom environment'.[1] Despite these pretty spot-on observations not being kept a secret, the world and more is still expected of schools in all societies – they are seen as the enablers of parents' and children's dreams for a great future and the impetus for an ascent out of poverty. They are expected to feed hungry children, to straighten them out and instil discipline if these have been lacking in the home and/or the community. They are meant to act as a levelling force in society, spurring fairer treatment of the downtrodden, and performing assorted other tasks both lofty and mundane in the local and national community. First and foremost, they are there to ensure that children are learning the national curriculum, progressing up the class levels in lock-step year on year.

Yet, as I've endeavoured to illustrate vividly, schools aren't even managing the main job of delivering the curriculum in a competent way. Education experts tie themselves in knots trying to figure out why schools aren't performing and why efforts to improve things don't seem to work. Why doesn't this injection of materials and other supports mean that children now learn? Why doesn't that teacher training or accountability measure do the trick? In countless rigorous studies, it's acknowledged that the socioeconomic background of the child (roughly: whether the child lives in poverty or not, whether the family has any literate members, and whether there are any books in the household) plays a major role in learning, but also in their health and ultimately their later lifestyles and careers. The researchers seem to know this, and yet they note it and then discuss the findings of their studies as if they thought that, actually, schools *should* be able to make up for virtually all deficits in a child's life. Perhaps it is because they are interested in schools and what makes them tick, or else the range of possible policies is not broad enough to deal with the root problems, so they simply ignore the deficiencies of the child's circumstances.

Even when the background of the child is acknowledged, and a few words are said about how poor children are unlikely to have space, time and light with which to study in the evening, little is ever said about *how* growing up in poverty militates against a child's chance of excelling in education. This chapter sets out to make up for all of the overlooking of this important aspect in children's learning that happens in most writing about education and why children don't learn in schools. I choose to write declarative statements because it is easier and because what I will describe is so very common, but of course, there are many cases where poor children might live in perfectly healthy, although poor, homes with perfectly functional families and communities. It is just easier to write without all the hedging and toning-down that is the norm to avoid accusations of generalization – but I would like to get it across that these statements indicate common situations, not universality.

***

Starting from the basics: to grow and thrive in good health, children need the right environment and the right support. Poor children are up against it from the very beginning, from their time in the womb. Poor women don't get the best nutrition and medical care, and they live in stressful and often polluted environments – all of which have ramifications for a developing foetus. Once born, similar assaults on the child's development continue, including poor nutrition and possibly under- or even over-feeding (the latter with the wrong types of food), and the stress they experience at home connected with their family's poverty. While air pollution is something that even the rich cannot get away from with all the air purifiers in the world, it is usually a whole lot worse for the poor. And it is not just in the air; poor children are more likely to encounter pollution in the land and water where they live. With poverty comes great stress, decreasing a person's ability to focus and make good decisions even as adults.[2] Hunger is often commented on as something that really impedes children's ability to concentrate, and under-nutrition does more than just make it more difficult to concentrate in the moment.

Then there are all of the other issues that are often commented on – the lack of time to do homework when the child has to help in the household after school, either by doing domestic work or by helping in the main earning work of the parents. Houses are unlikely to be terribly conducive places to study in the evening, and light is expensive and possibly difficult to come by. Added to this are the distractions of the neighbourhood, when other children are playing and not studying, or when neighbours are fighting or just talking loudly all around. The home set-up of many of the children in many of the places that I have studied in my career is just not right for fostering the northern type of studying and homework completion that has become a globalized norm. Our Northern educational model is therefore brutal, expecting legions of non-square pegs to be rammed into square-shaped holes. The circumstances are not right for this model to work, and yet still it seems to be the only model for learning and moulding young people deemed acceptable to audiences Northern and Southern alike.

*****

Before I started researching the development of very young children back in 2014, I had no idea how things worked in a child's developing brain or how important the first one thousand days from conception are. It was surprising to learn just how 'plastic' and adaptable the brain is. The more positive stimuli a child receives, the more connections (or synapses) develop between the cells (or neurons) in the brain. There has, up until relatively recently, been debate in the academic scientific literature as to whether humans continue to develop or grow neurons, but the consensus currently seems to be that humans are born with nearly all of the neurons they will ever have, up to about 100 billion of them, while some do develop after birth during infancy. They are then there for nurturing – or for killing off. The synapses that develop between the neurons in the brain are formed when a child regularly receives loving touch, hears many and varied words, poetry, song, and involved adult conversation around them, learns new things through their own physical efforts fuelled by their curiosity, and breathes clean air. At the time of birth, a baby's brain has about 100 billion neurons and about 2,500 synapses per neuron, or connections to other neurons, and after just a few years this increases to 15,000 synapses per neuron,[3] and this continues to increase into adulthood. The brain, as we develop, becomes like an ever-denser spider's web of connections, and the more the connections, the better.

The earliest years of a child's life might look pretty laid-back but it is actually a period of great opportunities and risks. Middle class parents lavish their children with picture books, language, music and experiences while poorer parents tend to lack the time and resources to do so – they are likely to be working all the hours possible just to make ends meet. When things don't go well in very early childhood, synapses develop in much smaller numbers, so such a child will start out at a disadvantage compared to their richer peers who likely benefitted from much more and much earlier stimuli. This is true the world over, and in some cultures it is looked at as an oddity when mothers speak to their babies. While some people find it quite normal to speak in full sentences to their cat or dog, a colleague of mine was told, 'You know, he can't understand you', when she was speaking to her baby while out and about, at home in Turkey. There are even international aid programmes targeting early childhood development that, as part of mothering education interventions, provide information to mothers about the importance of speaking to babies and engaging in what might look like very simple play on the floor with just basic household items. Very young children are highly vulnerable, and there are apparently aspects of the earliest brain development that, if they don't happen when they are meant to, can never be recovered or made up for – the quintessential missed opportunity. The foundational building blocks must be in place from the start.

Some things are within the control of parents but far from everything, and where the family lives also really matters. Particulate matter pollution in the air that we breathe impacts brain development, and in poor communities, it is not uncommon for cooking fires using various types of fuel to be lit inside the home, polluting the indoor air. In rich and poor countries alike, the poorer the family, the higher the indoor exposures.[4] Poor families are also much more likely, even in rich countries, to live on or close to very busy roads, polluting the air both inside and out. Children in any setting can come into contact with an array of nasty chemicals. Children in farming communities are exposed to fertilizers, pesticides and other agricultural chemicals. Children in polluted urban environments are exposed to water and soil polluted with chemicals, rubbish and human and animal waste. Even children in the rich suburbs of the Global North come into contact with herbicides and pesticides used in garden maintenance, while some children in the very wealthy Faroe Islands are fed highly polluted whale meat.

When I am in India, I am in a tiny, remote rural hamlet where air pollution is much less than in the city. Yet the air is often still polluted through particulates blown across from different areas, but more immediately from the burning of rubbish due to the lack of any system for its collection. Farmers burn stubble from their fields after harvest, watching the carbon from their own precious soil go up in smoke, contributing enormously to Delhi's air pollution problem every winter. Home cooking fires also pollute the air in the household, even when these are outside, as they invariably are in villages. With no chimneys, the smoke just tends to linger. Worse than this, however, are the chemicals that farmers use to increase yield and control pests and diseases. They often use these with no protective equipment at all, and some of the family members doing this work are adolescents. Parents use the chemicals and then come home and contaminate their children and things in the household rather than carefully washing and changing first. Some babies are even born 'pre-polluted' through the placenta and after birth the transmission continues daily via breast milk. From their first to their last days, the chemical exposure continues through insect repellents, contaminated fruits and vegetables, and from play that exposes them to contaminated soil, air and water, as well as through inadvertent contact with chemicals stored or just dumped near their home.[5]

It's not just a good guess that this chemical exposure is bad for children – it is established through scientific research that has found that organophosphate (pesticide) exposure during foetal development is linked with poor cognitive, behavioural and social development in children. Outcomes associated with exposure include 'abnormal primitive reflexes in new-borns; mental and motor delays among pre-schoolers; and decreases in working and visual memory, processing speed, verbal comprehension, perceptual reasoning, and IQ among elementary school-age children'.[6] Children so exposed are also at increased risk of attention-deficit/hyperactivity disorder and autism spectrum disorder, with all such risks found to be greater for the children of farm workers. One of the authors of the research study that the above quote comes from explained in an interview what this all really means. Whyatt explained that the type of neurological damage that happens is linked with 'working memory', meaning our ability to retain and act on short-term thoughts and new information. 'A child might only remember one or two parts of an instruction such as "open your science textbooks to page 37 and begin exercise number four"'.[7] Children can clock-up to two years' worth of developmental delay, showing slow motor speed, coordination and visual memory as well as having lower IQs and working memory.[8] What is even more unfortunate is that the exposure doesn't need to be enormous to have serious impacts, with children with low levels of pesticide exposure experiencing neurological and behavioural issues.[9]

For those breathing in dirty air, the effects are devastating. Children have a higher breathing rate in relation to their body size than adults do, and the natural barriers that develop in our lungs as we mature are much less developed in young children, meaning that they are more sensitive to the dirty air that they breathe in. Of course, their brains are affected by this source of developmental assault before they reach school, combining with the effects of chemical exposure. Vehicular pollution in particular is linked to frontal executive function deficits in children ranging from age two years up to the early teen years, and this has been documented in a range of contexts including India, China, Spain, Japan and multiple sites in the United States.[10] This study noted impacts on the same functions as already mentioned here, but also on their information processing speed, verbal abstraction, executive function and visuospatial and motor skills.[11] Our lifestyles are battering our children's brains invisibly, and then we expect great things in terms of discipline, application and learning outcomes. And while we know this much already, a major UNICEF report summarizes that 'As yet, we know the minimum – but not the maximum – extent of the harm. The variety of types of pollutants that are in the air across different environments make it difficult to determine the full impact of air pollution. But this growing body of research does provide an indication of the scale of harm.'[12]

Clearly, these are all impacts that have serious knock-on effects on how well children do in school. I have not even dwelt here on the more obvious illnesses in the respiratory area that can flare up and settle down again, and can become full-blown pneumonia or bronchitis. Every year in India, I see doctors on the TV news talking about how chest X-rays of urban teenagers are showing black lung. This is well established and self-evident, so it is the hidden barrage on the young, vulnerable brain's development that I have chosen to examine more here. And indeed, the cognitive deficits can be bigger than the physical ones:

> *Human development does not occur within a vacuum. The environmental contexts and social connections a person experiences throughout his or her lifetime significantly impact the development of both cognitive and social skills ... SES accounts for approximately 20% of the variance in childhood IQ, and it has been estimated that by age five, chronic poverty is associated with a 6- to 13-point IQ reduction. Disparities in cognitive development outweigh disparities in physical health, possibly contributing to the propagation of poverty across generations.*[13]

****

So much for children being well prepared to learn at school based on a healthy upbringing. Once the child has grown a bit and is of the age to enter school, there are further factors related to the child's family background, upbringing and home surroundings that impact on her ability to thrive in school, and truly learn. These factors are not easily mitigated, and are a reflection of the wider society and its values. There is also pretty much a consensus now that poor children get stuck going to worse schools than their richer counterparts in different neighbourhoods.[14] Even worse, when poor children are essentially kettled in these schools, things deteriorate with 'ghettoization', creating something like a downward spiral, with no 'positive influences' from people of a similar age.[15]

Stratification is everywhere. There's the gap between rich and poor, between urban and rural, and between private and government schools, and many of these categories overlap. Rich(er), urban and private schools go together quite neatly. However, there is also stratification within private schools just about everywhere these exist in numbers, within wealth levels within communities, and even within government schools. Private schooling in most countries is 'gated' first and foremost via the school fee, and once that hurdle is crossed, towards the upper end of the schooling spectrum, academic ability and other family factors start to enter into schools' admissions policies.

But back to the lower ebb of education – the schools that serve poor children, mostly in the South. One of the key factors in children's academic success is whether their parents are at all educated. This enters into so many areas of a child's learning, such as understanding the rhythm and regularity required for a successful education. Understanding the importance of the child attending regularly and showing up on time, fed and ready to learn. The importance of the child having the writing materials needed to do writing work in class. The importance of being supportive of the school and showing interest through coming to interact with teachers. There are many aspects of supporting a child in school that uneducated and illiterate parents find difficult or impossible, if they are even aware of them. My own mother-in-law shunned interaction with her children's teachers in the 1980s and 1990s, because of her negative feelings regarding her own lack of education (beyond the primary level) and her inability to speak English. She never went to school to interact with anyone there, while she placed enormous importance on her children's education.

There is a social 'distance' between poor parents and teachers in schools. Illiterate parents can feel it is an impossible idea to go to the school to discuss educational matters, and in my own research when I have asked parents about their interactions with schools, the responses have been illuminating. Parents have told me in Nigeria, India and Ghana that their interactions with government schools have been a waste of time, and it's just the way it is for them – but at least some do try. I have also interviewed Indian government school teachers who have expressed despair with regard to parents and even contempt for them – you can't help but understand them to a small degree when they are faced with a changing cast of characters in the classroom as different children are missing every day and often in great numbers. In such circumstances, how does one move the class forward through the curriculum? In Ghana teachers have not had much to report when it comes to interactions with parents. At private schools in these and many other countries, the school managers are clear – for the most part parents only come to inquire about the fees that the school charges, and nothing else. Sometimes after joining the school there might be a complaint about corporal punishment – usually that it's been excessive. I have done many surveys at cheap private schools in poor areas in the Global South, and no head teacher has told me that parents ever come inquiring about the qualifications, experience or other attributes of the teachers, or anything to do with how and what children are taught. It is all about the fees, and whether there are any discounts available. Illiterate parents don't know what to ask, and don't have any sense of their rights as parents to ask questions and seek greater understanding of what their children are going through when they go to school. In Tanzania, some people expressed the belief that schooling was something done *by the government to children,* and so it was a realm in which parents didn't have a role or a place; but I am sure richer parents using well-to-do private schools in Dar es Salaam do not have these same compunctions.

Once children have started going to school, poor parents don't know how to help their children with homework, although I have been told about assertive, motivated illiterate mothers who make sure they are right next to their children while they do their homework. However, the mother must take it on trust from the child that the work has been done. It's not just help with homework that poor parents can't provide, but also a space in the household that is conducive to a child's quiet, concentrated study. When you spend time in a rural village in Ghana at night, you see that life and activity are all around. Children are playing, and adults are walking and talking, sitting and talking, preparing food, arguing with a neighbour; it is all very social, very active, and it all takes place outside once the sun has disappeared and taken the worst of the heat with it. People have stopped working and things really come alive after dark.

When I've been sitting in such a situation interviewing parents, I have noticed that it would take a very strong-willed, determined sort of child to be inside, using expensive artificial light of whatever source, to sit and study, when most other children and the rest of the family are outside, living life. Our old culture of learning just doesn't fit with this setting – nor does it fit with the urban slum setting, similarly teeming with life and distractions. But traditional systems are so committed to the accepted necessity of homework that parents have come to expect it, even if they have not been to school themselves. It's now common practice for certain countries' school systems not to assign homework, such as in Finland and Scotland, because there is apparently no research-supported relationship between a child's spending hours poring over books and doing written work, and their actual learning over time. But traditional parents, even on low incomes, have certain mental models about education that they would find difficult or impossible to shake. To dispense with the assigning of homework would be considered to be short-changing children, and treating poor children negligently. Teachers would be viewed as shirking their duties by all concerned (except maybe for their grateful students).

Another aspect of the traditional, colonial school model that doesn't fit with traditional societies is the incompatibility of school schedules and calendars with times of peak farming activities, or the social importance of days-long weddings in India. Also, in a country as large and diverse as India, there are regional festivals that won't be celebrated in other areas but might hold major significance to local people. Those in charge of schools who have come from outside, or who have spent too long growing away from their roots, brush up against local cultures and don't understand them, viewing parents as careless and thoughtless with regard to the education of their children. Gaurav has felt this strange form of clash of cultures in his ancestral village, running the school that we started in 2004. He has spent considerable time every year in the village since he was born, and yet, city-educated and internationalized to some extent, it took him time to back down from his position of rigid adherence to the educational calendar. He continues to find it difficult to balance between recognizing people's valid desire to observe local festivals, with fighting against these events getting longer and longer each year. When school staff are committed and treat the education of their students with utmost seriousness, it is difficult to take into account the erratically diverging and then re-converging priorities of parents. Yet at the same time, even teachers live with similar pressures from their own families.

But it's not just parents who suffer from the existence of social distance with teachers – the students themselves are often worried about expressing their lack of comprehension in class when they haven't understood something. Questioning your elders, particularly much more educated and otherwise socially elevated elders, is frowned upon in many Southern and Eastern cultures, and it verges on unthinkable in many countries. So even when teachers ask their students if they have questions, the answer is likely to be 'no', or just silence. When they ask if anything is unclear, likewise, the answer is 'no'. 'Have you done all of the examples/exercises/reading/writing?' The answer: 'yes'. But when teachers look over the students' work, they will often find evidence to the contrary, and getting to the root of students' lack of understanding can be nearly impossible. At the same time, many of the unskilled teachers working in schools lack new and different ways of explaining things to students. When it somehow becomes clear that one or more students don't understand, the teacher often doesn't know what else to do but to repeat their previous explanation, which might not do any good.[16]

Students who want to keep flying under the radar become masters at hiding their problems, and when they do this, less-motivated, less-dedicated teachers collude with the hiding. It's not just when teachers ask students if they have understood; I have witnessed students doing a pantomime of following along, just repeating what is said by the teacher but not really understanding. Many skid haphazardly across the surface of understanding, and considering the challenge before the teacher, that of helping students who are behind, as well as teaching the rest of the class, most of them are probably only too happy to allow students to get away with their pretence of understanding. On the occasions that I have been observing a class and the teacher has been confronted by a clear and obvious lack of understanding on the part of a student, I have usually witnessed the needs of the confused students falling to the wayside, or else the whole class grinds to a halt to deal with 'the problem', which is also not fun for anyone. What has been most painful is to see a child asked to read aloud, and for the child to struggle so much that the teacher simply skips over them, eager to make progress with the rest of the class.

No one in these situations is necessarily to blame. Students might have had bad experiences in the past with expressing a lack of comprehension, or they might simply know it's not going to go anywhere good if they do express themselves. Many teachers are so terribly under-educated, under-prepared and under-skilled that they are not best equipped to deal with a student's problems. This latter challenge is then multiplied many times over because they are in a classroom filled with first-generation learners who need significant extra help that they are not prepared to give. Some students will likely be able to follow the material of the lesson just fine, and it is these students who are easiest to deal with, and to whom the lion's share of the teaching is usually pitched. In Northern schools, there would be special classes or at least some targeted support for students coming from special circumstances, such as newly arrived immigrants who do not yet properly speak the language, and teachers would revolt at the notion that they would teach significant numbers of such children with such needs alongside those who were prepared to sail through the curriculum. It just wouldn't work well for anyone. In many poor contexts, these are not special children; they are just the norm, and it would be hard to overstate the challenge to the students and the schools trying to teach them. Poor children from minority language households with no one literate in them can be viewed as immigrants to the land of schooling. Many of these most marginalized children must grapple with three languages, one of them a colonial one, by the time they are half-way through primary school.

These problems combine and overlap, so a child who lives in a remote, rural location is unlikely to have any choices and will be lucky to attend a local government school. The household won't have any concrete ways to support the child's education, and the parents may well think they are doing their bit by (usually) sending the child to school and (usually) feeding them first. These children are most likely to lack school supplies and to miss certain meals – something not unheard of either in the UK or the United States. During my research in Ghana, I was surprised to learn that parents would usually just give their child a coin to buy some food from a woman who would prepare and sell breakfast by the side of the road, often close to school or to the bus stop. Children said that when the parents had gone to the fields early and hadn't been able to leave a coin, they wouldn't go to school at all. This surprised me as they were at least given lunch at school. Getting back to the various obstacles – poor girls are somewhat less likely than poor boys to be supported in their schooling, although this is more a South Asian issue than an African one. Poor areas far from the gaze of the government education authorities are most likely to have schools that are severely lacking in crucial inputs. All of these disadvantages overlap, combine and reinforce each other to mean that children might have a very low chance of really getting anywhere in school, and they will have nowhere to turn for help when they don't understand.

***

The truth is that the lion's share of a child's success or otherwise in school is explained by the background of the child.[17] No matter what the country setting, parents make an enormous difference, even if they are illiterate or if they are not well-off; if they are utterly determined that the child will be disciplined and do the best they can in school, this provides a key enabling element in the child's circumstances. It makes sense here to set out the various lines of defence that parents can stack up between their children and the risk of failure – and so, how important money is. We can start with the fact that if they can pay for a reasonable school setting where the child stands a fighting chance rather than being lost in a sea of faces, and if they can provide the books and stationery needed for the child to make the most of class and homework, these are factors in the child's favour. Additional private tutoring on top of better schooling is not uncommon, further supporting such relatively lucky children.

The next lines of defence are more costly and very often out of reach for many parents struggling to make ends meet. If they can provide a home with space, lighting and quiet for children to do their homework, insulating them from the distractions of the neighbourhood whether urban or rural, one more defensive line is in place. If this last is secured, then it is also likely that where children go to school and where they live, they are probably mixing with peers from families with at least somewhat similar views and motivation levels regarding their children's futures. Where children are more sequestered in even slightly better-off residential areas with schools within them, then the circle of relative privilege (to whatever degree) is complete and will have made a difference to the child from long before she ever set foot in school. A very significant defensive wall is added thereby.

A benefit of this last line of defence is that a home setting conducive to learning may well also have provided the conditions for the child to grow up healthier, farther from the particulate matter, air pollution and other threats from the air that they breathe. The poor often live uncomfortably close to enormous roadways and other sources of terrible air pollution. When driving in Delhi, it is common to see tent encampments for the workers building or widening roads or working on building sites next to the road, with babies and young children present with their parents, breathing in exhaust fumes and dust day and night and toddling about close to the traffic. Such children are unlikely to even attempt to become educated – this is their lot.

Ways of defending children from assaults on their chances of success in school are very often real, tangible and physical. Their delicate physicality needs to be protected in order for it to develop and grow. In well-off communities, it is taken for granted that a healthy diet plays a role in the child's development and ability to concentrate, but so too does the parents' ability to protect the child from toxic stress and anxiety. Along with a protective and nurturing (although this should not be taken to mean a stifling) home environment comes less anxiety for the child to personally experience; anxieties about the physical, financial and emotional safety in and for her family. At the opposite extreme, toddling about by the side of a six-lane road means a life that is precarious in every possible sense.

***

I see many of the negative effects described here at work in the children who attend our school in Uttar Pradesh. While the foregoing is an oversimplification of how life and human communities work, what leads to success and what means failure, there is a validity to it, and we see it over and over reflected in the real world, often in cases where one or two of the protective factors are in place, but not all. Just some of the positive factors being present does seem to make a difference. In our Indian school, it is never a surprise when the daughter of parents who show themselves to be serious and committed does well. In fact, we find that children of such parents almost invariably do well, while some especially determined children thrive in spite of having parents who are not as dialled in to what it takes to succeed in school. But for the most part, we see the children of non-serious parents not doing terribly well. In the settings of my research in so many urban slums in large African cities, families could provide the living conditions only to the extent that that particular family could manage it, but the most motivated parents who dreamt of an escape for their children would provide the moral scaffolding and the concrete support to the child's education, for example by ensuring they sit down and do their homework, and by enrolling the child at private school and possibly in private tutoring as well. Many of the other factors were well out of reach and they either did or did not manage private school fees, although the wish to do so is usually there.

So, these very tough environmental and background factors play a key role in the extent to which children are able to learn, before we even get to considering factors related to the school. Much of this will feel familiar to rich country audiences – there is the ubiquitous TV and cinema trope of the kid 'from the wrong side of the tracks', and the youth who 'ran with a bad crowd', leading to his not doing well in school and in life more broadly. Bad peers in a bad neighbourhood lead to bad outcomes in life and cause the parents of their better-off peers to not want their children to mix with said problem youths. The trope, while overly simplistic, is rooted in reality.

***

The challenges of growing up in less advantaged surroundings are tackled in places like Finland by dedicating extra funding to support children who are struggling. And of course, Finland does not actually tend to allow much in the way of severe poverty to exist, and fee-paying schools are illegal. In what is meant to be the richest country in the world, the United States, the response is the opposite. Poor children typically live in poor areas, where things can be really bad in terms of safety, security, access to decent food and accommodation and freedom from stress and even recruitment by gangs. These areas pay much lower property taxes to the relevant government bodies, and it is this much smaller local tax revenue that funds local schools. So the ethos of that society is to consign children living in poverty to local education systems that have lower funding and are much less well-resourced than schools in richer areas serving much more supported and advantaged children, who are therefore less likely to need extra help or support. Schools in poor areas have the least experienced teachers, who try quickly to get transferred out.[18] Their system is designed to maintain and even increase educational inequity and inequality, which in turn stems from the extreme economic inequality prevailing in the country. The country has ample wealth to follow a policy more in the direction of Finland's, but it is their choice not to – if you are poor, it is because you didn't drag yourself up by the bootstraps; it is your fault and your children are consigned to the fate you endow them with. But it is a myth that it is purely personal choice that enables such bootstrapping.

Countries in the Global South don't have the same degree of choice in policy approaches; they don't have the wealth or the tax structures required to make up for the deficits of poverty, and there are untold millions with such needs. The rest of this book explains the problems that these countries face in struggling to provide a basic education system, and all of these issues related to building and running such a system are magnified in a daunting fashion when it comes to running a system full of disadvantaged children, many of whom are first-generation learners.

***

An estimate for India puts the share of non-school determinants in learning levels as high as 70 per cent, meaning that what schools can make up for amounts to less than one-third.[19] Children start off with disadvantages from before they are born. Learning about the forces assaulting the brain development of children who live in far from ideal circumstances is disheartening, and writing about it is extremely uncomfortable. It feels like straying into some kind of essentialist area, as if the argument is that poor children grow up with their brains damaged so what can we ever expect of them and why should schools be bothered trying especially to reach these children? This is not the intention of this chapter at all. There are myriad examples of children who have grown up in terrible situations in terms of their home and community environments, full of pollutants as well as toxic stress, but who have gone on to excel and do great things in life. My best student at the University of Edinburgh was a young man from Makoko, Lagos. Equally, there are those who grow up in ease and privilege who do absolutely nothing with their advantages. It is an entirely unknown share of any individual's trajectory in life that is determined by the particular fire within them.

So, there is no intention here but to highlight the terrible challenge of just getting through life and reaching adulthood in good shape, especially when growing up in difficult circumstances. As I said earlier, education researchers tend to be very focused on education itself, what happens in schools, what goes wrong in education systems, and they tend to scratch their heads to figure out what intervention or system reform will work to turn things around. More ludicrously, they consider what 'policy levers' to pull that will suddenly put the system in gear – imposing 'coherence' on an unruly situation.[20] The challenges of the child herself, all the baggage she brings to school, and all the assaults on her health and wellbeing[21] that have happened along the way are given something like an honourable mention, but are not really factored in, in any meaningful way. Fine, so we can't really do anything about these factors when working in our education and schooling-focused silos. Education people focus on the education part, but in the bulk of the analyses I have read, and in the bulk of the advocacy that takes place around education, the assumptions seem to revert back to some default setting where schools are failing, teachers are rubbish, and we want to get all children up to this particular minimum learning level when everything is mitigating against this happening. The media across the world is happy to propagate such messaging too. It's not even taken into account that vast shares of the people who have turned into the rubbish teachers that need training, corralling, controlling and motivating were children themselves not that long ago and grew up with all of the same deficits as their students.

I chose to write about this because it's not fair to the children and the schools to just mention in passing the lesser-known and vastly under-estimated beast that is 'socioeconomic status', and not delve into how it affects educational efforts; it's not fair to schools and teachers to expect them to move mountains, and it's not fair to the children and their families to expect so much of them when their societies have let them down and allowed them to grow up poor as they have. Each of the chapters of this book ultimately ends up shining a light on society and not the schools that are the boils on the skin, reflecting the disease inside. The schools are a manifestation of societies in which children grow up poor and assaulted from all sides; where nothing is fair and there can be no level playing field. What teachers could succeed in these conditions – never mind the poorly educated and unprepared teachers so common in the Global South?

5

The Crisis Response from the Community: Cheap Private Schools

'Teachers at government schools don't teach'; I have been told this in almost identical language, countless times in India, Nigeria and Ghana during interviews with parents, both urban and rural. Parents can see that if nothing much is going on at government schools then their children won't gain anything by turning up there. However, the extent of parents' mental engagement with what is happening (or not happening) at school varies hugely from one family to the next. Some parents are so consumed and exhausted by the effort needed just to make a living that they have no energy to worry about anything else. Other parents believe deeply in the power of education to one day free their children from poverty, so they are willing to scrimp and save in order to pay for something better than a failing government school, *cutting their bellies* to do so. The lengths that I have known parents in Lagos and Abuja to go to are heart-rending. Some mothers hide money from abusive or just controlling spouses, while others sell every single item in the household before they are willing to give up on paying for a private school. A parent might just look for a local person willing to do some informal teaching of literacy and numeracy. It often starts with some tutorial sessions with just a group of children gathered in a spot somewhere in the community. The demonstration effect kicks in, and more parents bring their children to this group.

So much of life is lived outdoors in hot countries that it will soon be noticed what's going on, and how actively the person in charge is teaching. More children come, parents get the impression that their children are learning more in this way than they do at school, and eventually the parents ask, even beg the 'teacher' to turn the afterschool sessions into an actual school with grade levels and all the core subjects, using the official school curriculum and associated textbooks. From these tiny seedlings have grown countless small, cheap private schools, starting from a small collection of pre-primary and primary 1 and 2 children, to separate classes for each grade level, with a class added per year. For some time the enrolments might not justify a class teacher per grade, but this does not hold these schools back. If the teacher is doing something right and keeping the costs low enough, it is only a matter of time until the school grows to the point where full classes run from the pre-primary level to the end of the primary cycle. From there, space permitting, some decide to expand to the lower- and then upper-secondary school levels, but there will always be more schools serving just the primary and pre-primary levels.

This is how the cheap private schooling phenomenon got its start, with most of the earliest school owners I have met describing their beginnings in this way. Again the demonstration effect has kicked in, not just among parents, but among people who feel able and willing to start up a small school of their own. When the appetite among parents becomes stronger and ever more evident, more people see opening a small school as a good way to make a bit of a living while doing something for the community. In many places opening a private school in the neighbourhood has been seen as a good way of employing educated adult children within a family, because regular jobs are so hard to come by. Once things start to take off, some actual investment will happen, building something of a structure to enable expansion beyond a single spare room in the household, or beyond the space borrowed from the local church.

In some cases these developments happen because there's precious little teaching happening at the government school, but in other situations it is because there is no government school anywhere close by. Many cheap private schools spring up, totally unplanned and unregulated by the government, in low-income neighbourhoods that would generally be classed as slums. Governments often have development ideas for these areas that do not involve accommodating low-income people, meaning they don't want to lend legitimacy to occupants by bringing schools, roads, sewage systems, electricity, clinics and the like. The people of the slums are not to labour under any misapprehension that they are welcome to stay where they are settled, despite their servicing and smoothing the lifestyles of the wealthy. This state of affairs means that government schooling is often quite a trek from home in the slums surrounding major cities. In many poor communities, children have to take risks to traverse dangerous roads and neighbourhoods to reach government schools beyond the slums. The alternative is to come up with something closer to home, and that's what the local educated person does when she starts a small private school that will ultimately grow. The neighbourhood private school provides schooling places for local children otherwise neglected in government planning, and it provides informal sector jobs for educated young adults for as long as it takes them to find something more in line with their ambitions. What it doesn't do is provide education of good quality, or education for very poor children.

On this basis a developing-world Dickensian back-alley breed of private schools was born, just like those that ran in England in the nineteenth century, called 'ragged schools' and even earlier, 'dame schools' were filling the same need in preceding centuries (more on these below). In England, the legislating for government schooling that took place in 1870 led to the redundancy of the ragged schools and dame schools. In the Global South people are still using cheap private schools, waiting for some development to render them obsolete. Strangely, *it is the legislating for universal private schooling that led to the phenomenon in the poor countries* while legislation wiped it out in the richer North. So, having sketched out how these schools developed 'organically', one-by-one, to become a phenomenon, it's worthwhile to try to provide a picture of what the schools are like now that this 'market' has been developing for quite some time and is relatively mature, especially in parts of Nigeria and India.

***

When I tell people from outside of my working life about these schools, even though I call them private schools, they don't realize what I mean, and I have to clarify along the following lines. No, there is no NGO involved; there is no church mission; there is no Northern charity instigating, funding or overseeing the thing. These schools are formed by local people within their local communities, and the schools live and die on the backs of the local people choosing to send their children there, and others who choose to work there as teachers. School owners are usually individuals, but sometimes act in partnership with a spouse or other family members. In some countries, schools might be run by two or three individuals in a business partnership. It is distinctly non-affluent parents who fund the schools, paying tuition and other fees by means of long, hard toil, although it has to be remembered that communities are not homogeneous (and neither are schools), so some people struggle more than others to pay for a cheap private school. The schools are so comprehensively private, that governments often don't even know they exist – and the schools like to keep it this way because of the burdensome nature of government oversight.

The lowliest schools that I have seen in eerily similar form in Abidjan, Abuja, Kampala and Delhi (and many points in between) take on a very poor form indeed, existing in the shadows of the informal sector. They inhabit all sorts of shacks and back-alley hovels, often comprising just wooden struts holding up a corrugated sheet roof and walled with bits of timber, flattened packing crates complete with 'this side up' and accompanying arrows printed on them, or even just thick plastic sheeting. Inside there might be some poor wooden benches and maybe desks, and sometimes there are sufficient, reasonable-looking desks and benches for all. Invariably, the only teaching-learning equipment is the blackboard and chalk. A lightbulb receiving electricity would be a rare luxury, and a ceiling fan almost unheard of. The stifling humidity of Lagos and the horrifying stillness of the air in tiny, unventilated schools tucked between larger buildings without a breath of air movement have made the sweat course down my body while I tried to interview head teachers about their work. The languid atmosphere that resulted from these circumstances was entirely natural; it was difficult to imagine having to really work and try hard in such conditions.

In Lagos I have followed on the heels of a local along cat walks of wooden planks over foetid flood and lagoon water, to find such schools, tucked away in all manner of circumstances. One day in Makoko, my research colleagues called me urgently to where they were, to visit a school whose circumstances they clearly felt had crossed some invisible, undefinable line and were inhabiting the educational and physical depths. The school was approached along a relatively wide and open path that was strangely springy underfoot – the footing had far more 'give' than it should have had, if it had been solid earth, and the 'give' was entirely different from the instability under foot of mud or sand. This particular place on the edge of the Lagos Lagoon had a quality to it different from other places I have spent time – what we were walking on was a sickening mix of food packaging, the ubiquitous flimsy, single-use small plastic bags that come with everything you buy even if the thing is for immediate consumption; these items were mixed with all sorts of rubbish and waste, mixed with mud and sand and God knows what else to make this strange, ugly, springy, unstable ground. No one could build a solid structure here. This corner of Makoko had a dispiriting, post-apocalyptic air to it, and as we approached the school on the left, we came to a large dumping ground directly opposite it.

The school itself was a simple makeshift structure with a pitched roof of corrugated sheets, as so many had. The front was made of plywood sheets whitewashed, and there were no windows. The door was shut against the stink of the dump. We entered through the unmarked door into a fairly large open space inside. Some of the sides of this school had thick plastic sheeting for walls, the slick black making the place feel somewhat hellish. There were blackboards on stands on the unfinished, earthen floor roughly dividing the space and there were children sitting in tighter or looser knots between the blackboards. Some had the languid posture of loiterers and it was not always clear who was a teacher and who was a student, although this latter difficulty was far from unique to this school. In my career of visiting hundreds of these schools, it was one of the most depressing for its air of chaos and abandonment. There were a few young adults pottering about, and we spoke to one young man who appeared to be a teenager but who informed us that the school was under his charge.

Throughout my career of private school hunting, no matter how poor the structure, some element of organization and effort on the part of teachers usually made it clear why parents would choose to spend money to send their children there. But on this occasion I struggled with my own inner dismay and turmoil, having to present a calm, un-wondering and professional demeanour. I wondered what could have prompted parents to choose *this*, when, in this dense, urban setting there were private schools all over the place. As part of the research project my team and I were going back to schools that we visited, where the staff had been interviewed, to hold further interviews but this time with parents of pupils. I had to keep my composure when asking the question from the questionnaire I myself had designed, 'how did you decide to send your child to *this school*, out of all of the schools in the area?', when inside I was incredulous: '*why on earth are you sending your children here?!*' The usual answer to the straightforward question is to do with perceived good quality, proximity to home and affordability of the fees. But sometimes a relationship with the head teacher emerges as a factor, as it did in this case: they said that the owner of the school was the pastor of their church, and the young man in charge was the younger brother of this pastor. I was relieved that there was at least *a reason* of sorts, and that these parents hadn't chosen this school on its 'merits' – they chose it for relational reasons, despite the depressing air in the place, and the horrific and unhealthy location. And it was why the young man could get away with allowing such a chaotic situation to prevail without even seeming to be embarrassed – his brother would not sack him, and the loyal church congregants would fear making too strong a statement by switching schools, or even complaining. This is not the 'positive choice' of school choice proponents' dreams, but there was a logic, and it serves as one of the many ways that school choice might not benefit the child in question all that much – as well as hinting at a largely unaddressed issue, that parents make bad choices for their children not infrequently.[1]

***

What becomes clear from so much time spent walking the slums of so many cities – and rural villages too – is that there is great variety in terms of the conditions in these schools. To outsiders they look poor in every sense – the quality of the infrastructure and facilities; often the demeanour of the teachers; and the children who attend them. They very often lack anything like what an objective imagining of a school, even a modest one, would include. But there is a vast array of schools that differ in their facilities, equipment, staffing, clienteles, popularity, size and degree of seriousness. While I visited many that made my heart sink as the pastor's school did, equally there were many others where the owner and the staff were doing their very best with terribly limited resources, and there were schools at every point on the spectrum in between. Teachers would be with their classes, mostly doing what they could under challenging conditions – some utterly inspired, natural teachers; while others appeared jaded, bored, and wishing themselves anywhere else. Most private school teachers wish to be employed in the government system where little work would be expected of them, and a higher wage with no accountability or oversight, as directly told to me by serving private school teachers.

In densely populated urban environments, cheap private schools exist in what is as close to a pure market as it's possible to get in education: there is a range of options at different price points, there is no monopoly provider, but the element that is lacking is information. There is no transparent way of assessing the 'goods' on offer – in this case the goods being the skill and efficacy of the teacher and management. School owners have to pick and choose between potential candidates for teaching jobs without much to go on save their school certificates and then a trial lesson or two. Teaching qualifications mean little in quite a few countries, where teaching colleges are either 'ghost' institutions or don't offer training of any value, or certificates can be faked. In some places teacher training is better (for some idealized classroom setting), but may or may not prepare teachers for the real world of the type of classroom they will actually face. Ultimately, there is no way at all for parents to judge objectively anything about school quality, and they do not even ask about teacher qualifications. It's something I have taken considerable interest in, how parents make up their minds about a particular neighbourhood school, especially when there are several. Of the hundreds of interviews with head teachers that my research studies have entailed, it is virtually universal that prospective parents come to ask about the costs, and of course in the process, they can have a little look at the school, but nothing is ever asked about the teachers, such as experience, certification or anything else.² To stress this point, *I have never uncovered evidence of one instance of parents scrutinizing the educational quality on offer.*

The employment market for these teachers is not much different from finding someone to do any other sort of casual labour, such as domestic work or working in a shop. 'Teachers wanted' notices are posted on the walls, and word is spread along the grapevine. There is no verifying of qualifications or background checks; there are no contracts and no benefits, no protections for either side, no notice periods and no minimum wage. The bargaining power of schools and teachers depends on whether it's an employer's or a worker's market, and where it is more the latter, teachers change from school to school on a whim, at any time of the semester, and often for a negligible increase in their pitifully low wages. The interests of their current students are not a consideration. Where it's an employer's market, teachers can be dismissed easily for being late or absent, or breaking any rules of the school. However, replacing teachers is a hassle, even if there are many applicants, so too much has been made of teachers' lack of job security in these schools. If teachers are doing even just alright, the school has no real incentive to sack them.

It is hard for outsiders to swallow the fact that teachers – people we like to regard as having near-hero status (at times, when not blaming them for all sorts of things) – can be paid a pittance with zero job security. How can these people be responsible for educating and shaping young minds? How can they be entrusted with the care of children in all their vulnerability? Note that I have not even mentioned child protection – the saving grace here usually being the small size and openness of most schools and the constant oversight of the owner. *How can it happen that this is the best anyone can come up with when such a high priority is put on education, globally?* The simple truth is that where corruption is rife, government services do not function, and people are left to fend for themselves. No one else is looking out for the interests of children, so someone spots a niche to fill, opens a school for local children and parents decide to use them. Tiny, local initiatives have caught on and spread, as it proves immensely popular to be able to bring children and leave them there all day with a teacher who knows their name, and will try to get them to learn something, while the parents go out to earn. The schools look terrible, but they look no more terrible than the communities of which they are a part. As I tried to make evident in the last chapter, children live this way, in poor housing with no sanitation, no water, no power, no rubbish collection, no government-maintained roads, and they go to school and socialize and play in similar conditions.

The reason the conditions are so bad in these schools is that the funding available is so small and often irregular. The parents paying the fees (often late, and often piecemeal) work in the informal sector themselves. Yes, despite being classed as 'middle class' or 'lower-middle-class' in this context, they make a precarious living selling things by the roadside; employed in small shops or running small shops of their own, or doing domestic work or other manual labour. Their wages depend on whether they can get work or whether their hawking brings in money on any given day, and their erratic incomes mean that they tend to buy the necessities of life in tiny, daily-use quantities as and when they can afford to. As in richer countries, poverty is very expensive. The better-off can shop around and buy things like laundry detergent, rice or cooking fuel in bulk. They can buy the materials their children need for school in more cost-effective multi-packs, rather than buying an exercise book here and a pencil there. I was told with wry humour by my colleague in Malawi that a day's-worth packet of charcoal for cooking was called a 'walkman' because it could easily be carried home on foot. Similarly, in Accra, I found pay-daily schools, where parents were charged a few coins per day for their child to attend; on tight days when those coins were not forthcoming, the child would have to follow the parent to the market for the working day to play and sleep under the market stall, or stay home. These daily-fee schools cost more over the course of a term and were no better than schools charging a termly fee, but once again, poverty costs in so many ways.

Ultimately, these schools are clear products and reflections of the contexts from which they have emerged, with all the diversity of the context. I must labour this one point: people living within one 'slum community' are not uniformly poor or deprived while visitors from richer countries seem to see such communities this way. In reality, there are those who live a less precarious life, choosing not to take the risk of moving out to a more expensive area, and there are those fighting to cling to the bottom rung of a ladder they may eventually lose their grip on. Pro-market cheerleaders point enthusiastically to proof that 'even the poor' can afford private schooling, when in actual fact these people, considered the lower-middle class in their communities, struggle terribly to afford the fees and costs – *cutting their bellies*.[3] Fighting tooth-and-nail should not be regarded as reassuring or encouraging because of the stress it brings. The nuance of the picture is everything, and various aspects of this nuance are just wallpapered over to suit particular worldviews – and potential market opportunities.

On the other hand, the child rights and pro-education lobbies argue that these schools are a bad thing: they are of terrible quality, exploiting the hopes and ambitions of poor families as well as exploiting the dearth of opportunities for the poor people who become teachers there. Treating education in this way – as this sort of sacred cow – makes no sense when we international commentators do not get up in arms about other forms of small, informal sector operations that employ people and also take people's hard-earned income. Education is apparently so sacred that no one must make a profit from it – yet corporations across the globe rake in millions from education either directly or for support products and services. Other things which should be considered a human right are the subject of endless profit-orientated transactions, such as the sale of food, housing and healthcare. Indeed, I would argue that the perversion of 'food' that we see daily in the arrays of highly processed junk food that rewires the brains of children and pushes them towards obesity is a far more egregious way of making profit than simply charging a fee for primary schooling.

The key redeeming attribute of these schools, as I would argue the case, is that they are from and of the community, for the community. Even if a person starts a school with the settled intention of making a small profit from it, to support their own living, or to provide employment for family members, the money paid in fees comes from parents in the community and it passes through the school into salaries for teachers who also are part of the community. Those teachers then use their wages to pay for their living expenses in the very same community, and ancillary local businesses earn from the existence of these schools – tailors sew uniforms, local shops sell notebooks, pens and pencils; local builders erect small school buildings. If these schools don't measure up and are unworthy of the child, then the same must be said of every aspect of these children's lives (and correctly so), and the poor conditions in which families currently live must be altered. It is not schooling that is a problem – it is the fact that poor people are, often for systemic reasons, consigned to poverty. We can then zoom out, from the most micro of levels, pulling out for the wider view of a community, to a city or state, to a country, region, continent. There is then the entire international system and the formal rules and arrangements that govern how countries interact, and these rules are stacked against smaller, poorer countries. If we as outsiders have problems with the way these children live and are educated, then we can do something about it by injecting more fairness into international systems that govern trade, and now that also govern how the climate catastrophe is being addressed – but too slowly to be effectual.

***

People often ask what is actually happening at these schools, and what they teach. Poor private schools teach whatever is the prescribed curriculum wherever they happen to be. They have no incentive to teach something different because parents want their children to progress up the educational levels, or at least hope that they might, which means they will one day have to sit national exams. Sometimes there are exams at the end of primary school, but more usually these happen at the end of lower- and upper-secondary levels. Students can only sit such exams if they have learned the national curriculum. Much is made of the potential of private schools to 'innovate', but in all of the poor private schools I have been in, I have not witnessed anything other than traditional teacher-focused 'chalk-talk' methods, where teachers lecture and write on the board and then ask what are usually very simple questions, checking rather superficially for understanding. Questions posed to the class are rather closed-ended, yes or no questions, or questions involving simply repeating back, in a sing-song way, what has been recited repeatedly by the teacher. There is nothing sophisticated or innovative as is often expected of the private sector – just because it is private. There is little change from what has happened in school rooms for decades and probably centuries, with the teacher the key source of information.

Textbooks are a less-common sight than they should be in the classrooms of poor private schools because parents spend all their money on paying school fees (and often these are not paid in full), leaving nothing left over to buy their children essential books and supplies. In the absence of textbooks, children look only to their teachers for knowledge, and this, it turns out, is a dangerous thing because the teachers at private and government schools alike tend not to know very much. Of course, things differ somewhat from place to place, but when researchers from aid organizations or NGOs or universities test teachers, they tend to find that these individuals struggle to pass tests of primary school-level subject content; that they have little idea of pedagogy and don't know how to explain material in different ways when children struggle to understand the first attempt at explanation.[4] Indeed, these teachers do not even know how to figure out whether their students have understood something or not.

As in government schools, a lack of textbooks means much time is taken up with teachers writing on the board things that they need the class to copy into their exercise books. I have spent hours in private school classrooms marvelling at just how little subject matter it is possible to cover over the course of an entire lesson, and how little engagement there might be with students. What is key is that teachers are present and trying, no matter how little might get done. Children seem to find their way to literacy somehow, and to some basic level of numeracy (even if late) – achievements that they might fail to manage at government schools. Conversely, I have been in lively and engaging pre-primary classes in cheap private schools in African (but not Indian) contexts, and by 'classes' I mean dancing, singing and playing – things I have never witnessed in a government classroom at that level.

The generally abysmal state of things comes down to the poor quality of education prevailing in the system as a whole. These cheap private school teachers will have had their own 'education' of whatever sort from somewhere, and when most schools are serving up terrible quality, it means that these schools pay this poor quality forward into the future, educating the teachers of the next generation. It is rather a hopeless situation that defies solutions particularly considering the enormous scale at which these solutions are needed. From my own experience of campaigns in the Global North for social causes, the image that is perpetuated is that money is the problem. The reality for schooling for the poor and lower-middle classes is that not even with money can one buy good-quality education. All the international aid funding in the world would not be able to create, out of thin air, an army of well-educated, well-prepared, motivated teachers to staff all of Pakistan's or Nigeria's schools. Maybe algorithms and robots will provide the solution (and of course people are out there working on that).

***

I've already mentioned them in this chapter, but I stopped cold when I first read Charles Dickens' description of a 'ragged school' in *Our Mutual Friend* of 1865. He describes one such school as being housed in 'a miserable loft in an unsavoury yard, crowded, noisy, and confusing [in which] the teachers had no idea of execution, and a lamentable jumble was the upshot of their kind endeavours'. I instantly knew the smell and the feel of the school he described because, 150 years later, I had been in so many myself – just not in Victorian London. Untrained teachers fight their way through the day, hampered by the entire circumstance of the school, yet for these unfortunate children, there is nothing else, and many are clueless even about how *to be in school* all day – how to sit, how to compose oneself and how to hold a pencil and exercise book, until they, of course, eventually become accustomed to the daily routine. But I have certainly witnessed many a 'lamentable jumble'.

For the three decades leading up to the 1870 Elementary Education Act, which brought about government provision of more uniform, recognizable schools in England, the ragged schools were the only option for the children of the 'perishing and dangerous classes'. They were utterly individual efforts, not comprehensive in what was taught, and did not use trained teachers. They operated in just the types of premises that I have visited schools operating in, in the twenty-first century. They offered a lifeline to many of the children served by them, as there was no other option in their poor, urban environments. Even before ragged schools were required in the ever-denser urban environments brought about by industrialization, the 'dame school' was a common form of private education, started by a literate woman in her home, serving local children. This again is exactly like the modern cheap private schooling phenomenon.

So, the similarities are striking between the English ragged schools and today's poor private schools in so many poor countries. There was the London Ragged School Union, a sort of association of these schools, which is echoed in private school associations specifically for cheaper schools today, and some that specifically serve to stand up for unregistered, illegal cheap private schools, such as Lagos's colourfully named Association for Formidable Educational Development. Back in Dickens' day, the fact that these schools were the only show in town for the children of the poor bothered many social reformers who felt that these schools were not good enough; that they needed to be regulated; that they needed trained teachers and other interventions to uplift them and what they offered. They needed materials, school feeding programmes and better facilities.

And so the similarities continue, with many objecting to the conditions in the poor private schools of the present. The more extreme in the human rights lobby wish for the regulation-to-death of poor private schools, never mind that in many communities, like the ragged schools of 1840–70, it's the only show in town. Those defending ragged schools pointed out that strict regulations would not work in the conditions in which the schools existed. They also pointed to some ostensibly positive aspect of existing beyond the control of bureaucrats and regulators, being down to the drive and determination of individual efforts, which were responsible for the positive aspects of these small endeavours. The head of the London Ragged School Union, Lord Ashley, the 7th Earl of Shaftesbury, argued that 'much of the great effort that has been produced by institutions such as these is attributable to this, – that they have been undertaken by voluntary agents acting upon their own principles, guided by their own judgment. I am sure that nothing could be worse than to have all brought down to a uniform system'.

He felt that under the 'icy touch' of regulation, the schools would wither away, and so the Union held to the position that it was better to operate under limitations than risk an 'unhappy remodelling' through externally imposed regulations.[5] And so the ragged schools went on for some time, for as long as they could before the 1870 Act came into force. Those that could and wanted to struggled to meet the regulations and became elementary education schools. But many were unable to meet the new regulations and so transferred their students elsewhere and closed their doors.

Dickens loved a good ghost story, and when I read the history of educational efforts from the 1960s, the 1860s and even earlier, it makes current developments seem like walking with ghosts – like the ghosts swirling around us that we do not see, whom Jacob Marley temporarily renders visible to Scrooge in *A Christmas Carol*. What is happening today is but an echo of things that have already been, like the ghost of schooling past, and we appear to be doomed to repeat history over and over without learning from past mistakes. If only those engaged in the struggle over education could be visited by education's version of Jacob Marley, to jolt us into listening to the lessons we should already have learned but have turned away from.

Whether or not there is any hope to be taken from what transpired in Victorian England is unclear. What is clear now is that the ragged schools provided a crisis response to a need born out of poverty and neglect that was not being filled by public efforts at that time. Then, as now, those suffering in poverty were put there and kept there by the wealthy and industrial, wielding power over them. In Victorian Britain, as pressure to act built, the government finally came through to provide schools that must have eventually proved sufficient in quality and accessibility. Poor private schools today are the crisis response in poor countries to governments' failings in a situation where international systems do not help them to rise economically. Another parallel keeps coming to my mind in the single-track dirt road that used to serve Gaurav's ancestral village in rural, western Uttar Pradesh, to the nearest paved road. My father-in-law had decided that he did not want to deal with a road that would often turn into a mud bath, and so decades ago he bricked the road so that it would remain at least passable all year long, including during the monsoon. It was bumpy and certainly not up to 'standard' for a public road, but it helped bridge a matter of decades, until just recently, in 2021, the road was finally tarred over by the government. I think of these schools – the ragged schools of 180 years ago and the cheap, poor private schools of today – as a very imperfect stop-gap or interim measure (like the bumpy, bricked road) until something better is ushered in, and it seems this would usually be the preserve of government (just as they were behind the proper paving of the road).

However today the challenges are many times greater; they are immense. As I have mentioned, there are nowhere near enough well-educated people to become teachers worthy of the name, and the population pressure on schooling systems in terms of expanding the offering and expanding the budget to meet it is more than what governments can withstand.[6] Many parts of the world are experiencing a demographic transition, but in the poorest places on earth, in Sub-Saharan Africa, populations are still growing, and so countries fall ever further behind in terms of the numbers of good teachers available in relation to growing numbers of children.[7] These challenges are daunting indeed – much greater than simply getting the funds, men and equipment together to pave a narrow road – and are almost never accepted fully by those interested and acting in this strange field of international education and human rights advocacy. There is no quick fix, and the key area where the parallel lines of ragged schools and cheap private schools suddenly diverge is the fact that the former were a response to no attempts at all to provide universal education. Today's cheap private schools, on the other hand, have grown up in response to efforts to provide universal access but which have failed miserably. Where do we go from here when no sudden effort under the auspices of a new Education Act like that of 1870 can save the day?

***

Something that has not been expanded on yet is how these schools appear in rural villages, which they do although much less frequently than in cities. Suffice it to say that they are largely similar, though much less common and perhaps even more rudimentary than they are in towns. Village schools only have competition from other schools to the extent that there is a sufficient number of local children to support more than one school, something that is much more often the case in India than in sub-Saharan Africa. I have hunted for these schools in rural Ghana, Nigeria and Ivory Coast, with varying levels of success. For the rest of the book, the basic image that the reader should bear with them is of a small, rough school with a few teachers, often unqualified (or qualified but not in a meaningful way) and very often under-prepared and under-paid, doing what they can with manageably sized classes but few materials and little pedagogical and even subject knowledge. The picture varies quite considerably depending on several factors, but is nevertheless a valid, basic image to hold.

6

Damage and Loss: What Empire Did to Education in India

And how did countries get where they are today, with the non-affluent pushed to search out private solutions to what is considered a public problem (education)? Why do people in the Global South seek and struggle to implement effectively a shape and system of education that is culturally alien? Europeans managed to over-run great swathes of the world with superior transportation and firepower, in search of riches, originally through trade but ending in the human catastrophe of empire. William Dalrymple's recent work, *The Anarchy*, sets out the road to Imperial India, from the origins of the East India Company, started in London in 1600, to government-run 'empire' in India by 1877, which would last until the middle of the twentieth century, well into the lifetimes of my parents. From these days formal religion seems to have stuck in Africa and elsewhere, but perhaps less universally than the near-religious fervour for education in the form that we envision it today.

What happened through the process of colonization was that local ways of educating young people and initiating them into adulthood, which were the accepted, context-appropriate practices for people, came to be viewed as unworthy in comparison with the limited education systems the rulers instituted to staff their colonial administrations with 'natives'. The exclusivity of these schools, which came to be seen as the avenue to more comfortable, better-paid work in the bureaucracy, helped lend cachet to this form of schooling, and what was done locally now looked a distant second best. The elephant in the room is the obvious dearth of office jobs that are expected to result from pursuing education, often leaving the educated young adult with a second- or third-rate certificate or degree that has rendered him or her mentally unfit to fall back on farming or any other traditional, artisanal way of making a living.

***

It's commonly told that education was largely introduced to the colonies by religious missionaries. However, the picture is more complicated, with much missionary schooling following eventual decisions by the colonial authorities to allow this to happen. As Carnoy states, 'the spread of schooling was carried out in the context of imperialism and colonialism – in the spread of mercantilism and capitalism – and it cannot in its present form and purpose be separated from that context'.[1] Carnoy discusses in detail how the structure of the schools introduced was not dictated by religion, but based on the needs of the colonizers' investors, traders and culture; those of 'the metropole' or 'the centre' as various writers refer to the colonizing and dictating powers of the past and today.

> Western schools were used to develop indigenous elites which served as intermediaries between metropole merchants and plantation labour; they were used to incorporate indigenous peoples into the production of goods necessary for metropole markets; they were used to help change social structures to fit in with European concepts of work and interpersonal relationships; and, within advanced capitalist economies such as the United States, schools were used to fit white workers and, later, disenfranchised minorities into economic and social roles defined by the dominant capitalist class.[2]

And yet formal education is now portrayed as a liberating force, while the earlier veneer of saving souls through bringing the Bible, or the 'civilising mission' of empire was all added later.

Philip Coombs wrote in the 1960s that the 'social demand' for education in colonized countries was growing wildly in the post–Second World War era, through to independence and beyond. This growing demand built from foundations laid during early colonial administrative takeovers has resulted from the 'demonstration effect' of people seeing a very small number of their peers become literate; learning to speak the language of the colonizers; getting jobs with them and entering what is perceived as the inner circle; thereby removing themselves from hard toil under a hot sun. The allure of education grew from a tiny kernel, based on the fact that it is a necessary condition for a person to get a steady salaried position with the civil service, which developed a sophisticated and privileged mystique. But of course, while it is necessary, it is far from sufficient to guarantee the winning of such a role. But the chance was enough, and this very demonstration effect and many individuals' irrational hopes against all odds continue today, demonstrated through the lengths people will go to secure civil service employment. The allure of schooling has endured, despite the unlikelihood of succeeding in steady civil service employment, and the casualties are those who don't make it, but become mentally unfit for traditional occupations. Their great expectations and adjusted mental models bar them from ever going back.

***

The historical case of India is in equal measures fascinating and tragic. While all colonized societies had their ways of doing things that were undermined and sometimes eradicated via colonization, India had what we can recognize now as a system of education that was sophisticated and also highly contextually and culturally relevant, because it was created from within the society to prepare young people for life. The British Empire ended centuries of educational tradition, choking it off and eventually stamping it out. Today's depressing and dispiriting education system in India resulted from what the British did, and it is very hard to see any way out of the horrors of today's terrible government schools, and the mind-numbing profit and exams focus of middle-class and elite private schooling.

Having lived in India, having worked in education in India, having done my doctoral fieldwork in India and having married into an Indian family at the age of 25, I never applied my mind to the question of what had existed, educationally speaking and otherwise, before the British arrived. Gaurav frequently railed about the loss of the ancient universities, such as Taxila (approximately 3,600 years old), which were burned by earlier invaders. The library of one ancient university was said to have burned for a month or more due to the enormous store of priceless documents it contained. It strikes me as quite bizarre now that, despite knowing this story, I never thought about what sort of education children would have experienced to prepare them for university-level education over three and a half millennia ago. It is likely that the international education and development industry is stacked with people like me who never thought or worried about what our ancestors had pushed aside in their hubris and ignorance. Perhaps they would have thought, well, there is no use crying over spilt milk, and now we have to deal with the situation as we find it now: people want education; their governments are too poor, corrupt, unmotivated, unaccountable or incompetent to give them what they want. Cue: White Saviour Mark II (or III? There have been several iterations). But there is a fatal error here. We cannot know how to avoid repeating terrible, criminal mistakes, when we do not know what our forebears did.

***

Strangely, I have found that I was only one step removed from a great historian of Indian education, society and colonial administration, Dharampal,[3] who spent extended periods of time in the archives in India and Britain to dig into what the British had documented about Indian education that was thriving at the time the British first came to the sub-continent. The British started to concern themselves with questions of education long before the territories held by the East India Company were taken over by the British government, which may seem surprising when education would ostensibly appear to be outside the remit of a commercial entity – but then, no more so than taxation and military matters would be.

An interesting entry point to the meat of the story Dharampal tells is via another graduate of St Andrews University who completed his degree in 1774,[4] one Reverend Dr Andrew Bell. It is through his work that we learn that cultural exchange and learning from other parts of the world have not always been one-way, from 'developed' North to poor South, or West to East, colonizer to colonized. Dr Bell travelled to Chennai (then called Madras) in India in 1787, later to bring back an educational method that was already centuries-old by the time he encountered it in Madras – the much-used Indian peer-learning method of primary education which he dubbed the Madras System (or the 'monitorial system', an off-shoot of which was called the Lancastrian System, for use in Britain and Europe) to be applied in British schools. He also went on to found Madras College in St. Andrews in 1833, which exists to this day, and which I used to walk past on a regular basis when I was studying in St Andrews. Even had I guessed that Indian communities were providing an organized and systematic form of education to their children for centuries at the time that the British were slowly gaining a stranglehold on the sub-continent, I would not have guessed that the method might have been so effective that it would be considered good enough for British children and applied back home.

But Dr Bell was not the first European to encounter and document Indian education at work. A Portuguese traveller to Tkkeri on the Malabar coast wrote in his travel journal on 22 November 1623, about the classes that Indian children were engaged in. Dharampal wrote that other sources document this method of learning having been conducted for two thousand years previously, meaning that it was contemporaneous with the ancient universities of India. This only stands to reason, as children would require good school-level education to be prepared for university. The schools of 1623 and later, when Dr Bell arrived, consisted of four classes under one teacher. In each of the four groups or learning levels, those who had learned the material most thoroughly supported the others. Early writing practice was done using a stick or finger in fine sand spread over a board starting with letters only; as children's skills progressed, so they graduated to using increasingly more sophisticated writing materials. Literacy and numeracy were mastered, along with crucial skills of keeping accounts, measuring land and many other subjects (including key religious texts) and skills.

Children would join the school for the first time ranging from age 5 to age 8, usually spending years in this primary phase of their education and spending many hours per day in school. Beyond this phase, there were elementary schools and colleges of higher learning, providing a staggering array of subjects. A large number of British commentators cited in Dharampal's work note that it was 'widely known' or acknowledged that there were (primary) schools in every village and several in the larger villages. Elementary schools and colleges necessarily meant that students had to travel further or live away from home, much like today in many places. Contrary to a common perception of how caste works in India, children of lower castes participated with those 'above' them in caste status in schools. For the most part, only boys attended these village schools, but girls and women were far from left out of learning; they would be educated in the home just as in Britain at that time – Hindu and Muslim alike. British officialdom acknowledged at the time that participation rates were similar to those prevailing in Britain and other European powers, while the amount of education each child received (in terms of years but also the length of the school day) was apparently considerably greater in India than in Britain.

The village schools had originally been supported through what we would call tax revenues gathered at the local level (mostly to pay the teacher), while most did not have a school building as such but were granted space within the village to meet. Of course, in rural India, and (I am sure) even in towns in centuries past, the vast majority of living is done outdoors, so the lack of a formalized school building would not have been something to remark at. Some schools were given funding or grants of land from the local nobility or king. The teacher would also receive support from the parents of his charges in the form of grain or small payments. Dharampal notes that 'the sophisticated operative fiscal arrangements of the pre-British Indian polity' made this possible; 'through these fiscal measures, substantial proportions of revenue had long been assigned for the performance of a multiplicity of public purposes. These seem to have stayed more or less intact through all the previous political turmoils and made such education possible. The collapse of this arrangement through a total centralisation of revenue, as well as politics led to decay in the economy, social life, education, etc'.[5] These arrangements were not able to survive the British with their excessively heavy taxation that removed the financial foundations for these complex and fairly comprehensive pro-social systems – and of course, the British were interested exclusively in financial gain. They overwhelmed a society in which learning had historically been extremely important. In describing the people of the Malabar region, whose learning was apparently more 'limited' than that of the 'central people' of India, Dharampal writes:

> They are particularly anxious and attentive to instruct their children to read and to write. Education with them is an early and an important business in every family. Many of their women are taught to read and write. The Bramans [sic] are generally the school masters, but any of the respectable casts may, and often do, practice teaching. The children are instructed without violence, and by a process peculiarly simple. It is the same system which has caused so much heat and controversy, as to the inventors of it, in this country and the merit of which was due to neither of the claimants.[6] The system was borrowed from the Bramans and brought from India to Europe. It has been made the foundation of national schools in every enlightened country. Some gratitude is due to a people from whom we have learnt to diffuse among the lower ranks of society instruction by one of the most unerring and economical methods which has ever been invented. The pupils are the monitors of each other, and the characters are traced with a rod, or the finger on the sand. Reading and writing are acquired at the same time, and by the same process. This mode of teaching however is only initial. If the pupil is meant to study the higher branches of learning, he is removed from these primary schools, where the arts of reading, writing and accounts are acquired, and placed under more scientific masters. It is to these elementary schools that the labouring classes in India owe their education. It gives them access, from the introduction of the system into this part of the world: advantage which the same classes in Europe, only now partially conferred on them a superior share of intelligence and placed them in a situation to perform better all the duties of life.[7]

Four-hundred years ago, and two centuries before the British would adopt the Indian method of education, Peter Della Valle published an account of this mode of instruction in Malabar. He wrote from Tkkeri, 22 November 1623.

> 'In the meantime' he says 'while the burthens were getting in order, I entertained myself in the porch of the temple, beholding little boys learning arithmetic after a strange manner, which I will here relate. They were four, and having all taken the same lesson before the master, to get that same by heart, and repeat likewise their former lessons, and not forget them, one of them singing musically with a certain continued tone, (which had the force of making a deep impression in

the memory) recited part of the lesson: as for example, 'one by itself makes one'; and whilst he was thus speaking, he writ down the same number, not with any kind of pen, nor in paper, but (not to spend paper in vain) with his finger on the ground, the pavement being for that purpose strewed all over with fine sand; after the first had wrote what he sung, all the rest sung and writ down the same thing together. Then the first boy sung, and writ down another part of the lesson; as, for example, two by itself makes two, which all the rest repeated in the same manner; and so forward in order. When the pavement was full of figures, they put them out with the hand, and if need were, strewed it with new sand from a little heap which they had before them wherewith to write further. And this they did as long as the exercise continued; in which manner likewise they told one, they learnt to read and write without spoiling paper, pens or ink, which certainly is a pretty way. I asked them, if they happen to forget or be mistaken in any part of the lesson, who corrected and taught them, they being all scholars without the assistance of any master; they answered me, and said true, that it was not possible for all four to forget or mistake in the same part, and that they thus exercised together, to the end, that if one happened to be out, the other might correct him. Indeed a pretty, easy and secure way of learning.[8]

An early nineteenth-century observer of India, cited in Dharampal, noted 'no people probably appreciate more justly the importance of instruction than the Hindoos [sic]; hence instead of offering obstacles or creating opposition to the establishment of schools, they have formed institutions themselves to meet various cases of ignorance and misery. They are not averse to a spirit of enquiry and discussion. All they wanted was a government that would not check and discourage this spirit.'[9]

At the time that the East India Company was moving in on India, some of those participating in and influenced by the Edinburgh Enlightenment, presumably including men like Dr Bell, felt a drive to engage with and preserve indigenous knowledge. Indeed, William Dalrymple details in his book White Mughals how the early British in India were prone to 'going native', adopting Indian customs and not infrequently marrying Indian women and starting families with little drive to return to Britain.[10] However, this early instinct gave way to the more forceful interest of financial gain. Presumably, allowing sympathy, empathy and even regard for local people to creep in would have meant difficulty in extracting as much profit from the country as possible. As the British grip tightened on India, and as much more uptight and self-righteous Victorian sensibilities succeeded those of the Georgian Enlightenment era, the authorities decided to exert more control over affairs outside of mere trade.

Yet it was the entrepreneurial spirit that indirectly dealt the slow but fatal blow to India's schools, which numbered, apparently, just about as many as India's villages and possibly more as larger villages were said to have several schools. When the British started squeezing tax revenues out of India, the local tax funds that had hitherto gone to supporting schools were diverted to a foreign, private corporation with an army, and so India's schools were slowly starved to death.

It is several decades into this shrivelling process that we find the first hard data on the existing education system that Education Management Information System specialists like me (as I was titled for my first job in Nigeria) would recognize as 'school census data', indispensable to education system planning everywhere. The data collection that took place across the 1820s and 1830s was spurred by a long-running debate in the House of Commons in 1813 regarding a clause in the India Charter Bill relating to the 'Propagation of Christianity in India' – that is, the 'religious and moral improvement' of Indians. Our UK- and World Bank-approved approach of today was born in Colonial times: 'Before any new policy could be devised, the existing position needed to be known better',[11] which meant that some more formalized data collection was required. It would not be sufficient to rely on the reports of officials like Thomas Munro, who 'had observed that "every village had a school"' or Prendergast of the Presidency of Bombay who stated that 'there is hardly a village, great or small, throughout our territories, in which there is not at least one school, and in larger villages more'.[12] Prendergast was writing from the perspective that to spend money on educating the locals was undesirable, but his point was allowed to stand (in Parliament). Similar reports emanated from Punjab.

Dharampal's dive into the meticulous records of the British shows a vast coverage of village schools – referred to by some as 'the legend of the 100,000 schools' of remarkably high quality, providing for an educational situation in 1800 in India more advanced than in England at that time, considering that public education did not start in earnest until 1870. According to the collector of Madras, 'it is generally admitted that before they (i.e. the students) attain their 13th year of age, their acquirements in the various branches of learning are uncommonly great'.[13] In addition, what Dharampal terms in his understated way as 'a kind of revelation' is the fact that contrary to assumptions, lower-caste and 'low-class' Hindu and Muslim children were being educated alongside their higher caste and elite Muslim peers. Perhaps most crucially, to contextualize the account recorded by the British, Dharampal notes that by the time of the data collection, 'it is a greatly damaged and disorganized India that one is referring to'.[14] This is because decades of slow starvation and squeezing of India's systems of taxation and public services had already taken place, with funds systematically siphoned off to Britain to build stately country houses and the elegant Edinburgh New Town,[15] from which I am writing these words.

It is the destruction of this system from around 1750 onwards (the destruction gathering steam in the 1780s[16]) that meant that by the time the British collected their schooling data in the 1820s and later, what they were cataloguing was a system already much diminished. In Madras in 1826, while girls were mostly being educated within their family settings and data on this was not collected in detail, the estimate of the share of boys receiving education at school was around a third while another estimate was that the number of boys educated at home could be up to five times the number attending school, a figure to rival or surpass the reach of education in Europe at the time.

To be clear about what Dharampal documented, at the time that the British arrived in India, there was a functioning, largely publicly funded but decentralized, locally managed education system in India that allowed those able and interested students, even from amongst the poor, to study to a high level in a wide range of subjects. Those who participated in the more basic levels of education finished their learning well-equipped with the skills needed for their daily lives – including work. At this point, the British desire to squeeze as much profit out of India as possible led to the destruction of the system of people and institutions getting funding to perform various public tasks such as teaching, medicine, feeding pilgrims, etc. Taxes were raised by the British while at the same time the amount that these original assignees of revenues received was greatly reduced. The fraction (in some cases as low as 7 per cent of the previous sum[17]) of what they used to get meant that they were no longer able to perform their public tasks in the manner they had been performing them only some decades previously. Some had their funds entirely removed and were reduced to beggary. Many of the old functions like teaching and medicine had to be given up because of want of fiscal support, which led to British officials estimating that the numbers of village schools had shrunk considerably by the time of their data collection. Collector A.D. Campbell of Bellary provided a detailed and damning indictment of East India Company misrule and its effects in August 1823. In a lengthy report, the first seventeen paragraphs of which are used partly in stating that the imitation of Indian pedagogical methods in Britain was well-founded; partly in describing the current defects in the system, he continued thus[18]:

> 18. I am sorry to state that this is ascribable to the gradual but general impoverishment of the country. The means of the manufacturing classes have been, of late years greatly diminished, by the introduction of our own European

manufactures, in lieu of the Indian cotton fabrics. The removal of many of our troops, from our own territories, to the distant frontier of our newly subsidized allies, has also, of later years, affected the demand for grain, the transfer of the capital of the country, from the Native Governments, and their Officers, who liberally expended it in India, to the Europeans, restricted by law from employing it even temporarily in India, and daily draining it from the land, has likewise tended to this effect which has not been alleviated by a less rigid enforcement of the revenue due to the state. The greater part of the middling and lower classes of the people are now unable to defray the expenses incident upon education of their offspring, while their necessities require the assistance of their children as soon as their tender limbs are capable of the smallest labour.[19]

19. It cannot have escaped the Government that of nearly a million of souls in this district, not 7,000 are now at school; a proportion which exhibits but too strongly the result above stated. In many villages, where formerly there were schools, there are now none; and in many others, where there were large schools, now only a few of the children of the most opulent are taught, others being unable, from poverty, to attend or to pay what is demanded.

As B.D. Basu wrote, wherever the British had 'swept away the village system, there the village school has also disappeared'. It is hard to truly grasp the scale of the British pillage, to reduce India to this level, when it had contained the richest place on earth, modern day Bihar, which is now considered a basket case of under-development.

***

But not to worry, the British were keen to fix the mess (the mess of their own making) and, in fact, fix it in a way that was better than what 'the natives' had before. Into the breach steps possibly the first model of the often-spotted international education consultant,[20] and certainly a candidate for providing the early but enduring pattern of the 'development professional', Sir Thomas Munro, Governor of the Madras Presidency from 1819. As part of the revenue consultations of the government, in 1826, Munro outlined his plan for education over the course of nine sizeable paragraphs taking up four modern printed pages. His 'minute' outlined the need in terms of the estimated number of children to be educated aged between five and ten years. He outlines the gaping holes in provision which he ascribed to 'shifting of the population, from war and other causes' – quite the euphemism for the ravages of the British and French. He outlined strategic or planning flaws, stating that the large number of village schools that had existed meant that no school would really excel in terms of quality, and stated therefore that it would be preferable to have fewer schools that would then be able to attract more students and better-quality teachers through competition (yes, indeed, he noted that the better teachers would attract more families willing to pay fees in his planned 'cost-sharing' model; and yes, this is an 1820s civil servant, not a 1980s World Bank staffer). He decided that 'better quality' teachers were needed, trained in British teacher training colleges to be established as part of his plan. These fewer and better-quality teachers would also be better-paid through British tax revenues (collected locally of course – supplemented by whatever fees the teachers could collect).

There is much concern in the document regarding the anticipated costs of bringing a more British-style education to the natives, despite the tax revenues in question being extorted from the local Indian population. But something that is curious is the insight that Munro showed as a side issue in the consideration of the funds necessary – he stated that 'this expense will be incurred only by degrees, because it will be long before a sufficient number of qualified teachers can be obtained'; furthermore, he cited, with approbation, the assessment of the Calcutta School-Book Society that the operation of the new system 'must therefore of necessity be slow; years must elapse before the rising generation will exhibit any visible improvement'.[21]

This plan of a newer, more British model of education, with 'proper' school buildings and professional teacher training, was instituted extremely slowly, as predicted by Munro. The British 'reforms' (following on from the slow starvation of the system that had started in the mid-eighteenth century) devastated Indian schooling participation, with numbers enrolled recovering back to 1822 levels (i.e. an already much-contracted level as compared to the pre-British era and as reported by Collector Campbell of Bellary) only after 1890. This was possibly the first needless demolition of a system that was serving very well the needs and wants of the people. It is likely the first time that 'white saviours' swooped in to save people impoverished by the saviours' own policies that had rendered the victims unmoored from their historical foundations. It is this early instance of 'development assistance' and 'aid' and its abysmal failure that led Gandhi to speak these words at Chatham House, London, on 20 October 1931:

> I say without fear of my figures being challenged successfully, that today India is more illiterate than it was fifty or a hundred years ago, and so is Burma, because the British administrators, when they came to India, instead of taking hold of things as they were, began to root them out. They scratched the soil and began to look at the root, and left the root like that, and the beautiful tree perished. The village schools were not good enough for the British administrator, so he

came out with his programme. Every school must have so much paraphernalia, building, and so forth. Well, there were no such schools at all. There are statistics left by a British administrator which show that, in places where they have carried out a survey, ancient schools have gone by the board, because there was no recognition for these schools, and the schools established after the European pattern were too expensive for the people, and therefore they could not possibly overtake the thing. I defy anybody to fulfil a programme of compulsory primary education of these masses inside of a century. This very poor country of mine is ill able to sustain such an expensive method of education.

The prescience of Gandhi's words regarding the future of 'education for all', based on the experience of his own country, is chilling. As I write this, there are seven years left until a century will have passed since he spoke the above words at Chatham House, and recent years have seen only a decline in true education amongst 'these masses' in India, with all those who can afford to do so, jumping ship from government schools to private schools of possibly only slightly better quality. But what Munro surprisingly got right in his misguided plan to 'fix' what his colleagues even more misguidedly broke, and a century before Gandhi's speech, was this: that education should only expand as and when properly able teachers can be found or educated, and then prepared for the role. There is no suggestion in his writing that speed, scaling up and urgency should outweigh the drive to do things properly (no matter that he was ill-equipped to pass judgement on education matters). *This is a crucial point*: India's 'indigenous' or original education system had 'scaled', but had done so over centuries and likely millennia and as a result, it really worked. Furthermore, he observes that what the Calcutta School-Book Society, however misguided they too will surely have been in meddling where they did not belong, said was correct: that the course of education runs slow, and that one cannot expect quick results in and from education.

So, our modern international education and development consultancy industry has much to learn from the colonial trailblazers of two centuries ago, and yet this history is mostly hidden, and we are doomed to repeat the same mistakes – adding new ones as well. I would argue that, first and foremost, the aid industry has no hope of success, just as Munro's plans were destined for failure. My Northern people have, for the most part, laid the foundations for many of the problems that need fixing, in a formidable case of *déjà vu*. A new plan to leave well enough alone would, of course, need to be based on the recognition of the fact that rich countries continue to cause problems in the countries that they meddle with.

The clearest historical parallel with the last twenty years from what Dharampal catalogued is what Indian parents did when their collectively funded schools ceased to serve them after the British choked off all support. Those who could afford to do so paid the school teacher to keep going. So, the village school became a small private school like those we see today. This meant that the numbers participating were small, and they were drawn from the better-off in society only. Those who could not pay were simply left behind – and it must be recalled that there will have been many (most?) who could not pay due directly to the impoverishment that happened to them at the hands of the British, for example, through the ruination of their hitherto world-renowned textile industry. James Tooley, a one-time enthusiastic writer and commentator on the subject of cheap private schooling, highlights this issue in his book that he named after Dharampal's work: *The Beautiful Tree*[22] (in turn borrowed from Gandhi). He provides an incorrect interpretation of the evidence from the later times (well into the nineteenth century) when a much-diminished number of schools was forced to run on user fees because their funding had disappeared. He ignores that this, as with today's cheap private schools, was only a crisis response and that the best era of Indian education, when there were one or more schools thriving in almost every village, was one of *municipal funding*.[23] Before the British there was nearly full coverage of schools funded from revenues. In the time of crisis that ensued, the only functional schools were those running on user fees. *This is exactly as today*, except there hasn't been any recent, modern era where collectively funded schools were both functional and ubiquitous in India.

***

India provides the prime example of the destructive legacy of colonialism – this legacy has affected the very form of the constitution of the country, language and culture, and the core institutions of society, including education. There was a complete dislocation in society. Colonial destruction is such that the developmental paths that people across the world were following, appropriate to their own environments and cultures, are lost forever. There is no going back to a world pre-globalization, a process that probably started meaningfully with the early voyages by sea for exploration and then trade. The intricate, reciprocal trade relations and connections between peoples on the African continent that were appropriate and mutually beneficial were destroyed by the terrible draw towards the coasts due to the distorting and degrading curiosity of trade with the Europeans, bringing guns and booze in return for souls to be transported across the ocean. The destruction to societal ways and systems meted out by the British in India far surpassed, in a relatively short time, what change and destruction were brought by the Mughal invaders, who at least settled in India and made a future there and so didn't want to comprehensively destroy what they found in India. Indeed, Britain's impoverishment of India meant the introduction of child labour when families were desperate, and when schools had ceased to function anyway – a legacy of shame for Britain.

So then, here we are, well into the twenty-first century having sold a very Eurocentric model of education, along with other forms of governance, to the countries we messed up through our own rapacious greed – we now continue the interference rebranded as 'aid' or 'development assistance'. The breadth and importance of this situation is enormous, and this chapter is able only to scratch the surface of it. It had to be explained here to show how the twenty-first century is not the first time that small fee-dependent schools emerged as a response to a crisis largely instigated by meddling rich countries: history is repeating, in the form of today's cheap private schools, and the meddling of outsiders in this situation.

7

Well-intentioned (?) Blundering in 'Advising' National Governments

The last chapter has shown historically what came of the interference of outsiders who thought they knew better and had better ways of doing things than local people. As Gandhi stated in 1931, the British 'came out with their plan', and decreed that every school needed to have 'so much paraphernalia'. He highlighted that to meet the specifications set out by the British would cost an enormous sum – much more than the locals' economical ways of doing things – and that it was too much for India to bear. The implications of this for today's practice of education planning, governance and aid donors' roles in doling out advice are many, varied, and significant, but mostly unheeded.

In the face of the challenges and contradictions already outlined in this book, the next question is, what have the governments of these countries been advised in their post-colonial incarnations by their supposedly more knowledgeable counterparts in the North? What assistance have countries been given to address the extreme mismatch between the aspiration for education and modern sector work, and the countries' current capacity to supply these? It could be supposed that caution and restraint might be advised, and that the virtues of planning and laying proper foundations for any development might have been noted. It would not have taken a particularly sharp analytical mind to perceive that if mass education has not yet existed, and the average educational level of the population is very low, then the finding of suitable teachers would most likely present a conundrum.

I know of several senior colleagues in the field who are now academics or practitioners who were, in their young adulthoods, teachers in countries in Africa. My father-in-law received his university engineering training from German academics who came to teach at Indian universities in the 1950s. There was clearly a perceived need for bringing in suitably educated people to serve as teachers where there just weren't enough people who had been through the colonial type of education that everyone now wanted to see expanding at breakneck speed. I have already cited various reports written by Western commentators in the 1960s who observed the dearth of suitable teacher candidates. Even the colonial authorities in early nineteenth-century India realized that the key constraint to educational expansion was the availability of proper teachers. And yet countries have not been advised caution – that accepting unqualified people into what is *a profession* would dilute whatever quality existed and drive learning levels down. Nothing in this chapter should be read as denigrating the capabilities of people in the countries I have been lucky to have worked in. They have inherited exceptionally difficult circumstances after decades of exploitation and impoverishment, to emerge onto an international scene that favours already rich and powerful countries. These countries face terrible odds with many still facing significant population growth that means that every year more teachers and more budget is required just to stand still, never mind to make progress in education. I don't shy away from describing problems truthfully, while I have appreciated every moment of my career that has brought me to the countries that I write about.

***

Indeed, rich countries advised the officials in poor countries to expand access, piling on the pressure like beings demented. All children should be in school – irrespective of whether the schools teach anything; whether they teach anything relevant and of value to the children and their future life opportunities; whether there are any suitable jobs to 'absorb' people whose expectations have been raised through schooling participation; and whether or not any foundations for such a mass system have been laid. Words like 'crisis' and 'urgent' are bandied about. Daft estimates are deployed to try to get the attention of the public, no matter how flimsy the basis of the various numbers – such as the percentage increase in all sorts of positive life outcomes that are meant to result from X number of additional years of schooling for every girl (or boy)[1]. On the one hand, the extreme lack of learning amongst school-going children is acknowledged and noted; on the other hand, it is absolutely necessary to get all children into schools – now – schools that can't even cope with the students they already have.

There has been a relatively sudden latching onto the idea of formal education as a way into a more 'modern' or westernized way of living and working for some pretty large segments of societies globally. On the other hand, there have been very large numbers of people whose children never see the inside of a classroom, for example, the children of pastoralists in northern Kenya. When I was involved with the planning of a new UK-funded programme of educational support for Kenya, the big question was how to get the children of pastoralists into school. Their way of life was simply not compatible with attending school in a fixed location for nine or ten months of the year, and planners tied themselves in knots to figure out how to square this circle. There was the added complication that population growth was affecting even such communities as theirs: they were finding that – possibly also partly due to climate change – their traditional way of life simply could not support successively larger generations. Some children from most families would have to leave the community to make their way in the world elsewhere, perhaps by migrating to Nairobi or Mombasa, and it is likely that at least some basic education might help them on their way. This was a particular problem that I could not see any clear solution for.

In northern Nigeria, there are also pastoralists, but the majority are more settled peoples. For reasons related to their own particular contexts, many children there continue to fail to attend school, and even more fail to learn even if they have seen the inside of a classroom. Different variations on the same story repeat and repeat from one place to another – while the particular detail and nuance of each story are vital to finding a way forward. Should all these children be persuaded into classrooms and any financial impediments to their schooling participation be removed, the glaring problem remains and even becomes worse: where are the teachers to come from? But this is only a glaring problem if we care about whether or not children are *actually learning*. Especially for public messaging, the working assumption has been that children's key barrier to learning and future success has been failure to make it into school. To explain things, I have to delve into the past a bit, in order to explain how donors and advisors counsel countries in the Global South today.

***

To start with, in the development industry, there is no regard for history. In fact, history is remade in the image or the idea that we hold in the present of what has come before, and one of the biggest myths that the international community uses is to say that education leads to all sorts of national development and the Holy Grail of economic growth. In actual fact, the two things are associated rather than one being caused by the other. More education within a society is, broadly speaking, associated with better living conditions and better health outcomes, but there is almost no evidence that more education causes these improvements to come about. A similar situation is described by Cambridge economist Ha-Joon Chang, who builds the case that rich country academics' and commentators' assertions that they got where they are today thanks to free trade are untrue. Lower trade barriers and less protection of domestic industry seem now to be associated with greater national wealth, but the truth is that such protective measures fell away as countries became strong and able to compete, so the causal relationship appears actually to flow in the opposite direction. Protection and tariffs enabled industrialization to take off within the national boundaries.

Chang writes about Tudor England's wool industry ambitions to illustrate how rich countries became wealthy through industrialization built on a foundation of infant industry protection and encouragement, not through the commonly peddled notion that they engaged in free trade, with no financial and other controls. Industrialization and wealth were not achieved through a free-for-all; it took an inordinate amount of planning and policy continuity over decades, with one ruler after another seeing the wisdom of the chosen path[2]. There is no reason why we should think about education as being all that different, and yet the rich countries bullshit the poor ones by insisting that all children should be in school now, even when they really shouldn't waste their time if the teachers and the conditions that could lead to actual learning are simply not available.

When poor countries are advised to open their markets and let international investors do as they like, bringing investment in and then pulling money out of the local economy as the direction of the wind changes or as the United States decides to raise interest rates, can it be any surprise that they make roughly equivalent (in their counter-productiveness) recommendations when it comes to education policy and planning? As far as I have been able to make out during my career in international education and development, development projects are things that basically *happen to* the 'aid recipient' or 'beneficiary' country. In my experience, there is a pretence of efforts to ensure local participation and local buy-in or, to use the most fashionable term, local 'ownership' of the project or programme. However, in the end, what happens as part of the programme is very much determined by the donor. It is arguable that with advocacy and pushing on the part of rich donor countries, governments start to take steps in the 'right' direction with regard to services for their citizens: health, education, water and sanitation, infrastructure and the like. But does this really happen? Is positive pressure really exerted?

Within the realm of education specifically, most governments seem to have come round to the idea that education is important, based on whatever evidence or lack thereof, and based on their own people's views on the matter. But how much education? When should children first go to school and how long should they continue for? In the poorest countries, children will usually enter school no sooner than the level for which fee-free education is provided by the government, and likewise they will usually not continue any later than the last year for which this is the case. At the same time, poor countries where the citizenry are most in need of free provision are also the least likely to have the tax revenues necessary to provide as much education as they and their international 'peers' might like. One might wonder then, where is the line in terms of what donors should be advising and pushing for? Does it make any sense to encourage a country where there is hardly anything at all that is approaching true education, to start to expand downward to the pre-primary level and upwards, 'universalizing' secondary school?

Six years ago I found myself in what I considered a rather unsavoury situation, having been asked by colleagues at a development consultancy that I trusted to be part of a research programme focusing on early childhood education. I was to act as Team Leader on this project, and the brief was to examine the quality of pre-primary schooling in Liberia, and to document it. We were to look at what was holding back the system, and what was causing the country's severe problem of over-age enrolment, where children were getting stuck at the pre-primary level when they should have been well beyond that point. With children of all ages in pre-primary classrooms, it would be impossible to conduct age-appropriate, child-friendly programmes for four- and five-year-olds even if there were the necessary staff with the requisite skills and the required facilities. When our research was finally carried out,[3] we found (in our most extreme case) someone aged seventeen years enrolled in a pre-primary class due to being illiterate, never having attended school before their mid-teens. Such a young person should have been enrolled in a 'second chance' or 'catch-up' programme for the development of basic literacy and numeracy, not in a class for four- and five-year-olds.

To fully understand this quite extreme situation requires some background. Liberia suffered the ravages of a long civil war and then, quite recently (at the time of the project concerned, 2016–17) the Ebola epidemic. The education system was on its knees as were the crumbling government buildings and other infrastructure. The country's government budget was heavily subsidized by international donors, principal among which was the United States, with government ministries fighting over crumbs. It turns out that there was no budget of any kind for pre-primary schooling in Liberia. Yet, the World Bank decided it would make sense for us, a team of expensive international consultants, to come in and study the 'system' (what system?) and measure learning (what learning?).

An obvious question: having found out that no learning was going on, who could possibly be surprised and what could possibly result? What could government people do when no more funds were forthcoming from the finance ministry?

The situation in Liberia was unlike anywhere else I had been. Schools were officially to charge a fee to parents for enrolling their children at the pre-primary level, but this level was not part of compulsory education (though it ostensibly took place within primary schools). Primary schooling was fee-free and compulsory, as in most other countries. However, the cash-starved state of Liberia's schools, coupled with the official policy to charge fees at the pre-primary level, meant that no matter what a child's age when first presented at school for enrolment, the head teacher would want to enrol them at the pre-primary level so that fees could be charged for two or even three years, to supplement the functioning of the school. On top of this situation is another layer of complication with parents bringing their children to school far older than the officially mandated age of 4 or 5 for pre-primary and 6 for primary 1. So, bring an eight year old to school hoping the child will enter compulsory schooling right away (meaning fee-free primary class 1), and the head teacher will put them in pre-primary for a few years instead – no matter that the parent had the right to enrol the child in primary 1. In the end, the child will be ten years old or more by the time they get to primary 1, four years 'over age' and now many times more likely to drop out.

Yet the pittance that parents could or would pay did not go to providing an extra teacher or anything relevant for the pre-primary classes that were not funded by the government. How schools managed was to stretch meagre resources. They would combine a couple of primary classes to free up a teacher and perhaps one of the primary classrooms. But there was nothing in terms of resourcing for any class; virtually no furniture and no books or other materials. In such a parlous situation, how could any learning be taking place? Yet measurement of learning was what our international donor backers would have us do there. We were also to investigate the causes of the over-age enrolment problem, and my special task was to do a costing of a proper pre-primary section at primary schools, based on the required equipment, as stated in the government guidelines. None of this was required. There was already evidence of the poor state of the country's education system, and the low level of learning at primary school and beyond. A small amount of survey research might have answered any questions about over-age enrolment, and the remedies for the problem were fairly obvious. Nothing could be done to fix the main education system unless parents were encouraged to bring their children for enrolment at younger ages and unless the already over-aged in the system were provided separate accelerated programmes to equip them with basic literacy and numeracy.

I would never have accepted the job had I fully understood what I was getting into: too close engagement with World Bank staff, the World Bank being an institution that I would never choose to work for, and for which my own father had suffered during a career of many, many years. Even worse, working uncomfortably closely with them to carry out truly absurd work (which will not have been a unique situation for the World Bank and many other donors[4]). However, having signed up for the role of Team Leader, I found that our team was being expected to use a learning quality measurement tool that the World Bank had been working on with an apparent expert from the University of Nebraska, formerly of UNESCO. They had made it seem as though we could choose how we would go about conducting the research, but at an initial meeting in Washington, we found that this was very much not the case. Learning to use this experimental and highly complicated tool that would be very unlikely ever to be used in the country after we were gone was arduous (for us 'worldclass' consultants) and felt quite futile. Much effort went into preparing the local research team for this highly complicated experience that they would never repeat. However, probably the most awful task was arriving at a costing for 'proper' pre-primary provision based on official requirements.

The list of equipment that each pre-primary classroom was supposed to have was preposterous, and very obviously copied straight from some rich country. It stipulated the furniture, the books, the toys, and even a proper 'dress-up box', complete with disguise wigs and glasses, etc. To cost this was a painful exercise, a piece of work that was deeply embarrassing for me to do, knowing as I did that there wasn't even a budget for a room with some nice floor mats and a few games and materials. I chose quietly to throw out items like excessive numbers of toys and the dress-up box. I scaled back the furniture requirements. Despite my best efforts, doing a 'light' version as well as one slightly closer to the spec, the cost per school and per student (which varied depending on various parameters that I manipulated) was still pie-in-the-sky. The estimate was so large as to feel nearly insulting to present to my government counterparts. The pre-primary schooling department within the Ministry of Education would continue to put in requests for government funding – some (or whatever) funding they could get – to be included in the proposed budget for the entire education sector that would be forwarded on to the Ministry of Finance. As happened every year, the department's requests would be cut out (entirely) before the whittled-down education budget request was sent from the Ministry of Education to the

Ministry of Finance. So dire was the money situation that not even the Education Minister would submit a budget asking for some allocation for teaching the youngest children. To get pre-primary schooling on the agenda would require a champion within the government, if not an Act of God, as my counterparts told me.

As for us, the team of expensive foreign consultants supplemented by one local for good measure, we wrote a very long, very fancy report[5] providing numbers for what the average parent was spending on education, evidence of the terrible state of learning in schools and the cost of providing a proper education system. We provided insights into why parents brought their children to school over-age, although our local colleagues seemed to know already. I heard that the World Bank swiftly shelved the measurement tools that we turned Liberians into guinea pigs for – the Nebraska/UNESCO expert continues to try to earn money by convincing whoever will listen that such measurements are needed. Of course, foreigners would continue to advise the government to provide fee-free education, to fund it properly through government sources and to keep boosting quality. Get over-aged children into catch-up programmes. But what was the point of all this? The World Bank got to report that it spent (the UK's) money on education in Liberia; we consultants got paid; we got an academic journal article out of it[6] (the World Bank had demanded publications should result from the programme), and I got to go to an expensive conference in Oxford, on the World Bank/UK's tab, to present what we did. I got to have a great time, catching up with old friends after having done my best during my presentation. I'm very sure that nothing changed for Liberian children.

The only hope for pre-primary education in Liberia would have been for the government to deploy an extra teacher per school and perhaps some floor mats to sit on; a teacher guide with guidelines on making simple learning materials out of common objects; some slates and chalk and a blackboard; and a roof over their heads for when it was raining or too hot. If I had costed this, I would probably have been accused of suggesting terrible conditions. It was blindingly obvious that the crazy specification and list of required objects, furniture and learning materials demanded of a pre-primary classroom was the fault of outsiders – some consultant had drawn it up based on what happens in rich countries, and this sort of thing happens all the time. A more achievable 'make do and mend' approach, while actually providing a classroom and a teacher specifically for the pre-primary section (at no small cost, just these two 'inputs'), would be deemed discriminatory and second-best. So the only alternative is a pie-in-the-sky goal and getting nowhere near it.

Rich countries are brilliant at advising poor countries to expand, improve and ensure equity for the poor, the otherwise marginalized, and most importantly, for girls. They don't advise caution or any pumping of the brakes to stop whatever modicum of quality from being diluted to extinction. They advise measures to stimulate such things as a desire for accurate data for planning purposes, while broader incentives within the education sector and also more widely within government and society are not aligned that way. They advise teacher training and continuous professional development, and practical day-to-day or week-to-week support from mentors who would observe practice and suggest ways to improve teaching. Such ideas may sound nice, but where is it all supposed to come from? If there were sufficient people who had the requisite skills and expertise and who were motivated enough to become great teacher trainers and mentors, but who were just not being deployed, then there might be scope for short-term action. But what about all of the other things that are required? The funds to facilitate training and the moving around of mentors, to get to schools to provide support and guidance to teachers during their practice. Even old-fashioned school inspectors whose job it is to go around and 'inspect' schools, checking their record keeping and what teachers are up to, even they do not consistently carry out their duties in many, many countries, and particularly with regard to schools in remote, rural areas. It is often schools that are more easily accessible – read: less painful to get to – where inspectors tend to go. Alternatively, it is where the inspectors expect to get the best reception – read: lunch and bribes.

Just accessing some government schools in the countries where I have worked is an arduous, even excruciating experience, and from a major city can easily entail an over-night stay (see Chapter 3's description of getting to rural Ghanaian schools). To visit one would make visiting others on the same trip more efficient, but to do this without a vehicle and allowances to cover accommodation and food is all but impossible. Without having travelled dusty miles in a clapped-out car with no air conditioning, weaving madly across the entire road surface, if it can qualify as a road, in hot conditions, to turn up at a school that hasn't been visited by anyone responsible for countless months, to experience the air of neglect, inertia, abandonment ... without such experiences it is difficult to understand the scale of the challenge and the unreasonableness of our 'advice' that mentors and teacher support staff should be showing up consistently and for extended periods. Teachers posted to remote areas complain that there is nowhere for them to stay long-term, and forget any guest house accommodation within easy reach.

Yet still consultants working on education and development projects continue to advise that poor country governments keep expanding access to schooling while also improving the quality of that schooling. In Liberia, what could we recommend other than that the government should provide catch-up programmes for the children who were so dramatically over-age for their level (or lack) of learning? They should provide pre-primary schooling for all children to get them well-prepared for the start of primary schooling. They should run awareness-raising campaigns among parents on the importance of enrolling their children in these pre-primary classes at age four or five. They should monitor practices at schools to make sure that teachers are not charging fees for pre-primary schooling, and therefore keeping children in a holding pattern at this level. We could advise that the Ministry of Education should put together a well-thought-out budget accompanied by a clear rationale for getting more funding for the education sector (but the overall government pot is limited, largely consisting of foreign aid). But developing a well-regulated, well-run, well-staffed education system simply cannot come about through being advised – and it did not require wasting tens of thousands of pounds on studies to inform this advice.

Yet project after project gets commissioned by rich country donor agencies, and the consultancy companies tasked with carrying out the programmes just go along with the insanity as their existence depends on these projects. It is really difficult being on the receiving end of a set of ToRs (terms of reference) for a project, and as a team on the side of the bidding agency, you have to sit down and think of ways to fulfil the requirements of those ToRs, and how to do this cheaply enough for the consulting company to make some money on the deal. The last time I was (half-heartedly) involved in such a bid, I was floored to find out that the UK's development agency wanted the programme to result in improvement to learning outcomes *within seven months of starting up*. Education is slow work, and improving systems and teachers' abilities and motivation levels in a real and meaningful way requires time and a whole lot of work in myriad different areas. It's not possible to improve education by tweaking this over here and pulling that lever over there.

When donors impose these ludicrous and unrealistic demands on implementing agencies, all sorts of crazy, distorting, unsustainable things happen in order to bring about the desired outcomes in the targeted schools. To return to Liberia, this sort of thing happened when the government, with donor funding, instituted the 'Partnership Schools for Liberia' pilot project. Private sector 'partners' were to take over the management of existing Liberian government schools, and somehow turn them around, raising learning levels (this is discussed in more depth in Chapter 10). For my own pre-primary education research project fiasco that was happening at the same time, 'systems thinking' was all the rage, while this 'partnership' idea was meant to turn around particular schools as well as positively affect the whole system. In desperation, the education minister at the time said that he wanted to have tried everything to improve things, leaving no approach shunned on ideological or other grounds, even if it seemed to indicate a move towards the private.

DFID said similar things about its work in Lagos, Nigeria. At the same time as they had a programme to improve conditions in the state's 12,000+ private schools using a 'making markets work for the poor' approach, they were also giving money to a foreign corporation, Bridge International Academies (now NewGlobe) to aid their entry into the Lagos market. When asked why they would do the latter while using an approach that is at odds with subsidizing a particular player, thereby distorting the market (as the pure markets people would view it), DFID officials indicated that they wanted to be seen to have tried absolutely everything to improve how things functioned in Lagos with its thousands of tiny, individual schooling efforts, plus the 1,600 government schools. But the Lagos schooling market was far too big to be influenced by such a drop-in-the-ocean programme.

In the end, it is hard to understand what the point was of donors like DFID recommending really anything to governments whose material conditions are so inimical to carrying out the received advice. In late 2022 I decided to read the website of the UK government's current Nigeria programme, the one for which I had worked on a losing bid to boost learning levels in just seven months. It brought me wry amusement in reading that their sample activities include to 'improve teaching and learning in performance-focused schools and colleges – leading to the use of evidence-based teaching and learning approaches and better management'. Secondly, they would 'assist stakeholders in upgrading their systems to better incorporate human and financial resources, ultimately allowing them to run their operations more efficiently. Better-managed systems should lead to better results for students'.[7]

The first statement sounds very much like Partnership Schools for Liberia, where insane levels of inputs were poured in to raise learning from almost nothing to just more than almost nothing, and the levels of spending were far and away more than the government could ever have hoped to sustain after the pilot programme ended. Equally the statement could have applied to the preceding Nigerian education programme that I had worked on; it is just empty rhetoric – nearly meaningless in real world practice. Sadly, there is nothing more credible in the second statement. I know from my own time there that 'human resources' of the right skill level to be good teachers were sorely lacking. Financial resources were likewise in very short supply. The mention of running systems more efficiently is touching, and it is topped off by the optimistic phrase that all this *'should* lead to better results' – these statements are practically a copy-paste job from previous programmes, the documents from which I learned were now stacked and locked away in disused classrooms in Lagos State, doing no good to anyone.

Knowing what I know about these projects, it is amazing to me that anyone has the heart to keep a career going in this way; trotting out the same hackneyed old crap again and again and calling oneself a 'development professional'. I wonder if they keep cycling in and out people with just enough continuity to make sure that the same type of nonsense is produced and staff do not revolt about the endless futility of it. The continuity of the staff of the development consultancies that carry out the bidding of the donors is often similarly low – something the industry seems to have in common with cheap private schools. Another similarity: along with good intentions sometimes comes no relevant experience, specific skills or cultural knowledge of the context. As for myself, I had only the best of intentions when I went to Nigeria as an EMIS (Education Management Information Systems) State Specialist, despite all my lack of experience at the time, or knowledge of the Nigerian context. What I lacked in experience, I tried to make up for in enthusiasm, commitment, and sincere, hard work, but none of this could make a highly flawed basis of work and reason for being there make any sense in the end.

Some others I have known in the industry were not so benevolent; they were in it for the earnings and for a particular lifestyle that they could not afford back home in Europe, Australia or the United States, rather than to be able to help countries do better by their citizens. Some consultants would work on multiple programmes at a time, working all hours and billing more than one project for the same day, having worked fifteen or sixteen hours on two different projects. This was the type of consultant (exhausted, jaded, bored) who would copy and paste from one project report to a document for another project, and would forget to replace the country name with the correct one, or forget to change 'health sector' to 'education sector'. Of course if the IMF can reach for 'off-the-rack' policies,[8] why can't consultants just copy and paste too? These variously motivated individuals have managed to achieve dubious and limited outcomes through working with and advising national governments – usually dangling the carrot of aid funding.

Now, just try to imagine the situation of the 'beneficiary' country civil servants who have to deal with this succession of projects and their associated representatives; sometimes there are familiar foreign faces who return to work on the next one (after the previous project), which can feel a bit like a friendly reunion of colleagues. But it can't be any wonder if civil servants end up jaded, and operate in ways that seem disingenuous when they are forced to listen to foreigners *whitesplaining* to them the problems their education system faces. As a young consultant, I have watched senior British colleagues explaining the leakage of money from the system – death by a thousand cuts, or, in this case, the slideshow included a visual of a bucket pierced on all sides with water leaking out of the many holes. I remember being amused by this at the time, but knowing what I know now, it is hard to fathom how people must feel about having these well-known and well-understood issues explained to them in this way by some foreigner. Yes, there is corrupt 'leakage' of funds. But civil servants don't need this explained to them, they know it, and they know why it happens, but what no one knows is how to stop it from happening; how to fix the problems with the system to get to a situation where people don't feel the need or the right to whittle away at the available resources. The 'leakage' problem is fully enmeshed with so many other issues far beyond the education sector. In the end, people have to be able to make their ends meet, and someone has to be the first one to start to forego the opportunities to whittle, and this first person needs to inspire others to change too. It is all beyond some dinky little donor-funded education project, working away in its silo for far too short a span of years, to make any impact.

On my last job in the education/development sector, in Accra, at my favourite Ethiopian restaurant in the world, a colleague on the project, whose role was to foster or broker 'partnerships' (in this case, between the government and various donors with regard to pet projects the latter wanted to fund/cajole the former to try, like our friends, the Liberian guinea pigs) spoke of his frustration. He said that it was difficult to persuade people in the Ministry of Education to go along with things suggested by donors (i.e. by him) that were not accompanied by any budget. His frustration was due to his own day-to-day struggles that were ultimately caused by these difficult locals' refusal to swallow any and all suggestions sent their way – and certainly unaccompanied by $. In some cases, what was being suggested was very obviously correct. On the big Nigeria programme that I was part of, there were two consultants who were tasked with wrestling with colleges of education in Kwara State. Just one (of the three colleges), in fact. They found that graduates of dubious (or no) quality were being churned out by the hundreds, while the number of worthy graduates needed was very small. There were countless other issues, but the key stumbling block with regard to making progress was that all of the incentives in this dysfunctional situation were aligned to taking loads of students in order to bring in funding through fees. There was no incentive to shed unnecessary staff and scale back the operation to suit the demand because no one wanted to lose their jobs, and there was no one wielding an axe to make these tough decisions. When the most powerful stakeholders are orientated around protecting their jobs, some of which are gained through systems of political patronage, what on earth can be done? The leaders who would bring real reform are always cornered and compromised by their need for support from people whose jobs might well be axed.

It is a safe statement that in the end, no 'project' can save a country's education system; no amazingly effective pilot programme can dazzle people through the example it sets and get them all to work that way all the time. The status quo is strong, as is the effect of inertia. Instead of ill-conceived meddling and advising, it would be best for rich country representatives and advisors to focus on un-rigging the rules of the international game that are keeping these countries poor. Even if we would not leave these countries alone and properly level the playing field just because it is the right thing to do, it doesn't make sense to waste everyone's time with bogus development projects and boatloads of wonderful advice. But then what it is all really about is providing philanthropic cover and soft power so that rich countries can keep the same old situation going, and call on countries' support during crucial votes at the UN (as well as bringing funds home again in the form of consultants' daily rates). So, sadly, there are things we have in common with our friends at the Colleges of Education in Kwara State. We all just want the gravy train to keep rolling, and none of us want to be the ones left standing when the music stops.

8

Bad Advice Regarding the Regulation of Cheap Private Schools

Rich country aid programmes advise all sorts of idealistic things for schools in the South, like better-trained teachers and teacher mentors to support them, as I described in the last chapter. They round out the picture by advising all sorts of things to do with minimum standards for both public and private schools. From their standpoint, because children in poor countries are as worthy as children in rich countries, the standards of teaching staff and infrastructure *should* conform to some approximation of our own idea of what is right for a school, and for this, there is a need for clear regulations, properly enforced. Of course, this is a lofty view that is essentially correct – if we assume we know best for people in other countries. But there are innumerable 'shoulds' floating around, without a lot of consideration of who will pay the bill for better standards and for their enforcement. Even more salient, it is not clear where proper teachers will come from, money or no money.

The point has already been made in this book that the cheap private schools I have studied can be quite dispiriting. The buildings are often dark and depressing and, in quite a few instances, hardly merit the word 'building'. The furniture is poor and rough, and the only teaching equipment is a black board. There is often an insufficiency of textbooks in the classroom because parents can't afford both the fees and the books. The teachers, many of whom have only recently finished school themselves and might be taking university courses of dubious quality, are often so young that you might mistake them for students.

With such schools so common in so many places, certain questions arise: *where are the school inspectors? Aren't these schools regulated? Why are they allowed to operate in such a sorry manner?* The clear visual evidence of the poverty of these schools' circumstances is enough for people within the education and development industry and the NGO world to decry the existence of these schools in the form that they take. Unluckily for the middle and poorer classes in the countries where I have worked, it is really only the private schools serving the upper-middle and elite classes that would have a hope of meeting any ostensibly reasonable set of regulations.[1] Those fighting for the human rights of children feel that cheap private schools are an affront to their pupils, violating their rights to free education, good quality education, a safe environment … I could go on. Yet the terrible government schools are considered something that we can work with; places we need to urge and chivvy children to flock to for enrolment – quite inexplicably. But cheap private schools, as violations of the rights of the child (and also of the teachers who are exploited there as low-wage, informal workers in what should be treated as a profession), should quite simply be regulated out of existence. This is the view of people who sure do know human rights and could probably rattle off provisions from the many international conventions, but who likely know almost nothing of substance about cheap private schools and how they operate. These people are idealists and purists, out of touch with grinding daily reality – something that I have had occasion to explain to such idealists on several occasions.

But what about the position of government personnel? I have always found this issue somewhat more difficult to parse because the individuals, as well as the institutions, tend to come down hard on cheap private schools, even though they themselves would never even consider subjecting their children to the government system that they supposedly work for. And there is a strange conflict here: while they are probably well-off enough to avoid using the very cheapest private schools, their desire to escape the government system that they clearly agree is failing should, one might think, mean they have some understanding of the demand for *cheap* private school places, no matter how poor some of the schools are. Yet they are united with the international human rights brigade in wanting to deny low-income households from availing themselves of a non-state alternative. As far as I could tell, discussing the issue with people from ministries of education, it seemed that they have to toe the line and go with the notion that private schools must have a long list of high-quality facilities, while government schools are allowed to run in any manner because it's a government service and the government is cash-strapped. (Never mind that cheap private schools are dependent on fee payments from low-income people, so are also cash-strapped!) Lastly, I felt that there could be an element of embarrassment to the issue when parents would do anything to avoid the schools that these officials work for/with. All of these currents, the national and the international, flow together to mean that the forces of officialdom and often of organized civil society are targeted at cheap private schools as a scourge and a menace.

Whatever one thinks about it as an armchair opiner, an education expert working in the field, a government official or a human rights activist, the fact is that there is no effective oversight of any of this. I am yet to learn of any country where cheap private schools are thriving and are effectively monitored, quality-assured, regulated and the rest. I've already said that schools have no incentive to improve the teaching quality at their schools because parents can't really tell the difference and do not exert their consumer muscle with regard to this issue. If there's no pressure from the fee payers, then there's no incentive for the school owner to do much more than make superficial, visible improvements to the building to entice more parents through the doors. Indeed, markets and competition for these fee payers do not mean endless striving for improvement – something that can even backfire for the school owner by driving teachers to change employers in search of an easier, less-pressured life. When people make well-intentioned suggestions as to how to improve schools, they usually don't understand the 'business model' and the informal sector context in which these schools operate, which means that there is a fairly low sort of equilibrium level of effort required of schools to remain in the 'market'.

***

So what are the current, formal regulatory regimes actually like? Why are schools hiding? As I went along in my research career, I gathered information on regulatory regimes in the countries I worked in, building a picture that was bizarrely consistent from West to East Africa and then in India too. Despite the differences between these countries, there were some startling similarities in how they approached private schools. Countries typically have a set of minimum requirements differing by the level of schooling involved, codified in a single document which would be available to prospective school owners either free of cost or for a fee. The regulations set out the minimum measurements and other specifications for school buildings, and they stipulated minimum teaching qualifications and staffing numbers. They also typically include a minimum land holding, numbers of toilets or pupil-toilet ratio and more. The requirements were typically extremely unrealistic, stating that proprietors must have this elaborate set-up in place before they have enrolled even a single student. Some regulations go so far as to require that the management has a bank account with the full salary bill for an entire year or two years stashed away.

Lagos State in Nigeria required an enormous auditorium, a large playground, and a sick bay with a qualified nurse on staff. Setting aside the sheer impossibility of non-wealthy parents being able to afford a school of such a standard, the size of the plot that the government demanded was largely unavailable or else eye-wateringly expensive. The only half-way affordable land to be had at the time I was working there was way out on the fringes of the city, and I was told that already in 2024 these areas were also densely built up. Where plots were available within the settlements where working people live, they would invariably be too small and often effectively outlawed for school use by the regulation that any school must be such and such a distance from a filling station or from a place where alcohol is served. In densely populated urban areas, such restrictions are just unworkable and have the effect of elevating the need to serve beer above the need for children to go to school (things which generally do not happen so much at the same time of day in any case).

What always struck me as being so very jarring was that whenever I chanced upon a school that fulfilled the requirements, or at least came close to this, the school was catering to the upper middle classes or the elites. Only at these socioeconomic levels are parents able to pay the sizable fees required to maintain the high standards in such schools, both in terms of the capital investment, sometimes initially provided through loans which must be paid back, as well as the monthly running costs, which are invariably mostly made up of teachers' salaries. The level of provisioning demanded by the regulations would, if enforced, have the end effect of requiring one (very high) standard for private schools, which can then only serve the well-off, leaving the lower orders to bad government schools, with cheap private schools effectively outlawed.

The incentives for government are confused and confusing. The major cities that I have worked in all have peripheral informal settlements where those of very limited means live, servicing the businesses and households of the main (wealthier) core of the city. Some cities also have interior slums. While many of the inhabitants leave their neighbourhoods to travel into the city every day for work, there are many who also stay local and work within their own neighbourhoods. Most of these people migrate from rural areas to find work opportunities in the cities; many are fleeing difficult or dangerous situations in their home areas, for example, people fleeing Islamist violence in northern Nigeria who move to Abuja and Lagos for safety and for jobs. For as long as there is no call (by richer people) for the peripheral land that these people inhabit, then their existence and occupation of the land are tolerated, often willingly because these communities serve as a source of cheap labour. But there should be no mistake that they are only tolerated for a time, and governments do not want to lend any air of permanence or legitimacy to these communities that could be implied by the provision of public services, utilities, roads or anything else to make life easier for the people living there. It is key to preserving the advantages of existing privilege that these slums should be cleared at any time.

At the same time, they have to allow people to put their children into school somehow. There are government schools just outside many slums, and those living closest to these might choose to send their children there, but they are not enough to serve all children. Then, because there is nowhere else to send children who would be rendered out of school if cheap private schools were forcibly closed for not meeting regulations, the authorities turn a blind eye, sometimes even denying that such schools exist. In other cases, inspectors do the rounds, visiting cheap private schools and issuing demands or at least strongly worded advice regarding improvements to be made, while usually taking a pay-out from the proprietor to allow the school to continue to exist.

Where closures are carried out, this is usually in a relatively haphazard way, while many illegal schools simply continue to operate. For many municipal and state authorities, the sheer volume of schools that they would have to try to keep up with is too much for them to manage with severely limited numbers of people on staff and with no funding or vehicles for site visits. Yet the chance to get their palms greased at schools means that visiting the easy-to-reach ones may well be worth the trip for government personnel – but only to certain schools. During my first study in Ghana, the poorest private school owners told me that government officials did not make repeat visits to their schools because they found that the cash these proprietors could offer was so paltry as to render it not worth their time. Without this opportunity to earn by visiting these schools, any concern for the quality of the facilities or instruction offered at these poor schools simply did not enter in.

∗∗∗

There is more to learn about the regulatory regime in poor countries than just the minimum requirements for running a school. There is a whole process to go through at the very beginning in order to gain official permission to operate. In general, governments require that schools apply for permission to run the school on a chosen site well before their intended start of operations. They must submit site plans and paperwork describing the school, and in some cases, a considerable amount of funds must be secured, as already mentioned. For small, cheap private school operators, this type of application process is impossible because it implies having a site secured (most governments demand that the school be owned and not rented) that is available for site inspection while the school is not yet running. This sort of regulation is a non-starter because no one in a low-income area could afford to buy or pay rent for a site, particularly in urban areas, that is not yet earning any income. The only way this might be possible is if the land is already owned by the proprietor. This does happen, but it is usually the case when the proprietor is starting a small school in their own residential premises – and such a plan will never pass muster with the authorities.

In the end, virtually no school operator waits to commence operations until after the relevant government person has inspected the site and approved the plans for the school, and as far as I can tell, no one really cares. The usual modus operandi is to dip a toe in the water by starting things up to see how it goes. There are fees to pay – both official fees and bribes – that no one will want to get into paying before they have seen whether they will be able to attract any students. Coming forward to make the government aware of the intended (or functioning) school's existence is a major decision, opening an enormous can of worms.

***

I repeat that I have never been to a country in which regulation of this type of schooling sector is done at scale, or done well even with only patchy, partial coverage. The abiding common features of failing regulatory regimes include a lack of person power and resources to visit schools, as well as corruption and unsuitable standards for the context. As a result, school owners avoid interaction with the government at all costs. Strangely, private schools are seen as cash cows, and school owners are perceived as raking it in, despite the obvious difficulties when serving lower income people.

I have been told countless times by government officials in the sub-Saharan African countries where I have worked that private school owners operate illegally, are disdainful of the law and exploit parents. They couch these critiques as being in the interest of ensuring that children are attending good-quality, safe schools – yet government schools are so very bad. The best I can say is that in Ghana at least I was told by school owners that officials give them some advice and goals to work towards (usually to do with physical structures) that are practical, while also expecting payment. In other cases, also in Ghana, I was told that government officials would say something like, 'move your toilets two metres further from the building', meaning pointless expense for no positive gain for students, when that money could go to teaching and learning materials or improvements to classrooms.

As for the school I worked with my Indian family to build in rural western Uttar Pradesh, we built the school with massive, regulation-size classrooms because we never expected to run our school without becoming duly registered. When the government registration inspector came for the site visit, he surveyed the scene and eventually made it clear that he expected payment. When remonstrated with, that the school was built to regulation, the unfortunate reply was, 'it's not my fault you followed the regulations; I still need to be paid'. And so the relationship started, and would continue, with contempt and a total lack of interest in the actual mission of education – and this carries on to the present time, as I make final tweaks to this manuscript. The government arbitrarily made our school re-register as if from scratch, despite having remarkable outcomes from our last class 12 students in their board exam results in 2024. All the usual bribes were necessary, irrespective of our length of service to local girls, the standard of the building, and how well our graduates have done.

***

It is not simply because they want to avoid wasting school funds on bribes that school owners try to fly below the radar. The worst schools, already described as the only hope for the relatively poor to access something safer and in some way better than government schools (or else just within easy reach from home), simply have no hope of ever meeting regulations or even coming close. Theirs is not a situation of working towards acceptable facilities that would one day be passable. Theirs is a situation of being beyond the pale, as I have described in previous chapters; beyond redemption. These schools will exist for a relatively short time in the big scheme of things until the general prospects of the local community perhaps improve to the point where such very poor schools no longer have a market. It is these schools that are the clearest target for school closures by government authorities, and the owners know it, so there is no use trying to interact with the government because it cannot end well for the school.

I have already painted a picture of a very poor school in Chapter 5. I have described how a community is built on a mixture of waste, human and plastic, and soil, sand and industrially polluted and blighted ground. The school I found was nestled between poor-looking houses that made the school not look all that out of place. Other schools I have seen exist on miserable wastes of otherwise unused land next to a filling station. Another school was in a flimsy shack that was half under water when I visited in the rainy season in Lagos, only ever fully dry in the dry season. The schools that are the worst of the worst are (or were) to be found in all of the contexts where I have researched this issue. The reason I say that these poorest schools will eventually wither and die, unless they manage to pull themselves up by the bootstraps and improve, is because I have seen the utter transformation of the cheap private schooling market here in rural, western Uttar Pradesh. When I did my doctoral work in the winter of 2005–06, there were schools that inhabited what would reasonably be described as the type of open-sided shed that one might expect to find livestock sheltering in. Children sat in lines on long runner-mats with a few materials in their laps, looking towards an improvised blackboard on the wall. There are no such schools anymore in this area and it would be impossible to find children sitting on the floors anywhere other than government schools.

When the enthusiastic pro-child-rights crowd says that these schools should be regulated with the aim of closing the poorer schools down, what they fail to see is that children at a low ebb are the ones who lose out. Never mind the poor local person trying to make some sort of living by serving local families via their small private school – it is the children who will have nowhere else to go if the cheapest fee-paying schools are closed by the authorities for failure to reach minimum standards. Perversely, the result will be the same for children if their schools improve and offer better teaching, because fees will inevitably rise and become unaffordable for those on the brink. So, my question for well-intentioned commentators is: *what regulation, what set of rules and minimum standards can ever work in favour of these people on the cusp of real, grinding poverty – the people the human rights crowd wants so desperately to protect?* And it should be recalled that I say 'on the cusp' because these issues do not affect the truly poor and the poorest of the poor, because fee-paying schooling will already have been far out of their reach. What happens if the schools on the lowest fringes of the private sector are prevented from operating is that the children teetering on the brink fall down into the lowest strata. The grim truth is that it is the almost-poor people who have to contend with the worst schools out there – these children get the rough end of the bargain no matter what the outcome of the debate on what to do with the worst, cheapest private schools.

If the government comes along and closes a private school, then the children thrown out would be able to afford to attend government school, but this would swell the ranks of children being badly served in the public sector. However, children in many other private schools would not be so 'lucky' as to find a government alternative close enough to home. One day in Kampala, I walked all day and found an astonishing twenty-seven private schools for just one government school. In many of the areas I roamed, small children would not have been able to walk to this one school compound; it was too far. So what then, if governments decide to follow the stellar advice of outsiders, regulating to death the small neighbourhood efforts picking up the slack for the public sector? What then? Well, nothing then. As one government official in Abuja told me, they had sought and gained through the courts the necessary order to shut down 550 private schools in low-income peripheral areas of the city. But this government official told me that they had no intention of carrying out the closures because there was nowhere to send the children who would then be out of school. So the court order goes unused and the matter rests.[2] The cheap private schools continue to fill a gap left by the government.

***

Human rights proponents, both foreign and domestic, feel that this situation lets down vulnerable children. The complete lack of affordability of private schools among the poorest is just another form the letting-down takes. They call vigorously for governments to regulate the hell out of these schools, closing many in the process because there should be no place for fee-paying schools in low-income areas. This is the view particularly when considering the level of schooling that is most used by the poorest segments of society, that is, the pre-primary, primary and lower-secondary levels. The message is broadly the same that comes from the multinational organizations that pride themselves on being concerned with universal human rights, writing reports and issuing various demands on people they will never meet.[3]

What the well-intentioned fail to note (at least publicly) is that if governments divert enormous amounts of person hours to visiting thousands of cheap private schools, this effectively diverts already scarce public resources, human and otherwise, away from government education. What would instead be most effective in making poor schools raise their game would be to focus with dogged determination on improving the government schools that any private school must stay one step ahead of in terms of quality, in order to stay 'in business'.[4] Ministries of education need enough people on staff to positively 'quality assure' thousands of schools, not just 'inspect' them – starting with their own government schools. This means that they should observe teaching and try to get to grips with how well the teachers are doing and so much more, as well as inspecting the premises and the record-keeping at the school. Many times, teachers have told me that they have never had any interaction with government inspectors because they come and simply stay in the office, where the records are kept and the bribing happens. This means that inspectors sometimes do not even see the whole premises, and they rarely see what happens in the classroom and how. Most school inspections are simply tick-box exercises leading to bribes. The only positive end result is in the pockets of the inspectors – this point should be clearly understood.

Yet negative end results can be much more far-reaching: the tick-box exercise can be enough to get schools closed down. I have argued strongly with Lagos Ministry of Education officials about their pointless attitudes towards the quality of school buildings and the precise type of toilets when the communities that the schools are serving are poor and the people cannot afford to pay for anything better. This happens in a context where the government was providing some 1,600 schools compared with well over 12,000[5] private schools. With the majority of the state's children attending private schools, the government was in a poor bargaining position indeed, and yet argue they did, throwing their weight around with arrogance. One more contextual detail: none of those state officials would ever have considered sending their own children to one of the few government schools (this applies in most places where I have worked, not just Lagos), and one of the people I argued with the most went off to work for Bridge International Academies (now NewGlobe) a few years later, although he didn't last long with them. It seems that things have improved somewhat since 2009–15, as a result of a pragmatic change of attitude on the part of the government, but it remains to be seen what the new government (as of 2023) will choose to do.

The end result of this situation, as I have already indicated, is that the poor and nearly-poor are left in the most miserable conditions in the poorest schools, and the government has no data on unregistered private schools to indicate that these children's schooling is even taking place or that children are safe. No international aid donor can engage with such schools to help them because of the optics of supporting schools that look just so terrible; but they don't understand the vital role the schools are playing. Governments are too embarrassed to work with these schools in a spirit of encouraging the head teacher to do whatever she can to improve the school's operations within the given constraints because they have this all-or-nothing attitude to school standards – while woefully neglecting their own (government) schools. This is how it will remain for low-income people unless and until their economic prospects improve, as in my little corner of western Uttar Pradesh.

***

There is no silver bullet to the problem of having far too many schools to oversee, but some things have been tried. At the time when I was living and working in Nigeria, I thought that perhaps schools could be encouraged simply to try on their own to improve themselves. The only UK funded programme that focused solely on private schools, the Lagos DEEPEN programme, came up with the idea that school proprietors would fill out a self-evaluation form, with the idea that a government inspector would come and validate the results, and between the inspector and proprietor, a 'school improvement plan' would be arrived at. The school owner would then work over months and even years to implement the agreed plan. This was the seed of a new way of addressing the issues, but while our government partners were initially willing, they eventually backed out. However, having given the schools ideas by simply having them fill out the self-evaluation form, we later found that they had already started to take action around various points that they recognized they were weak on. This suggested to me that it was within the realm of possibility that there could be a website for private schools that they could log in to, to get a range of materials that they could use for themselves. If trust eventually built up, then perhaps proprietors would become confident enough to supply the government with some information about their schools. Useful, actionable materials in exchange for data could be a mutually beneficial *quid pro quo*.

Time and again I tried to convince people that it didn't seem to be having any positive effect to have this binary categorization of registered (legal) and unregistered (illegal) schools. More governments could at least take the approach of Uganda's ministry in stating that a case-by-case approach was appropriate with respect to many aspects of schooling infrastructure and operations, but until corruption becomes less endemic and processes begin to be more rule bound, corruption will continue to detract from efforts to effectively regulate private schools.

Whatever way things go, the poor lose out. If government diverts resources to messing about with small private schools that are somehow managing on their own to operate with fee-paying clients, then they are taking resources away from the government school sector and its improvement. If schools are closed down, then relatively poor children are thrown into probably-worse government schools (or no school at all). If the poorest private schools are somehow cajoled and corralled into improving, then their fees would rise and they would become unaffordable to the somewhat-poor because let's face it, no industry can afford to drastically improve quality without having to pass increased costs on to the consumer. So, again, it is the least well off in this equation that always suffers, as in most things in life.

Informal settlements are vibrant and full of life but also full of severe difficulties, which I started to become somewhat familiar with when I began visiting Makoko in Lagos semi-regularly. Children attending poor private schools live in rough little houses, flats or just rooms, in cramped and difficult conditions, and their ragged schools are simply part and parcel of the place. They stand out in no way, and so the children there live, play, go to the shops, go to school and go to church in the same conditions that they have known all their lives. When I was sent to Nairobi by UK-DFID and met with people working in the slums to discuss whether it might be possible to implement means-tested benefits to reach the poorest within the slums, I learned a great deal about just how many strata of poverty there are in an informal settlement. A small encapsulation of what I learned is in the detail of the varying cost of housing along the slopes in Kibera. I was told that the further down the slope, the closer to the stream a house is, the cheaper the rent, because rents were inversely proportional to the amount of horror caused by rain. At the top of the slope, households would get essentially fresh, clean water falling on them. At the bottom of the slope, these poorest houses would receive the filth of all the houses above them, making rain a truly horrifying event that rendered the floor of the houses entirely unhygienic, bringing the risk of disease as a bonus. When people can hardly afford to live in such a terrible situation, and their children cannot walk for miles to some already over-crowded government school outside of the slum, then what sort of regulations could possibly allow for any reasonable type of school for these children to attend? What sort of strict and rights-based form of regulation can possibly help this community? Do you protect such a child's rights by closing her neighbourhood private school? And just who will better-serve these children from outside when people are setting up small schools themselves already, without anyone else's help?

To read of 'rules-based systems' and proper 'regulation' feels like a ridiculous joke when the systems needed for this are simply absent. Layered on top of this is the random cruelty of organs of government who conduct partial slum clearances with little or no warning. On a day of fieldwork in Abuja I headed with my small team into the informal settlements peripheral to the city centre, moving in the opposite direction of the rush hour traffic. 'They are like flies', driver Paul said about the okadas (the motor bike taxis) which ferry people out of the massive, sprawling settlement to the main road where they could get a bus into the city. This was another parallel to the phenomenon of poor private schooling. No buses would ply the streets of the settlement; indeed, they would never be able to manage the roads. As the main road crossed into the formally developed city, so too began the operation of a more regulated way of working and living. For the slums, though, the informal private sector solution to a lack of city buses was for young men with motorbikes to ferry individual passengers down the hill to the main road, or from place to place within the slum. Paul drove me, as usual, past a large and busy market deep into the settlement where I met the rest of my team and we did our day's school visiting and head teacher interviewing.

On the way back out of the community, and towards the city in the evening, we passed the smouldering wreckage of what had been the market. The sight was post-apocalyptic, like a bomb had gone off, and anyone not present at their stall at the time would have lost the stall and its contents in the demolition. I wondered what had happened, and we found out that the authorities had come along and levelled the place because there were plans to build a proper market with a paved floor and a massive roof over the top. I asked in shock if the construction would be starting imminently, and the answer, accompanied by laughter, was no. They just do this from time to time. Maybe one day the demolition will presage the building of that planned market. As the study progressed I found that interviews with proprietors revealed that this was a settled pattern, probably exaggerated in the case of Abuja, Nigeria's Federal Capital Territory, for which there was a 'master plan' drawn up and which was still far from complete. The entire area that the settlement inhabited was already planned out officially, although construction for that phase of the plan would not commence any time soon. The idea then was to keep the populace in a constant state of uncertainty, and to stop them from making major investments in building quality or from believing they might have some squatters' rights. The government was fighting a war against permanence for this community, so that it could come in and hand over the plots to developers (read: whoever would bribe them the most lavishly). In phases of the plan that had already been built, plots designated for schools had already been 'taken over' (quite the euphemism) by other people for private interests, as I was told by the Abuja government official mentioned previously. He told me that because it helped to explain the dearth of proper schools. In Lagos too, there have been pointless partial slum clearances that have never amounted to the scale required to achieve the desired goal of clearing the Lagos waterfront for upscale development. All that happens is that some homes are destroyed and already low-income people are pushed towards precarity, if they are not already there.[6]

In these contexts, then, what regulation can protect the interests of the poor? What can anyone do to ensure that the relatively poor have access to schooling of an acceptable quality? What has the Education for All movement, backed by UN bodies and coalitions of NGOs managed in this regard? Yet still the calls come: 'private schools must be regulated!' I realize that the schools I know most about, and have spent the most time in are a particular sub-set of private schools, and a sub-set of a sub-set in the diverse universe of 'non-state actors in education'. Clearly, the corporations of this world running private schools, such as Bridge International Academies/NewGlobe, need to be regulated stringently (more on them in the next chapter). To my mind there is a clear distinction to be drawn between a large corporation baking violation of regulations and laws into a plan for profit extracted at the very bottom of the pyramid; it is very different from a small school from the community, of the community, for the community, where all revenues are kept within that community.

The way I view the situation, government authorities would do well to act with humility considering the reason why things have gotten to such a pass – that people do whatever they can to avoid government schools. It would behove the authorities to act in an inclusive and accepting manner towards these schools, acknowledging that their failure has led to the need for private schools, and welcoming school owners to come forward to share experiences, challenges, and if nothing else, just school data for government education management information systems. But officials clearly relish the existence of unregistered and therefore illegal private schools as a cash cow for them – regular bribes are what it takes for a blind eye to be turned in perpetuity.

The bottom line for the poor and nearly-poor is that there is no practical help for them, coming from outside the community (from national or international sources). The well-intentioned want to mess with these communities' own self-support mechanisms in some sort of twisted attempt to save them from themselves. This is Victorian/Carnegie-style paternalism, more appropriate for a past century. Of course, I realize that to suggest that schools for the relatively poor be allowed to operate with very poor standards is 'problematic', as the message that this would send is that the children of the semi-poor deserve only so much. This is not at all what I mean, and it is far, far from ideal. But the strange thing is that this is what already happens, with most of the truly poor using supposedly fee-free government schools of very poor standards. The reality then dictates this: international and national elites are just fine with the truly well-off buying their way out of poor-quality schools into objectively acceptable and sometimes actually good schools. What 'we' are not okay with is those on low-incomes scrimping and saving to buy their children's way out of bad schools (the government school baseline) into something just slightly less awful. Dressed up as something else, something pro-equity, this standpoint achieves nothing good but rather the keeping of all of the poor and nearly-poor down, together, perhaps where they belong?

9

Thinking about Education the Way Starbucks Thinks about Coffee

What if education could be fixed via the roll-out of a cheap, standardized model that takes the determination of education quality out of the hands of poorly-educated, unprofessional teachers, and lodges it firmly in the corporate headquarters of a for-profit corporation based in the United States? Lessons can be centrally designed and fully scripted, down to the last detail, and pinged across the world to any able and literate person brought to stand in front of a class of children anywhere in the Global South. Like Starbucks outlets the world over, small differences might be observable from one country to another, but standardization would remain the order of the day. A Starbucks-equivalent schooling model would capitalize on the appeal of the cheap private school, while eliminating the vast variability in the quality of teaching and infrastructure found between schools.

The model that thousands of disparate, largely unconnected individuals have replicated in their local communities has been seized on by American entrepreneurs as a way to make money while positioning themselves as captains at the helms of 'social enterprise'. There are a few other international chains, but the most famous of these companies is Bridge International Academies (Bridge), rebranded as NewGlobe, the name of the parent company, while they were going through a child sexual abuse scandal. Bridge/NewGlobe was founded by people who 'wondered why no one was thinking about schools in developing countries the way Starbucks thought about coffee'. The reasons are quite obvious, but, not to be deterred, they posit that 'our biggest challenge is that we need to ensure we standardize everything. If we want to be able to operate like McDonald's, we need to make sure that we systematize every process, every tool – everything we do'.[1] Sadly for the child victims of abuse at the hands of their teachers, there is no way to standardize the conduct of employees outside of scripted lesson times.

A one-time ardent supporter of private schools, activist-academic-entrepreneur James Tooley (co-founder of the Omega Schools chain in Ghana) observed that the corporations running fast food chains had a deep understanding of how standardized processes lead to cheap and consistent burgers, from which lessons could be drawn for the cheap, private delivery of education in bulk.[2] And as it would turn out, the product is doled out quite analogously in each sector, even from the price point of view: McDonald's is not actually all that cheap for people in the Global South and has been for some time a symbol of foreign cool. Even more aspirational is Starbucks, which is certainly not cheap or accessible to the poor, and similarly, the supposedly low-fee or 'affordable' chains of private schools are out of the reach of the actual poor (as opposed to what we in richer countries view as poor). This much is true then – Bridge and Omega are likely to have equal claims to 'affordability' as Starbucks and McDonalds have, in the markets where they operate. It's always been cheaper to order a cup of coffee at an American diner or a British 'greasy spoon' than at Starbucks, just as it's cheaper to send your child to a small, locally owned cheap private school in a Kampala slum than it is to send them to a Bridge school in the same neighbourhood.[3]

International chains like Bridge and Omega Schools talked a big game at the beginning, projecting enormous growth, similar to many a Silicon Valley start-up. Indeed, because Bridge made a teacher 'computer' (actually just a common e-reader) central to its standardized model, they have even tried to don the tech company image of cool, efficient modernity, presumably in a bid to appear more exciting, innovative, 'disruptive' than they perhaps are. Indeed, EdTech has become a key avenue for the increasing insertion of the private sector into education. But the claim of Bridge being a tech company is probably about as far-fetched in many respects as a fast food outlet making a similar claim because they use a computerized 'point of sale' ordering system and other tech-enabled monitoring and central ordering systems. The two uses of technology could be seen as doing a pretty similar job – spitting out orders in the kitchen's prep or assembly area/classroom (delete as appropriate) and keeping tabs on the availability and sufficiency of the necessary inputs, to the easily-replaceable, unskilled non-professionals ostensibly doing the work of cooks/teachers (again, delete as appropriate).

At the present time, the market share that international corporate chains have captured is infinitesimally small – so why devote time and attention to them in writing, research and advocacy? This is a question I have grappled with, at first urging people to pay the likes of Bridge minimal attention because they were tiny and were unlikely to reach profitability. But the subject deserves light being thrown into its dark corners for several reasons. The most worrying idea is that the small attack mounted so far could be the thin end of an enormous wedge, a new and shameless avenue via which to siphon off money from poor countries. And this time it's personal, to millions of people in the Global South. To profit from the sweat and toil of low-income mothers and fathers dedicated to finding the best possible education for their children, exploiting their hopes and dreams, to repatriate profits to already-rich countries *is disgusting*. It is that much more mercenary than taking money from governments or from oil extraction or something slightly further removed from the common citizen, the ultimate grassroots level. It appears that much worse when you learn that the entrepreneurs involved travel by helicopter to their holiday house on the Kenyan coast,[4] even if their fat salaries are funded by clueless venture philanthro-capitalists rather than profits from their hitherto unprofitable corporation. It appears *even worse* when you learn that the company sought to cover up and frustrate the investigation into crimes against children that took place at and in connection with their schools, so that they could spread their model to additional countries before they got the fundamental issue of child protection under control.[5]

Expressing worry about the wedge slowly forcing the door open may seem farfetched, but I am a student of history, and one need look no further than the history of the British East India Company to see what horrors can be achieved by a small but ferociously focused band of people when the defenders' response is disorganized and when the ferocious band is severely underestimated and even discounted. William Dalrymple's *The Anarchy* sets out the threat as played out in history, and while NewGlobe may look like small potatoes now, so too did the East India Company at the beginning, and it took them well over a century to reach their zenith. The great history of Northern capitalist aggression shows that, like water flowing and finding its way into every crack and crevice, so capitalists will seek every means by which to extract profit from those in the South who struggle to compete with us with both hands tied behind their backs. There's another way these companies are getting involved in cheap private schooling in the Global South, public-private partnerships (PPPs), and it is to this avenue that Bridge/NewGlobe ultimately pivoted, discussed in depth in the next chapter.

***

The task of this chapter is to provide a picture of what it looks like to think about education in Africa the way that Starbucks thinks about coffee, and how 'world-class education' is allegedly being delivered under corrugated sheets over wooden-plank-and-chicken-wire structures through fully scripted and standardized lessons. The purpose of this introduction is to help limber-up the mind of the reader for the mental contortions that will be expected of it by the ideas of education entrepreneurs. It might be reassuring that this thinking is not confined to white Americans in regard to poor African and Asian children: indeed, a school chain owner in Sweden said that running schools as a business was just like selling fridges – you just have to know your sector and what the customer wants.[6] Only someone who has never tried to teach could have said this.

For Northern companies to feel comfortable establishing precisely this type of business model and to gain funding from their own gang of aid agencies, they need to be comfortable propagating the image of people in the Global South as being mostly poor. Anyone not living in a house that a Northern family would recognize as having the basic necessities earns these people the uniform label of 'the poor'. The fact that what is locally a middle or lower-middle-class family using a Bridge school can easily be passed off, particularly through visual aids, to Northern audiences as extending access to 'the poor' provides further avenues for funding from the venture-philanthropists/philanthrocapitalists. It's believable because surely only a poor person would send their child to a school made of wooden planks and chicken wire as provided by Bridge. And here the mental gymnastics begin – we are to believe 'world-class' education is taking place in such settings, while the children of the founders, Shannon May and Jay Kimmelman, are sure as shit not attending the 'world-class' schools their parents created.[7] These people must all be poor – we can just leave out images of where the school-aged children of the truly poor are (mostly in government schools, or out of school and working) and that is convenient for international chains to maintain the image that poverty is alleviable via market-based approaches where the consumer pays. Cognitive dissonance? No matter. The corporate fast-food-style chains can simply claim to be reaching that amorphous blob, 'the poor', and the corporate owners and managers can be seen to be 'doing well by doing good'. Everyone is happy – 'the poor' (the blob) are the recipients of Bridge's 'knowledge for all' while the rich have achieved the resulting warm glow.

***

There is a lot of talk about the private sector bringing innovation to a model of education that was designed well over a century ago, and designed in cultures radically different from those of the Global South in which this model is now being applied. Techies have been bemoaning the old-fashioned nature of the prevalent schooling model for years now, with various private sector actors making great claims regarding innovation. SPARK Schools in South Africa, not at all 'cheap', but somehow having been bundled in with them, in cooperation with a company that looks like a typo but is actually called 'itslearning', have 'announced one of the most compelling partnerships in EdTech with a common vision of creating the world's best learning management system (LMS) integration with G Suite'. They even find some American teachers willing to acclaim this as a 'game changer', with it heavily implied that there could be (positive) impacts on learning as a result. When I looked into this great innovation, I found that it was in fact just an online system for dealing with students' assignments. It may make teachers' lives easier, but it has nothing to do with classroom innovation.[8]

There are some interesting examples, such as the Khan Academy, which uses the idea of the 'flipped classroom', where children listen to lessons at home online. This means that they can pause and go back to things they don't understand the first time, and they can listen to the lesson all over again if they need to. Then, when it comes time to practise what they have learned, that is, by doing homework, they actually do this at school with their teacher on hand to help them when they are struggling to apply what they have learned. Presumably, they can then ask questions they might have raised their hand to ask during a normal lesson, in this case replaced by the video. This represents an innovative approach, using technology to deliver a lesson, and what some would say is a better use of the time a student has with the teacher. But arguably, there is very little left that is new under the sun, and so other approaches like collaborative peer learning approaches, well, as Chapter 6 showed, such approaches were being used in India for hundreds, and likely thousands, of years until the British copied and exported the model before doing away with its use in India. There is a vogue for bringing back techniques and ideas that have been used in the past and might have been discarded for some reason, and repackaging these approaches as innovations, to trot them out anew.

Rising Academies (a much less aggressive for-profit chain), for example, uses group work and peer learning, and trains their teachers in tried and tested questioning techniques that enable the teacher to really determine whether their students have understood the lesson content or not. However, it is difficult to pass off using long-established techniques or methods as 'innovation' just because you are doing them somewhat better than others, although where this is the case, it may feel quite novel when anything actually does go well. I have discussed the issue of pedagogy with John Rendel, who founded a distinctively different chain of very pointedly not-for-profit secondary schools in Uganda (PEAS), and he agreed that for now, getting schooling in its traditional incarnation to work well represents a major victory and should not be denigrated for lacking innovation. There are some things that require an extent of training that may be unrealistic to achieve in the medium term.

With regard to what the classroom looks like in most private schools, I have yet to see anything other than a largely traditional classroom set-up. Bridge, the most notorious for big claims, purports to be innovative, and yet when I visited their schools under the most ideal circumstances (i.e. with senior staff from the headquarters in Lagos – meaning that school staff were on notice and would put on the best show possible), what I saw was the teacher at the front of the classroom reading the lesson from the e-reader. She would ask questions of the class that they would answer. Children would use printed materials at times and would do exercises in their notebooks at other times. For mathematics problems, the teacher would go through them step by step with the whole class, allowing students to tell her what to do and if something was right or not. Nothing about this was new to me or in any way an innovative delivery of curriculum material. It certainly didn't seem to fit the bill for ultra-trendy 'learner-centred' approaches. The strangest thing was every single action of the teacher being dictated by the script she was following on her device; every single thing that was said and done, down to cues given to the class (often a snap of the fingers, which was quite strange – the one innovation, perhaps), and when to walk around and look at what the children were doing, and how many seconds to spend on this.

The Bridge operational theory posits that, at the same moment in a particular grade level, the same thing would be happening in each Bridge school within that country or state. This strict standardization was passed off as innovation, along with the centrally controlled management of the school, facilitated through the school manager's smartphone, streaming instructions to him or her for every minute of the day, and feeding data back up the chain to headquarters. It might be considered innovative too, then, if we could completely standardize all children's thoughts and behaviour, eliminating any variation and all individual character and personality, cutting down Bridge teachers' 'classroom management' burden. I have not had the opportunity to observe lessons at any of the non-Bridge corporate chains, but Bridge classes do not look any different from those that happen in locally owned private schools, with one exception being the hard-core classroom management techniques used, which are described in a later section of this chapter.

***

The least inspiring or 'world-class' lesson I observed at a Bridge school was one on 'crafting with paper', during which the children were told about all the wonderful crafts they might do with paper, if only they had the space and the materials. This type of lesson, one telling students about a practical thing that they would, ideally, learn-by-doing instead, is not unusual in resource-strapped schools in Southern countries. Long ago, I became accustomed to lessons on 'computers' where no computer is ever seen in action by the students; rather, they are taught through pictures and descriptions about what a mouse is, what a monitor is, what a keyboard is, and how to open, format, name, and ultimately close a Word document. It is only to be imagined what children make of such things and how accurately they can imagine the actual doing of the things they must passively learn about.

So, the Bridge lesson on 'crafting with paper' was no different in tenor and content than countless other lessons I have observed in infinitely less well-funded private schools. Rising Academies and Omega, now under the same corporate umbrella, both expanded at a much more modest pace than Bridge did in its early years. They seem to have paid greater attention to teaching practice, providing standardized materials but allowing teachers greater independence and arguably commensurately greater responsibility and professionalism while providing better support to teachers. Yet overall, from where the student sits, there is little that is remarkably different or innovative in these chains, as compared with the model employed in locally owned schools which may or may not be a bit less well-organized. The business of school education continues much as it always has with varying degrees of professionalism in different schools – the difference with the for-profit chains being that, if successful, the organizations will one day siphon profits from non-wealthy parents in the South to be repatriated to the United States and the United Kingdom. This is in stark contrast to locally owned schools, where revenues from virtually every part of the school undertaking and its ancillary services stay local rather than benefiting outsiders.

***

Central to school education is the teacher, with schooling being a very labour-intensive sector. Online charter schools are arguably the only ones that actually take advantage of economies of scale – as they will often have one teacher remotely monitoring the progress of hundreds of children in virtual classrooms at the same time, with dubious results. Looking at the low-tech classroom of the typical cheap private school, it quickly becomes apparent that teachers are the central challenge. People who would set up schools within their community realize that they have to recruit locally, and that, depending on the local population density and the level of pay that they can offer, they will have a smaller or greater pool of candidates to recruit from. Rather than addressing the trained-teacher supply problem, Bridge (especially) built its system to capitalize on the reality they were presented with, which allowed them to hire cheap and dispensable proxy teachers. If there's a script for every moment of the lesson and every word spoken by the teacher, then particular individuals can come and go, but the system has been 'teacher-proofed' or perhaps more accurately, 'person-proofed'. Unqualified secondary school completers are plentiful, cheap and easy to mould – but making teachers into depersonalized cogs in a machine could well have proven a factor in Bridge's child sexual abuse scandal.

The chains provide their employees with materials that guide them every step of the way, although the degree to which they do this differs from company to company. James Tooley has written about teacher-proofing the schooling process as though it is the best possible idea,[9] while having professed a sincere solidarity with individually owned schools. Paul Skidmore of Rising Academies also speaks passionately about what they do to ensure teachers are able to perform in the classroom, and Omega Schools and Rising Academies provide their staff with standardized lesson plans and support materials to scaffold their practice, at least treating them more like thinking people with agency than Bridge does. Overall, with these chains, teachers are to the extent possible rendered deliverers of material set for them from thousands of kilometres away. They are not expected or trusted to plan lessons or to determine how particular content should be delivered. Their role is to deliver as instructed from on high, and this system has been designed mostly by foreigners from outside of the context who evince confidence that they know best.

Now, before getting all upset, it is important to understand that there is certainly a logic to this: teachers are not some special class of people who organically develop the knowledge and skills needed for the job. Indeed, taking into account the schools in which probably the majority of the world's teachers were educated themselves, it would be a miracle if they ever developed these intellectual assets, through no fault of their own. The sad reality is that, in the places where they operate, the likes of Bridge are not wrong for assuming that the candidates available to them are not prepared to be the autonomous, sensitive (in terms of picking up on incomprehension among their students), proactive and responsive professionals that one would wish a teacher to be. It is for this reason that lesson scripts and systems of monitoring and control are developed. In their locally owned competitor schools, teachers rely on their own knowledge and understanding, supported solely by the chapters of the textbook that they work from. They are likely not equipped with the skills of questioning for comprehension and explaining concepts in different ways that good teachers need.

The idea behind Bridge's scripting of every minute of every lesson is to render the teacher into a fast-food burger flipper. The idea is that, should one teacher quit or be sacked on a random Tuesday, a ready Bridge teacher in their reserve bank of candidates can be slotted right in on Wednesday morning to deliver that day's pre-scripted lessons with a minimum of disruption or upheaval. The personal relationships between teacher and students are not factored in – after all, there is nothing much that any school owner or manager can do about this if a teacher seeks to leave – but at least the classroom and behaviour management and child-energy-channelling techniques used by the replacement teacher will be identical to those used by the outgoing teacher. No time is taken to ascertain where the class is up to in terms of the syllabus – it is all pre-determined by the e-reader. Whether or not children are managing to keep up is a separate issue.

What is wrong with all this? Where needs must, why not embrace the teacher-as-burger-flipper; teacher as standardized part to be slotted in and, inevitably, quickly replaced? After all, one issue with government systems is the lack of accountability of the teachers, so to get them to work, teachers must know that they will indeed be sacked if necessary. I have pointed out that teacher turnover is a factor for all low-fee private schools. I have pointed out the disruption that results, and it is inevitable that there will be some disruption at an individually owned school when a teacher leaves unexpectedly, before and after a replacement is found. So what is wrong with having teachers familiar with the use of the e-readers and the classroom management techniques ready to slot right in the next day to keep the thread of learning unbroken? What is wrong with minimizing disruption in the kitchen of a cheap, chain restaurant by having everything designed, frozen and delivered from a central office, for kitchen workers to unpackage, fry, and throw together in the prescribed manner?

What is wrong with it is what probably every reader of this book would feel in their bones to be wrong with it – none of you need to be told, and none of you would send your children to such a school. While it cannot be denied that many teachers will need some help and support in the absence of proper preparation for the serious work of teaching, this rendering of a teacher into the educational equivalent of a fast-food worker goes against the grain for human beings possessed of a spirit and a sense of their individual self. It may be just as effective, if not more so, than leaving an untrained person to it in the classroom armed only with a textbook and some rudimentary instructions from the school owner. But this is the crucial factor: what sets the Bridge model apart is the formalization, the institutionalization, of the highly informal response to educational need *by hiring unqualified people* and utterly denying the magic that takes place when a person whose vocation is teaching, teaches. Not only did Bridge originally hire unqualified school leavers out of necessity – indeed, *they favoured such candidates* as they were easier to shape and mould.[10]

***

So what does all this look like in practice? As already mentioned, the most extreme example and the one with the largest market share, Bridge, provides an e-reader to each teacher, which they call the 'teacher computer', and the teacher loads the week's lessons from the school manager's smartphone. The teacher then follows the script on the e-reader screen, and this script contains links to answers to each and every question (purportedly) that their students might ask about a given topic – for example, how to add fractions or how to conjugate a verb. Jay Kimmelman, one of the founders, was confident in explaining to me, in Kenya in 2011, that there are only so many questions that any child will ask on a given concept, and their lesson plans contain answers to them all, taking the pressure off the teacher to provide the right answer themselves.

Children's actions are tightly controlled too: they are to sit in a certain way, not touching anything on their desks, until told to pick up a pen or pencil and do a particular exercise or activity. Their hands, like suspected criminals, are to be visible at all times, with fingers interlaced on the desk. The only part of the classroom interaction that is not scheduled and scripted is anything to do with classroom management and dealing with children acting out or not paying attention. However, the way in which children are disciplined certainly is scripted, with teachers provided training on how to do this as part of their initial crash course. Children are instructed to, at all times, 'track the teacher', which was something that was alien to me until I visited Bridge schools in action in Lagos. After reading about charter schools in the United States, I connected the dotted line between this sort of practice and the American charter school movement. One teacher in the United States has written about how she regards the demand that her class always 'track her' as part of an 'oppressive and dehumanizing system of student management'.[11] It basically means that children's attention must be intently fixed on the teacher at all times, which strikes the observer as being akin to the distinctly not innovative 'teacher-centred' classroom, as opposed to being modern and 'child-centred'. Bridge schools borrow from the methodologies employed at charter schools, and when, in Lagos, the children in a Bridge classroom would let their attention start to wander, the teacher would interrupt the lesson script to demand that the children 'track' him or her. The children would chant in unison, in a sing-song way, 'traaack the teacher with your eyes and your body', which was accompanied by choreographed arm and hand movements. The lesson could then continue on its preordained track. I never witnessed what would happen if a class presented any more significant challenge to the teacher than simply not 'tracking' her.

At Bridge, I observed a teacher taking the class through a lesson on the addition of fractions. It was clear that this was not the first time that the class had encountered this concept, and by the end of the period, the class had gone through the addition of some fractions, and they were left with the fraction 7/8. The teacher, as scripted, asked the class if they could reduce that particular fraction at all or if this would be the final answer. Half of the class said 'yeeeess!' while the other half said 'nooooo!' The teacher looked at her device, which was clearly assuming the whole class would answer correctly in the negative, and so was prompting her to move on. The hung jury of students meant that she froze, embarrassed, and looked to the back of the classroom where I was seated next to a senior Bridge staff member (their local head of academics), our presence lending the scene a particular tension. She didn't know what to do and, at a loss, simply followed the electronic script to the next topic, without even indicating which half of the class was correct and which was in error. There is an emphasis on speed in this model, which was well documented in the Kenyan context first,[12] and it appears likely that many children do not catch on quickly enough under the tyranny of the e-reader. So, what happens to them? Clearly, more mental contortions and gymnastics are again required to allow the reader to accept all this as embodying 'world-class' education. Training and conditioning in gymnastics, as in any sport, help to move one up the difficulty scale, and so fittingly, we move on to more advanced feats of mental contortion to process and digest all this – whether these schools have a clear advantage in how much their students learn.

**

I was initially one of the credulous many, convinced that international school chains just had to be able to do a better job of getting children to understand and learn primary school material than the typical cheap private school with no outside support or investment. I had conversations about this with many people working in Nigeria or interested in private schools, and it seemed that, particularly the rather muscular and showy Bridge, with all its research and development, all its market research (in the subtext, read *all their foreign, Northern wisdom, systems, drive and efficiency*), must be able to do better what small, individual schools have to do on a shoestring. Even if they recruit from the same local pool of teacher candidates as every other school, even if they do not invest in serious pre-service teacher preparation, they have invested in researching and designing systems to support and scaffold this same type of teacher in her daily practice. So, one teacher left to sink or swim on her own with only a textbook and a blackboard would surely do less well than her chain school counterpart. It is ubiquitous that many teachers in the South are not equipped with the skills to explain curriculum material in various different ways; they are not equipped with diverse strategies, and they often are not even solid on the primary level subject content that they are to teach, which leads them to give incorrect replies to students when they ask questions. Therefore, with Bridge's e-reader supplying the answers to students' questions, taking the lottery element out of this aspect of the classroom process, it just seemed too plausible that these schools would be doing a significantly better job than government schools, for sure, but also other otherwise comparable private schools.

Focusing on the example of Bridge, it came as a shock to me to learn that careful research into the subject has not yielded the anticipated results. A UK-funded evaluation took place in Lagos, which was only possible because the company, despite being a for-profit market player, accepted a grant from the UK government to help support its entry into the Lagos market. Despite Bridge having dragged its feet throughout the process, the results were released in 2018. The evaluation sought to compare the contribution to learning directly attributable to the school a child attended for children at three types of schools: Lagos State's own government schools, the typical individually owned private schools and Bridge schools. The research sought to compare the learning across children from similar backgrounds, or in the language of economics, they 'controlled for' children's socioeconomic status to determine whether any learning advantage or disadvantage was due to the school itself versus being more influenced by factors outside of school.

It is startling that the evaluation found no advantage for Bridge schools over individual schools in numeracy, while they did have a statistically significant advantage in literacy (0.35 standard deviations, for those who like to read results in econometric terms). In literacy, then, Bridge schools were found to be superior to individual schools, which were in turn superior to government schools. But in the trickier subject to get right, numeracy which is necessary for any advanced mathematics learning, Bridge schools were no different from any other private school, while all of these non-state schools were superior to government schools.[13] Omega Schools and Rising Academies also did their own evaluations, finding advantages in relation to government school students, but no clear evidence of superiority over individual private schools emerged for Omega.[14] Rising Academies' endline evaluation report states that their students made significantly greater literacy and numeracy gains over three years than comparison private and government school pupils. However, in literacy, while their students exceeded a designated 'modest' learning target, they failed to reach even a 'moderate' target. In mathematics the picture is worse, with students failing to meet even the 'modest' learning target.[15] PEAS is another matter, with those schools specifically targeting the less well-off, and providing solid learning that is far more equitably distributed from a poverty and disadvantage perspective.[16]

What does this all tell us then? It shows that just a small learning advantage over individual schools accrues from enormous sums spent on research and development. The total expense of the chain school model just does not seem to be worth it. But a key issue to come out of all these studies and evaluations looking at the quality of various types of public and private schools is the importance of teacher characteristics. It is not often made explicit, although one in-depth and highly detailed study from Kenya makes this utterly so[17]: the teachers that teach in all of these schools are often highly similar. They likely have pretty comparable levels of subject content knowledge, although in countries where civil service teachers get better pre-service preparation, they may have better knowledge of pedagogy and different professional techniques. These teachers have, after all, come out of the same country's national schooling system as that which they are then employed to teach in (whatever the sector), so it makes sense that low levels of student learning go with low levels of teacher knowledge. The international chains accept the situation, as they must, and have fully understood it, having done the requisite market research, and it is for this reason that they invest more in the system around the teacher, or in the tech-delivered scripts that their staff will work from, so that the abysmal standard of available recruits will have the smallest possible impact on the final outcome.

And this is the key thing to be learned from looking at these chain schools: there is nothing that can be done to get around a lack of *real teachers*, if the end result will be a really good quality of education, with deep learning for the students. The tech giants and Silicon Valley philanthrocapitalists may wish there was a tech solution but there isn't. Gates and Zuckerberg have failed to make a dent in poor learning levels back home in the United States despite burning through $500 million (per year) and $100 million (over five years), respectively,[18] and in resource-poor settings in the South, tech doesn't go very far. The poor quality of teachers provides a firm and impenetrable ceiling to the levels of learning that can be achieved in a classroom. I have been saying this for years, but it was only when the assessments of the chain schools started to emerge that I knew I could assert this with confidence. And yet, why do we need published, peer-reviewed evidence to tell us what we know instinctually in our bones to be true?[19] Were most people in rich countries to be asked if 'world-class' education could actually be delivered with untrained people put into a classroom with a script to read from, and whether they would like to send their children to such a school (made of wooden boards, corrugated sheets and chicken wire), the answer would be a resounding no. And yet, some pass off such an arrangement as being 'world class' when served up for those people down there in those poor places in the South. As the centuries-old saying goes, you can't make a silk purse out of a pig's ear, and that is exactly what the corporate chains are trying to do with a bit of tech here and some scripting there with a large helping of surveillance.[20] And they want to make money out of this – or rather through their main efforts through public-private partnerships (see Chapter 10), so that another sector can be added to the range of economic activities that facilitate the siphoning of profits from South to North. Why should the education of children have some sort of sacred cow status?

Another important thing to note is that, unlike at other schools, there is no plan to make things at chain schools any better. They have no aspiration to hire better teachers in the future because, firstly, these are hardly available, and if they were, the salaries they would command would be out of reach. The whole point of their model is to engineer their way around the glaring teacher constraint. Lack of improvement in the actual teaching is baked into the design. Bridge seems to hope for improvement only in the materials provided to teachers, but from a dubious source: they have legions of extremely poorly paid 'fellowship' holders in the United States writing lesson plans and other materials, complaining about working conditions and exploitation on sites like Glassdoor.com.[21]

In light of the limitations of the model, it is unsurprising that the company had doubts about the performance of their students in their first schools in Kenya when it came time for high-stakes national examinations that schools are judged by. Peg Tyre, in a *New York Times* article, described Bridge 'trumpeting' its students' success on the Kenya Certificate of Primary Education exam in 2015, during which apparently 63 per cent of Bridge's class eight students passed the exam, compared to 49 per cent of other students. Tyre was told by ex-employees that this result was achieved at least partly through the flying in of teachers from the United States who held an intensive cram school to get students ready to pass the exam, while others who seemed less than likely to pass were asked to repeat a year so that their potentially poor scores would not drag down Bridge's pass rate.[22] Naturally, the company doesn't mention this 'cram school' in their PR materials, but even worse, I'd suggest that the resulting pass rate is not so impressively high as compared to other schools' as to be worthy of being 'trumpeted'.

***

There are myriad reasons to fear the encroachment of corporate school chains into the national education space of target countries. First, these chains zero in on countries where the public system is already weak and on the back foot, but where the groundwork has already been laid for them in the form of a thriving, cheap private school market, belying their often-stated side-aim of increasing access to education in places currently lacking. While some chains are content to be growing but not dominant players in a local education market, Bridge/NewGlobe only established its initial presence as 'proof of concept'[23] before entering into 'partnerships' with governments to quickly reach thousands and even hundreds of thousands of instant 'clients' who have no choice – a captive, government-paid market. They would then play a larger and larger role in a country's education system with the ultimate end of becoming 'too big to fail' or even to effectively regulate (not that regulation of individual schools is effective now …). The best defence Southern countries have against these chains is to allow their thriving local schooling markets to continue to thrive. With these schools, they will know that if any given operator closes down, there will not be any major systemic impacts. Their local economies will benefit by all of the revenues to the school and to support services such as books, materials, uniforms and food vending, which will all be kept in the local economy. There will never be any question mark over who owns the curriculum and whether materials are compatible with local requirements. Despite their currently small footprint on national education systems where they are currently operating, the threat of corporate entry will be underestimated at countries' peril – even from the other chains less rapacious than Bridge/NewGlobe.

To save the worst for last: in 2023, news broke of tens of catalogued allegations of child sexual abuse at the original Bridge International Academies in Kenya, and of the International Finance Corporation (IFC, the commercial investing arm of the World Bank Group) working committedly with NewGlobe's founders,

Jay Kimmelman and Shannon May, to cover it up.[24] Their main goal, established in September 2020, was to keep the victimization of children under wraps just long enough for parent company NewGlobe to convince more investors to back them and more countries to welcome them in. Trying to deflect, NewGlobe was keen to point out via a report that they themselves commissioned back in 2020[25] that child sexual abuse and other gender-based violence is a well-known issue in schools, with NewGlobe's target countries very much sharing in this problem. One might ask then, why they were not many times more robust on this issue in advance of opening so many schools in their chosen hotbed of child sex abuse (as they sought to portray it), Kenya.

In brief, in 2018 the IFC's own Compliance Advisor Ombudsman received a complaint from EACHRights in Kenya regarding myriad failings and violations of Kenyan labour and health and safety regulations at Bridge schools. For some reason, it took until February 2020 for a team to be sent to Nairobi to investigate, and while they were there conducting their interviews, they heard much more distressing allegations from the communities where the schools operate regarding the sexual abuse of children. The IFC investigator, Daniel Adler, who by all accounts seems to have been deeply committed and sincere, immediately informed the IFC of what he had learned. What would come out over the next few years is a despicable story whose zenith is a 12 September 2020 call between May, Kimmelman and two IFC staffers, William Sonneborn and Shannon Atkeson. This was a crisis call to figure out how to respond to the news that they received a few days prior, of a formal investigation having been launched into the disturbing allegations that IFC investigators had received seven months prior in Nairobi – an investigation they had done their best to forestall. Unfortunately for the call participants, someone was taking hand-written notes that were later leaked, along with the ensuing draft investigation report of late summer 2023. It was also revealed that Bridge had compiled a list of *at least 70 allegations of abuse*. The goal was to figure out how to keep things quiet until the company's 'Series F' funding round closed, which would facilitate their entry to several new markets, including Rwanda. 'The revelations would "spook investors" and undermine Bridge's expansion plans in Rwanda. "Time matters", as one person on the call put it. "Need to delay until Series F".'[26] To do this, a settled intention to 'neturalize Adler' was agreed upon, which the company would go on to try to do via outlandishly false allegations against him,[27] along with the commitment to 'gumming up the process' of the entire investigation.

In NewGlobe's world, anything goes, and no matter what claims they make, they seem to survive, shape-shifting as they go. It is probably no coincidence that in 2020 they chose to re-brand as NewGlobe, the name of Bridge's parent company, probably hoping that this would help them shed the reputation they earned in Kenya. As I have already said, it is no surprise that sexual abuse took place at multiple Bridge schools – it can happen at any school, and they ran several hundred schools at one time. What is appalling is how it was dealt with, with the leaked IFC report stating that child victims' families were left to bear the financial burden of getting medical and psychological help for their children. Neither the company nor the IFC thought it their duty to support children and their families to recover and move on, despite IFC rules clearly stating that remedy must be made when an IFC-funded project *causes actual harm*. Apparently, the IFC considered setting up a fund for the purpose of helping victims and their families but then thought better of it, as it has also refused to do with regard to other projects that have harmed communities.[28]

The IFC follow-up in Spring 2024 has also been terribly weak, setting out the intention to support services helping victims of abuse across society and leaving it up to Bridge's victims to seek out these services, rather than helping and compensating victims directly.[29] Needless to say, the core mission of May and Kimmelman was to expand their empire[30] and wheedle their way into the education systems of yet more countries, and their attitude to date has been to act like they are protecting state secrets, keeping their cards as close to their chests as possible, admitting almost nothing. In mid-March 2024, Ajay Banga, World Bank president, emailed all World Bank staff to admit that 'mistakes were made' with regard to the IFC investment in Bridge, and to express contrition for the trauma suffered by the child victims, on the eve of the publication of the Compliance Advisor Ombudsman's findings.[31] Banga also signalled that an independent investigation would take place, and two months later, in a 16 May press release, the Board of the IFC announced the start of their search for an outside firm to look into the CAO's investigation:

> The review will seek to confirm that IFC staff and management cooperated fully with CAO as required under IFC policies. This will include verifying that IFC provided complete access to documents and staff as requested by CAO; ensuring IFC in no way interfered in the CAO investigation; certifying that IFC took all actions required under applicable CAO policies; and making sure there were no actions to limit the effectiveness of the Bridge investigation.[32]

This language seems to indicate that they are looking for a company to confirm that the CAO investigation was flawless, rather than to get to something approaching objective truth on the matter.

I am very sure that abuse takes place at public and individually owned private schools of all fee levels, in all countries. However, a core difference between a Bridge school and the average cheap private school is that between the hired flunky that is the 'Academy Manager' at a Bridge school, whose every move and action is dictated by instructions delivered from on high via their Bridge-issued smartphone, and the private school owner whose everything is wrapped up and invested in their school. The Academy Manager and her 'superiors' back at HQ simply cannot be as invested in averting disaster for their client families via the predations of school staff as a person who has built their own school from the ground up, who keeps watch and scrutinizes teachers' actions every day, and who scrutinizes each individual hire. The school proprietor has serious skin in the game, while the 'Academy Manager' can just walk away. Teaching at cheap private schools, especially in poor informal settlements, can be a dispiriting and thankless task. Anyone who might claim that the people working in these schools don't perceive a difference in the scrutiny and level of personal, financial and emotional investment from a Bridge Academy Manager versus an individual school owner has no idea what they are talking about. Teachers at Bridge have reported being bamboozled into thinking they would earn all the extra bonus payments that Bridge recruiters said they could earn through a series of extra duties, mostly to do with recruiting additional pupils for the school. However, to reach the maximum possible salary plus bonuses entails work for which there is not enough time in the day, and one can speculate at the level of disenchantment and disinvestment a teacher might feel after they realize this.[33] It is unlikely that one can work for Bridge and not be aware of one's disposability. This may be true to an extent at individual schools, yet still there are much tighter relationships of management and accountability at such schools that may help to keep teachers' actions within the realms of decency.

As sure as I am that abuse happens, I am also sure that cover-ups occur at all types of school. Shame and embarrassment are strong, especially in certain cultures where girls, in particular, can come to be seen as 'damaged goods' or as having brought it on themselves. There are myriad ways that a school owner and victims' families might work through this, which will involve the police in some cases but not in others, sometimes because the family does not want an official case opened.[34] What is unlikely is that the proprietor will disavow the family or pay for the legal defence of the accused to get their conviction overturned, as Bridge did with a teacher put on trial and actually convicted in one particularly gruesome case.[35] What will not happen is a corrupt and uncaring school owner being enabled and promoted as so many investors did with NewGlobe, potentially impacting the lives and fates of tens or even hundreds of thousands of students through their callousness. As I have said, having much more invested both financially and emotionally in the local area, and having to face the reality that the buck stops with them, an individual school owner will have to work hard to make children safe or face ruin and shame in their own community. What is more, they will not have the backing of a key arm of the world's most well-known multilateral development organization, the World Bank, to help them cover up their staff's crimes and facilitate them to expand their operations.

It must be understood that allegations of abuse were rolling in from nearly the earliest days, certainly from 2013 onwards, and the IFC was explicitly made aware in 2013, 2016 and 2017, yet did nothing about it.[36] Unharried by this key investor, NewGlobe just carried on without instituting the necessary processes and mechanisms to address the risk to children in their schools: from the first intimation that they were not able to monitor teachers as needed, they transitioned from (possibly) being naïvely negligent to being wilfully so.[37] Scaling up institutions like NewGlobe means scaling up the risk and harm that comes with them, and they were just egged on by the likes of William Sonneborn, whose remit at the IFC is 'disruptive technologies', among other things. The company needed serious correction and guard rails, but Sonneborn, with such a remit, seems to have been more of the Facebook worldview, where it's cool, innovative and techy to 'move fast and break things', claiming to 'disrupt' things to *make the world a better place*. What is so galling about international actors of various sorts coming in and capitalizing on a schooling model that I can only see as a relatively long-term crisis response is that they are institutionalizing this crisis response, hiring teachers who are not prepared, illegally in the case of Kenya, where every teacher must be certified and registered with the Teachers Service Commission.[38] But in institutionalizing and concretizing this model, they are doing so in a depersonalized way where the buck stops somewhere way up the chain in some office building in Nairobi or Cambridge, Massachusetts. Education International published a report in which Bridge teachers stated that they didn't bother following the dictates of the company when their roving monitoring staff were not on site.[39] Trying to avoid the red flags that would result at HQ if the e-reader data suggested that the pages of the lesson plan were never used in the designated lesson time, they would just randomly skip through the pages of the e-reader lesson scripts, thereby sending nonsense data back to headquarters. But much more damagingly, the company's tech-based monitoring systems were not able to deter predatory staff members from abusing children. Clearly, they did not have a firm sense that they would be personally held accountable. Bridge schools and NewGlobe's founders and senior management failed in what must be the core mission of any school: to keep the children in their care safe first and foremost, with how much they learn or do not learn and any other consideration coming a distant second. They did nothing serious about it until after the major investigation into their systems started in late 2020, when they had already been entrusted with vulnerable children for well over a decade. Even then, they did nothing like as much as the IFC belatedly advised them to do. What did the World Bank do? They permissively hung back, enabling them to fail upwards spectacularly.

Kimmelman and May are now notoriously difficult to deal with. One colleague who was involved in the evaluation of Bridge school learning outcomes told me that at times it felt almost impossible to work with them, and I had been explicitly banned by them as a possible member of the evaluation team. They were similarly difficult with the team who would evaluate their work in Liberia (this will be discussed in Chapter 10), and in both countries, the evaluations were forced upon them, with considerable difficulty, as a condition of the funding they would receive. The UK government saw fit to gift £3.45 million to Bridge to help them enter the Lagos market,[40] as I mentioned earlier. British International Investment,[41] the UK government's development finance institution, that is, the British version of the IFC, is invested in NewGlobe through an intermediary, Novastar, which proudly states that it has been invested in Bridge since the very beginning, 'pre-Series A', investing again in 2014/15's Series D, and again in 2017, Series E, at which point they took a board seat,[42] meaning that they know all about the child sexual abuse, the IFC investigation and the attempted cover-up. In a condemnatory report of Session 2022–23, the International Development Committee expressed the view that the UK should not be invested in any private education project having 'unintended consequences for international development'.[43] They note that through Novastar the UK government continues to be (indirectly) invested in NewGlobe. Considerable shame is deserved by any Northern investors who are willing to maintain involvement in a group of schools so reckless of the damage caused to poor and vulnerable children. These investors seem about as accountable as the disposable teachers hired by Bridge in Kenya.

10

Seeking Billions from the Bottom Billions: Capitalizing on Aid Spending through Northern 'Partnership' Policies

As yet, no one has figured out a way to make a killing from operating cheap private schools, because until there are cheap and effective teacher-robots able to cope with very young children, there just aren't going to be the requisite economies of scale available in what is an extremely labour-intensive sector. NewGlobe, for one, would not be where it is if it had been left to basic market forces in the poor countries where they operate – it needed outside investment and now education-sector public-private partnerships (PPPs) to survive. PPPs exist globally and in many sectors, entailing private actors in all sorts of roles: owning and running publicly funded schools, providing management services, teacher training and countless other 'services' to aid in the provision of public education. The motivations for governments to enter into PPPs are various, including failures of quality and coverage of the public system and supposedly to increase efficiency or at least bring down costs. In Liberia, it proved the only way to attract more donor support to their education sector, while in other places it is seen as a way to drive improvement in quality or access. In rich countries, corporations have been making money through large contracts with governments (often involving self-dealing and other corrupt practices[1]), and now some companies are inspired to seek profit through contracts to serve a great number of the world's 'bottom billions'. The surest way to be able to do this is to latch onto a captive audience, the users of government schools – but this is not strictly the preserve of for-profit schools; non-profits and charities can get in on the action too.

    The World Bank suggests to client governments that if they just follow some simple rules and steps, then contracting out can mean better quality schooling at a lower cost. Instructions in their seminal 2009 tome[2] start with the Ministry of Education putting out for tender a contract to run schools, or some aspect of the schooling system. They would then receive proposals from a range of companies or organizations, with the best proposal earning the party the contract for a set duration, presumably to be extended or renewed if all goes well. There should be performance standards set out in the contract that the company must meet or exceed, and the idea is that the government holds the private entity to account through the mechanism of the contract. Missing specified milestones along the way would lead to penalties to get the company back on track, and possibly to termination of the contract if things go very badly.

In such models, there is much riding on the degree of strength and efficacy of the government's personnel and systems for overseeing and enforcing contracts. This goes far beyond having good contract lawyers, as they can only spring into action when it has been determined that the company or organization is failing to deliver as agreed. And how is this determined? Simple output measures might be relatively straight forward to deal with, but if it's about learning, it's an entirely different thing. What happens in schools that results in actual learning is often referred to as a 'black box' process that is impossible to definitively know. Therefore, even in a scenario where a country has an efficient, nimble, dedicated and switched-on administration, it can be difficult to decide that a contract has been irretrievably or even just partly broken and then to prove it, while companies tend to be tenacious in clinging on to a lucrative gig.

Now, imagine how these things go where poor-country governments have contracted out on the advice of richer countries in the mistaken belief that this will lighten their load. This occurs in places where the government bureaucracy does not have sufficient personnel of any kind and few or no personnel suited to establishing whether a company is living up to its contract terms. What if they do not have access to good enough evidence – credible data – to prove this one way or the other? In poor countries, ministries of education are often run on a shoestring, and there is no money for simple office supplies, drinking water, or any of the other things that allow a government department's staff members to do their jobs.[3] As for overseeing outsourcing contracts effectively, including the data collection required, and holding contractors to account? The capacity of poor-country governments to do this, even just in terms of person power and vehicles needed, is in doubt.

Corporate entities, on the other hand, are keenly aware of the need to have lawyers ready to act when needed.[4] What if there is asymmetry between a poor country's government and a northern corporation's degree of readiness to move to litigation? In this very-much-to-be-expected scenario, companies can simply coast, doing whatever is the minimum to be seen to be delivering, without much fear of being held to account. They can inflate costs for profit, and use legal bullying to keep their government clients in line. I have, in my writings and in public forums, asked repeatedly how these contracting-out models of public–private partnership can be suggested to be easier to oversee and quality-assure than a state system. In both cases, there are comfortable contracts shielding the people directly letting children down, whether civil servants in schools and ministries or over-worked corporate employees. All of these things happen in rich countries, so this will happen with entirely different dynamics in poor countries too. Scandals to do with government contracting even happen in much easier-to-assess sectors such as accounting, as the UK's Post Office – Fujitsu Horizon software scandal illustrates. There are all sorts of other considerations that swirl around and influence contracting relationships that affect whether a contractor is held to account for failures or not, and in the Post Office case, Fujitsu's saving face was so important that UK citizens running post offices were reputationally and financially ruined (defrauded), prosecuted and imprisoned for fabricated crimes.[5] There is no reason at all to suppose that contracting out will be any better and less-corrupt than government service provision.

***

The momentum behind the partnerships idea was building from the millennium, but governments and potential private sector partners may have felt especially encouraged from the end of the 2010s onward when, in 2009, the World Bank published something like an 'idiot's guide' to contracting out and how great this can be. In addition, certain organizations grew up to push the PPP idea both at home in the UK and abroad, such as Absolute Return for Kids (ARK), whose PPP wing was spun off into its own entity, EPG (Education Partnerships Group[6]), pushing PPPs and associated propaganda.[7] The World Bank's 2009 PPP tome[8] sought to provide comfort to governments with its checklist of things that it said needed to be done to make a PPP successful – but it reads as some sort of fantasy wish list when looked at in the cold light of day. The details, elaborated later in the chapter, are so demanding of government resources and organizational ability that I immediately wondered why any government would engage in a PPP when they could just turn these advanced organizational abilities and quality standards monitoring systems onto their own schools instead. Why would anyone need a PPP if they had the wherewithal to effectively oversee one? There are also the accompanying unintended consequences to consider, such as the myriad new avenues for corruption that putting out for tender entails – 'the corrupt official's best friend'.[9] Construction and other procurement contracts are like gold to politicians' cronies and supporters.

The pro-PPP spin seems to have been working for several countries and companies. Ghana, for example, recently brought in the Public Private Partnership (PPP) Act (1039) 2020 to foster PPPs in a broad range of service sectors. Private companies are certainly interested in government contracts: Rising Academies started out with its own for-profit, private fee-paying schools in Sierra Leone, and, along with Omega Schools in Ghana (which was later acquired by Rising Academies), became a player in Liberia (discussed below), as well as the far more rapacious Bridge/NewGlobe. Omega's ready-made chain of schools seemed to be the perfect partner organization, and Ghana has been of interest as a PPP target for international donors and the Education Partnerships Group. As with Liberia, such PPP plans tend to come under heavy fire from teachers' unions and civil society groups (both domestic and international). The fierce opposition in Ghana put proposals on hold in 2017, just a year after the Liberian experiment kicked off. The World Bank has pushed PPPs since the 2000s across a range of sectors in Ghana but did not succeed with an education PPP by the time of writing, while the United States' aid agency has run a programme to support the private school market in northern Ghana (likely the thin end of the wedge).

Three cases are illustrative for this chapter: one is Punjab, Pakistan, where a suite of PPP policies has been tried; the second is the case of Liberia's high-profile PPP; and the third is the case of NewGlobe's move to government support partnerships.

***

The list of donors that combined forces to push an experiment on Pakistan's Punjab province is long. The World Bank, Asian Development Bank, the UK's DFID, USAID, the Norwegian Agency for Development Cooperation, the Japanese government, various UN agencies and finally, the European Union were all involved. The provincial government had a policy cocktail pushed on it that included more PPP reforms than most any other country in the Global South, and it probably remains at the top of the charts.[10] The donors had a large hand in writing the country's policies, and ultimately Tony Blair's friend, Michael Barber, brought his brand of 'deliverology' to government schools while the PPP reforms were delivered with private players through the newly established Punjab Education Foundation (PEF). Seemingly, most schools – public and many private schools, existing and potential – were to get the policy makeover treatment. In 2015, *The Economist* dubbed Punjab the 'new standard bearer for market-based education reform'[11]; reforms which were meant to bring out-of-school children, the disadvantaged and under-privileged, particularly girls, into school.

The PEF threw everything at the wall to see what would stick. *Foundation Assisted Schools* would mean a school getting funding for each child attending, basically a capitation grant. The *Education Voucher Scheme* would allow parents to spend a voucher at the private school of their choice, a truly market-encouraging approach and the holy grail for Milton Friedman's ilk. The *New School Program* would provide seed money for individuals to establish private schools in unserved areas, probably the most pro-poor approach in reaching those not yet reached. Lastly, the *Government School Support Program* would mean poorly performing schools would be handed over to a private entity to manage in a US charter school-type set-up, something that might or might not work, depending on the individuals involved and whether the stars are aligned. It has been interesting to see how these different approaches were applied in different situations and to see whether one scheme or the other was more likely to achieve the aim of getting marginalized children into school. The voucher scheme could only ever have made sense in dense urban areas where there were lots of schools to choose from. The New School Program, on the other hand, successfully brought schools to locations where no one had bothered to set one up. This much at least makes sense: different approaches were chosen for different situations within the province.[12]

So, returning to the World Bank list of requirements for PPP success – and Punjab's arrangements seem to have been tailored to this list – firstly, we see that the donors successfully pushed the idea of setting up a separate body from the usual Ministry of Education. This is the autonomous Punjab Education Foundation. This ticks off number two on the list, *splitting the purchaser and provider role within the administration of the education system*, as the Foundation does not provide any schooling itself. The ministry would continue to handle government schools, but the PEF would be responsible for 'purchasing' the services of the private sector providers or 'partners' to take part in the various programmes.

Next, capacity is to be built within the contracting agency, the PEF. They did recruit some capable and qualified staff, at least at the very beginning.[13] Having established the separate foundation as a para-statal organization and tried to ensure a reasonable *capacity to carry out its functions*, the organization is meant to *design and carry out a transparent, competitive, and multi-stage process for selecting private partners*. This means putting out to tender the delivery of programmes, inviting private sector partners to submit proposals with a short list (possibly selected from an initial long list) selected for final consideration. Candidates to win a contract for service delivery would be selected based on competition between the providers based on their proposals. To achieve transparency requires that criteria for selection be clearly and publicly outlined in the public advertisement so that organizations could show how they meet the criteria. Decisions could then be made based on the proposals assessed against the stated criteria and also based on costs as proposed by the bidders (unless costs were already stipulated by the contracting organization).

For such processes to be fair, first, there would need to be enough personnel with the skill and knowledge required to consider the applications. Second, for the process to be considered competitive and transparent, there needs to be an absence of corruption. This last statement instantly torpedoes the entire idea of transparency and competitive bidding, as not even rich democracies are able to manage this – just consider how friends of Tory politicians in the UK managed to get contracts during the COVID-19 pandemic, just to take one small, recent example.[14] The difficulties in this area are also demonstrated by the secondary school level PPP in Uganda aimed at expanding access to secondary schooling affordably (for the government and for families), but which was not able to carry out the policy of selecting partner schools based on clear criteria and a fair process. The partnership was eventually closed down for all sorts of failures – largely to do with oversight and accountability of partner schools, as well as their selection.[15]

As part of the tender process and throughout the entire running of programmes an *effective communications strategy* is needed, which should communicate to prospective service delivery partners as well as to parents. Communicating openly with parents lets them know that there is a programme they can engage with by enrolling their children in PPP schools. Communication with service providers allows for the greatest possible number of tenders to be received. Lastly, communicating details of government spending and service delivery, whether delivered through government structures or through parastatals and private partners, helps to combat corruption.[16] Good communication can help to hold service providers to account – if community members know what private providers are meant to be doing within their community, then they have a better basis on which to try to hold them to reasonable standards.

The World Bank further stated that *appropriate performance measures should be established* which, if broadly known, could be used by the community to monitor service delivery. They further suggest, based on a particular view of what motivates various players in a market to perform at their best, that the *performance measures should be used to decide on the delivery of performance incentives or the application of sanctions* for failing to perform according to the PPP contract and the specified terms. For this, a broad knowledge of what should be delivered is crucial to holding providers to account, and in the World Bank's world view, getting schools to produce more learning on the part of children is a matter of carrots and sticks, appropriately applied. To continue to take part in the PEF programmes, schools are subject to regular monitoring visits to ensure a minimum quality of facilities, but more crucially, children must participate in the Quality Assurance Test. The QAT takes place every year in a multiple-choice format, which is a rather crude tool aimed at determining whether children benefiting from PEF schemes are learning. Schools are warned if they do not pass muster for one year, and if they fail again for a second year, then they are cut off from PEF support.[17] This threat is taken seriously because many schools would be unlikely to survive on their own.

***

The way the theory goes, this accountability mechanism means schools are well-run. It means that management ensures that teachers show up to school and remain at school all day. Yet, as I have found in so many countries where I have worked, this is only half the battle. Good school management means that teachers are not simply on school premises all day, but they are actively in class and teaching during all of their scheduled periods. Teachers know that their students will sit the QAT yearly and that if the school's students don't pass, then funding will go; parents will be unlikely to fill the gap, and in the absence of income, the school will shed staff. This 'stick' of accountability motivates teachers to do what they have the knowledge, skills and facilities to do well – to teach children who then learn as a result.[18]

The counter-factual to this type of management theory is that if funds make their way to the school through the relevant mechanism of whatever PEF programme, and the children are not tested and no one but the school and the families know how things are going, then teachers are likely to slack off and management might not care that much, provided that the funds keep rolling. According to the World Bank and PPP theory, it appears there is little perceived difference between government and private sectors in service delivery. While they would usually claim that private operators have to be leaner and hungrier to survive than bloated, lethargic government systems, they do not seem to have enough faith in this idea to trust it in the absence of a stick being wielded.

The last ingredient for the World Bank is to ensure the *generation of data on what is tried in such programmes by creating a framework for evaluating programme outcomes*. Through this means, it can be determined what type of approach works best and where, and what ingredients were present to ensure a particular result. Approaches to this sort of cataloguing of results from interventions are notoriously difficult to do honestly and objectively. If the organization assessing results has anything to do with the delivery, design or management of a programme, then they have incentives to give a favourable report. Yet the types of companies that take part in these programmes tend to have a vested interest in keeping the gravy train moving anyway, so they are often not terribly keen on giving negative evaluation reports. In the case of Punjab, there is a 431-page consultants' report on the state of education, spanning reform efforts of the public sector as well as those of the PPP, and this did not find much to report in terms of improvements to learning over time and reduction in the usual disparities based on wealth, location and sex.[19] In such a long report, there was *a single mention of corruption*, and many consultant-hours went into writing up entirely intuitive answers and anodyne conclusions. One thing that it did highlight was that of all teachers – public, private and PPP – those working at PPP schools had the poorest subject content knowledge, and yet they seem to reap somewhat higher results (amongst their pupils) than teachers at the other types of schools.

So how has this worked out in practice? Does the theory hold, and does private sector involvement mean better outcomes for children? The short answer is no. Western theorists, consultants and World Bank staff dreamed up a programme that essentially consists of an educational obstacle course that school owners must negotiate in order to receive the prize of funding. The stated idea behind the schemes is that poor and marginalized children, especially girls, are brought into school for the first time and are enabled to learn. Yet, this core equity and equality of opportunity goal is not something that is focused on in the monitoring of the programme. It also happens that poor and hitherto out-of-school children are the most expensive and difficult to reach effectively.[20] Schools do not relish the prospect of bringing in large numbers of such students, and for good reason, because they require enormous attention and extra support. The well-educated and prepared teacher of our imagining, standing in front of a class, would reasonably require at least one skilled teaching assistant to help where there are many severely disadvantaged students, but this is never the case in poor settings.

The real-world unintended outcomes flow very naturally as follows. Owners and managers whose schools participate in the PPP know that the school will only manage to keep hold of the funding if their students consistently pass the Quality Assurance Test. With teachers who have less than a 50–50 chance of actually grasping the curriculum material[21] and who have about a similar chance of ever having received relevant training, there are a couple of ways to ensure that the pupils pass the test. The most sure-fire way is to make sure that the children that are admitted and enrolled in the relevant programme are already highly likely to do well and pass. This means to enrol children who were already in school elsewhere if possible, and certainly enrol children who are fairly well-resourced at home. In essence, *enrol anyone but the target children*: out-of-school and struggling, marginalized youngsters.

A researcher for Oxfam has documented how schools navigate through the obstacle course to maintain their funding by testing children who wish to enrol and only admitting those already seemingly capable of jumping through the quality assurance hoop.[22] As one head teacher admitted, 'before admission we give a test. If the child performs poorly we don't admit them into the school. We do not want weak children because we have to pass the QAT'.[23] Some have even reported enrolling children on a normal, private fee-paying basis for a year to see how the children do before submitting their names to the government for funding. Either way, the end result for equity is the same: children benefitting from the PPP funding are very often those from more privileged and supportive households already able to participate and learn well in school, or those who are demonstrably able to pay private school fees already. School managers stated that there is no supervision of PPP schools to ensure that they are reaching the target audience of marginalized children and there is actually an incentive to avoid them if possible. As so often in the development industry, the incentives are mismatched with the desired outcome. Considering that the expectation of the programme is that classrooms should attract a large share of poor and marginalized first-generation learners, one might reasonably *expect* that learning levels would be poor, and it might actually be seen as *suspect* to observe test results that are too uniformly high or even just passing – given the context. But the quality monitoring tool pushes teachers' efforts in entirely the wrong direction, to focus on the least difficult or problematic children to teach.

Extra funding to hire teaching assistants or more skilled teachers would be a reasonable expectation (providing such teachers are even available) on the condition that the target audience is reached; however, corruption and creativity provide ways and means around all monitoring and quality assurance measures. If donors would just face this fact, it could well prove more cost-effective to simply support the schools and let them get on with it, rather than spending the time and money necessary to test students as a way of monitoring schools[24] because this simply leads to the exclusion of the target audience.

Another unintended outcome that is common across countries where there is test-based accountability of any sort is the narrowing of the curriculum as part of teaching to the test. This inhibits inquiry into areas of the curriculum or just general learning that is not on the test. To add insult to injury, head teachers in Punjab say that the test is not even appropriate for real conditions:

> We have understood now that QAT is everything and the future of the school depends on the results of that. We are trying to teach to the test. But there are many issues and my teachers struggle. If you look at the syllabus, we don't think it's appropriate, it's not according to the level of the child. They are testing certain things that need to be tested in a higher grade. This is not the educational standard in a rural area. Now also think about the teacher who has done only matric (grade 10) – how will she understand and teach the content herself, let alone teach it to very weak students?[25]

Remember the evaluation report that found that PPP school teachers had the poorest level of knowledge and skills? This is where this fact rears its ugly head. But as with so many standardized tests, there are prep books and materials available in the market and another of Afridi's interviewees indicated that schools routinely rely on these. This does not mean real learning, and the setting up of the obstacle course that is ostensibly aimed at ensuring learning in return for funds just ends up with education corrupted, aimed at just ticking boxes and letting funds flow. The business opportunities are plenty so it is only really the parents who might want to complain, if they had the knowledge, experience and confidence required. As for everyone else – school owners at least make a living as the PPP funding means a significant expansion on what would have been the natural client base; teachers are employed, although they may be struggling with the curriculum and the difficulty of the monitoring tests; publishers are happy because they sell textbooks and test prep materials; lastly, the suppliers of ancillary services are happy, including tailors stitching and selling uniforms and small shops selling writing materials. In short, money flows around the system, parents are freed from child care for a few hours, and school participation data looks a bit better on paper, but this doesn't mean any real improvement in the minds of these children. In addition to this, donor governments pay into projects supporting such partnerships, and consultants draw daily rates to design the programmes, and then they draw fees for evaluating them. Money flows home to the donor countries through their 'experts' sent abroad, and yet the cash also helps to make numbers on paper look better for the donor country when included in the amount of aid money spent.

Almost everyone involved is incentivized to make it seem like everything is going well, yet there is ample evidence that such policies with such accountability measures do not work[26] and the end result is that Pakistani children still struggle to read, as illustrated clearly in the work of Nadia Naviwala.[27] These policies find their bedrock in the assumption, in rich and poor contexts alike, that teachers have been holding back, not doing their best because they are lazy and/or unmotivated, and that their management is poor or non-existent. With the right incentives and accountability, they would suddenly be doing so much more. This assumption has no support in evidence in rich countries, and in poor ones like Pakistan, teachers actually struggle to cope with the primary level curriculum material, and children are expected to struggle with multiple languages.[28] They can be greeted with all the carrots and beaten with all the sticks in the world, and they won't become better teachers. International businesses are able to capitalize on PPPs in a number of ways, even when the delivery 'partners' are locally owned, as in Punjab. International consultancy firms come up with bright ideas for development projects based on theories of change that assume all sorts of things about the society concerned that simply are not accurate. Increasingly, we are likely to see international chains of schools and other types of education support companies bidding to deliver the services designed by international consultants. These consultants will then win contracts to evaluate how well the international chain and others delivered the service, comparing them with whatever other schools exist.

Government officials may or may not believe that there is real potential in the programmes, as designed, to bring about real change, but their sector gains in any case, as more funds flow, whether or not the government department gets any direct funding. High-profile programmes raise the profile of the ministry, and staff often get to take field trips that entail certain perks. Some staff will also be poached by one of the consultancy companies or chains of schools, where they will earn much higher salaries and leave the ministry denuded of good people. The consultancies evaluate what they have been delivering or programmes delivered by another company, but either way, there is no incentive to give a really no-holds-barred evaluation as all of these companies essentially want to keep the gravy train rolling.

***

In November 2015, Liberia's Minister of Education, George Werner, was invited to Kenya by Bridge International Academies' founders to see how well the model was doing there so that he would be convinced to enter into a partnership with the company. Along for the ride was Katie Meyler, founder of the now-defunct charity More Than Me. Bridge's founders convinced the minister that if they could run a tight ship in semi-rural locations in Kenya, then surely Liberia's schools wouldn't be a problem. The company was so bold as to claim that they could take over the management of Liberia's entire primary schooling system to reap much better results than the government could. Their seduction routine worked, and the government announced that they would go for it. There were international backers keen to see Liberia's teachers and children experimented on to see if a private management PPP would work any better in that poor setting than it has in rich countries.[29]

However, from the start, the scheme did not play out the way the company or the minister intended. Teachers' unions and civil society groups, both nationally and internationally, made such an uproar that the plan was significantly watered down,[30] and other organizations, both Liberian and international (including More Than Me, Omega, Rising Academies and others), were invited to submit tenders to take part in a pilot scheme, a trial run much reduced in size from the original plan of encompassing the entire primary schooling sector. Even worse than having to compete with others (from Bridge's point of view), the international donors backing the experiment were insisting on a 'gold-standard' randomized control trial whose results would be used to determine whether the PPP would be allowed to continue and expand. Bridge, despite their public professions of confidence in their model and their abilities, tried to dig their heels in, and in some media reports were characterized as 'bullying' the Liberian government and threatening to pull out and even possibly to sue the government for violation of the memorandum of understanding that had been signed.[31] Now that Bridge would have to compete with other providers to prove itself and was not going to be able to just slip into a comfortable donor-paid contract with a severely cash-strapped government that was out of options and would have no way of effectively monitoring contract fulfilment, the company came up with all kinds of criteria that whittled down the list of possible schools to be 'randomly' assigned for the pilot. This meant that the pool of schools that any of the pilot participants might be expected to manage was a very short short-list of the country's *easiest-to-access and manage schools*. Suddenly, this terribly confident and plucky corporation was no longer as confident when they learned that there would be competition and scrutiny: comparisons would be made and the spotlight would be on them above all others. In the first year of the pilot, Bridge was handed fifty schools to manage, while another seven providers divided up forty-five schools between them.[32]

An important factor was that it was only the management of the schools that was outsourced to private operators, with largely the same civil service teachers and largely the same students. Bridge, however, managed to get some changeover of staff, getting the government to deploy younger, newly and allegedly better-qualified teachers to be assigned to their pilot schools. At the same time, they capped class sizes at the officially designated class size (this official pupil-teacher ratio was routinely exceeded in government schools), pushing out some of the children that had hitherto attended the schools they took over. Poor teachers and excess children were simply pushed to a different part of the system rather than a solution being provided to support them.[33]

The evaluators found that after the first year of what ended up being a hugely expensive trial period for Bridge and one other provider that chose to spend outlandishly, there were noticeably more words read per minute and more sums done correctly, but from a catastrophically low baseline. The other participants in the pilot did not spend unsustainably – choosing instead to stick to the $50 per child provided by donors for the pilot, which the government might conceivably be able to sustain long-term, although even this was unlikely in the medium-term – and found little in the way of results. Bridge and British-run Rising Academies spent about twenty times as much as their competitors, and yet still, progress did not continue into years two and three. After the second year, there was hardly any difference from the year one results,[34] with some suggesting that progress fizzled because some of the international attention had been taken off the situation.

I suspect, based on the way the pilot played out, that outside actors would have achieved essentially nothing if they had been confronted with the *average* government school, never mind the worst, in Liberia. Most of the country's roads beyond some main, paved roads are simply earthen tracks, turning into impassable red mud baths during the rains. There was at the time no mains electricity supply beyond Monrovia, with whatever electricity to be found supplied by private generators.[35] During my own work in Liberia (on the research project discussed in Chapter 7), I found the atmosphere to be the poorest and saddest of all the countries where I had worked. Monrovia's buildings were in the sorriest of states, and there was basically no education budget beyond paying teachers (insufficiently). There are clear reasons why schooling is as it is in Liberia, beyond the explanations and simple solutions written by international consultants.

The country has also witnessed the cavalier attitude of 'white saviours', similar to and arguably even worse than what happened with Bridge in Kenya. Katie Meyler set up More Than Me[36] as a school scholarships organization, placing poor local girls, many of whom were coming out of sexual exploitation, into existing private schools. After winning a large grant, she then established the More Than Me Academy in September 2013, where her local fixer and partner, Macintosh Johnson, used school premises to rape approximately one-quarter of the school's students in just the first year. This was nothing new, however, but rather a continuation of what he had been doing to More Than Me scholarship girls before the school opened, at his own home. Meyler herself had exhibited a complete lack of awareness of what was appropriate to do with children that were young, vulnerable and not her own, taking them to adult parties in the middle of the night, taking them from their community without even getting guardian consent, and having them sleep in her own bed with her (with Johnson present)[37] – things that would have been deemed totally inappropriate back in the USA. It should have been perfectly clear they were inappropriate everywhere.

It was this disregard for proper behaviour that led to the failure to keep those children safe. In the months leading up to the Academy's opening, the person hired to be the country director for the charity quit, leaving behind a Risk Management document with suggestions for how the charity might avoid disaster[38] (little did she know that girls were already being raped). Her warnings were disregarded, the school opened and a sexual predator remained at the heart of the entire operation. By January 2014, a victim came forward to the school nurse to report being raped, but it was not until June that year that the school management was informed. Within days Johnson was arrested and later put on trial, dying of AIDS before he could pay for his crimes.

Despite these incredible failures in *basic child protection* on the part of the charity, and despite the total lack of regard displayed even by its founder in her treatment of other people's children, this organization became one of the implementing partners in the Liberia PPP, which kicked off in Autumn 2016. The scandal can hardly have been a secret in Liberia, as people came out on the streets to protest at various points. It was not until the astonishingly in-depth reporting by Finlay Young for ProPublica broke on 11 October 2018 that Meyler and her clueless board were to face consequences, with the whole charity being wound up by June 2019.

Clearly, there is no reason to assume that private actors are necessarily more honest and transparent than government ones. It is particularly telling that two organizations with catalogued sexual abuse of children in their records could become 'partners' for a country with governance structures as weak as Liberia's, with the blessing of the donor community. Added to this, the group conducting the randomized control trial carried out a survey of students in 2019 to investigate the effect of the programme on corporal punishment, sexual abuse and other matters. They found 3.5 per cent of children reported sexual intercourse with a teacher, while 7.5 per cent reported being molested by a teacher, with Bridge-managed schools having a *higher* incidence than others.[39] One of the biggest donors in the world, the World Bank, was aware of Bridge's record in Kenya but let it slide and may or may not have informed the management of the Liberia PPP; was highly likely aware of More Than Me's horrific story up to 2014 and did not raise this or Bridge as important issues for consideration, and never took the 2019 Liberia survey results back to Bridge to discuss what they would do to minimize risks to children.[40] The *prima facie* cavalier and uncaring attitudes of all of these organizations is breath-taking, with funders like the World Bank pushing the expansion of private service providers like Bridge/NewGlobe. It would be interesting to know the level of oversight that the World Bank exerts in regard to their funding of NewGlobe's partnership with the Edo State Government, in Nigeria.

Should a ten-fold improvement in reading levels in one year always be considered an amazing achievement, and is it worth so much effort, funding and salaries for so many Northern consultants? It all depends on the baseline, but if this is as horrifically low as it was in Liberia, it might at the very least sound like a cracking good start. Things look a bit different now that we know that progress did not continue beyond that first year, and the new-and-improved reading level was still far from functional literacy. The spending to achieve a meagre improvement was insanely far beyond what might be sustainable in even the next decade. On top of that, child protection remained an unaddressed issue, and progression to the secondary level was compromised; enrolments at this higher level actually declined in the communities 'served' by Bridge.[41] So, could anyone say that the whole thing was worth it? What the two for-profits said about their high spending in order to justify it was that if they were subsequently able to take over many other schools, then economies of scale would kick in. The spending was only so high per child because of sunk costs: systems had to be designed and tried on a small scale before they could scale up, and many of the initial fixed costs of designing materials for the Liberian context, etc., would not need to be repeated. Eventually, the 'unit cost' would come down when the number of children served was drastically increased (i.e. when the costs were amortized over tens of thousands of students). The spotlight has since turned away from Liberia, but at least the underwhelming results from the experiment are unlikely to mean that other countries scramble to follow suit, using a similar arrangement, at least for now, or until the next time, because this industry, like so many others, doesn't learn from history.

***

Bridge International Academies has followed a strangely similar path to an unsuccessful education company that started out in 1992 as Edison Schools, a chain of for-profit private schools in the United States. After failing to make a profit this way, they pivoted to become an 'education management company' running what are essentially public charter schools in the US, for profit. This didn't work either, with the company losing many public contracts, and now EdisonLearning provides various support services for government schools.[42] So has the Bridge International Academies trajectory been, rebranding under its parent company name, NewGlobe, in 2020 – probably not coincidentally the year that they finally faced scrutiny over hitherto hidden child sex abuse cases in Kenya.[43] It may be that the founders studied the case of Edison: an early investor slide deck shows Bridge apparently way over-estimated (at $64 billion) the 'parent-paid opportunity' (although this may have been intentional to demonstrate belief in the model), meaning schools that operate as normal private schools. At $179 billion, they correctly estimated that PPPs held enormous earning potential. On top of this, they were already then planning to monetize the large amounts of data gleaned from their tech-enabled systems. This would entail personal data use for assessing credit scores for loans and access to health insurance, among other possibilities.[44]

Their modus operandi has been to enter several African markets with their private school model, used as proof of concept,[45] and then go for state-wide[46] PPPs where they introduce and run their e-reader-focused model in government schools. The Liberia partnership model was just a stop along the way, just like with Edison's school management service. At the beginning in Kenya, they opened their fully private, fully standardized schools at a punishing pace. They soon went after opportunities to engage governments and donors, and in the case of their establishment in Lagos in 2015, they convinced the UK's aid agency to give them £3.45 million,[47] and the Lagos State government to bend the rules so that their model would work financially. This, despite Lagos being well-supplied with private schools of all fee levels. A senior member of their Lagos team told me directly in 2016 that had they been kept to the regulations as they were on paper, operating in Lagos would not have been financially viable. Their private school toehold in Nigeria has led to partnerships with the state governments of Bayelsa, Edo, Kwara, Lagos, and Osun states; they also seem to have had a four-year programme in Borno State from 2017.[48] To facilitate their entry into India, they convinced the state government of Andhra Pradesh to let them use dilapidated government school buildings, turning public infrastructure to private profit-oriented corporate use. They have now started a statewide programme in Manipur, which will surely be the first of many, as they are recruiting hard for staff in India, including in locations in Delhi, Meghalaya and Telangana. They are also recruiting for positions in the Central African Republic and Benin, indicating further expansion into these countries.[49] It seems they have also had an arrangement in China,[50] but I was not able to find details.

In Rwanda and Liberia, NewGlobe was able to skip the tedious private school operating stage and move straight to PPPs with the national governments of these much smaller countries.[51] The new PPP model is to act as a wrap-around support service provider to public education systems, having largely left the running of fee-dependent private schools behind. Strangely, despite the close working relationship of major donors – the World Bank Group of institutions, the Global Partnership for Education (housed at the World Bank), USAID, and the UK's Department for International Development (as it was known then) – no sharing of red flags seems to have taken place after reports to the IFC of child sexual abuse in 2014, 2016 and 2017. No issues were seriously raised as a result of public protestations from groups in Kenya, as well as lawsuits in Kenya and Uganda, that Bridge was breaking local laws and private school operating regulations.[52] No red flags were raised, signalling questions as to whether Bridge was a fitting partner for the Liberian government or, presumably, with Edo State, where the partnership is funded by the World Bank.

They are now so confident in their support-service-provider role that they have closed down 293 of their 405 Kenyan schools (or 72 per cent) about which they used to make preposterous claims of projected expansion and scale – and about caring for the children and families they served. In abandoning these communities, it seems they don't care so much, after all. They now state that as of June 2022, 95 per cent of the students they serve attend government schools.[53] In their new incarnation, things look a whole lot easier with regard to the crucial element of accountability for results: they do not have to run schools and hire and manage staff anymore, for whose success or failure they would be entirely on the hook. The PPP model means that they work with civil service teachers, only loosely accountable to the state – not to NewGlobe. Much research shows that sexual abuse of children in schools is widespread, but in this PPP model, the blame cannot be laid at NewGlobe's door. They also have no responsibility for school facilities, so no fear of being blamed when a child is electrocuted to death on school premises.[54]

Part of the service is to provide a full complement of textbooks for each child and e-readers for teachers to receive the digital, scripted lesson plans beamed to them from 'the back end'. They also provide crash-course training to the teachers, which is much more real-world classroom-orientated than much traditional teacher training in the countries where they operate – although it is based on using scripted lesson plans, which provide a significant crutch. The training also covers the one area of teacher practice that can't be dictated by the script: classroom management. They learn weird and wonderful ways of mentally straight-jacketing their students, which I have described in the last chapter. It begs the question of how well these methodologies hold up when applied in government school systems in Nigeria, where the poorest school-going children go, and in great numbers in each classroom.[55] Their proof of concept was created with parents well-off-enough and motivated enough to send their children to fully private, fee-paying schools – very different from the government school clientele.[56] NewGlobe also provides monitoring staff who visit schools and work with teachers to some extent. There is also a hotline for tech support for teachers who are having trouble using the NewGlobe-issued e-reader. The software and lesson plans, as well as the school management app, are all proprietary, meaning that for as long as a government wants to use them, this will attract a fee paid to NewGlobe. The printed matter, such as the textbooks for children, is also covered by the same copyright/proprietary, contract-bound rules.

Training local monitors at least gives something like a nod to 'system building', but the partnership is not like training wheels on a bicycle that can be used for a few years and then removed to take off on one's own. The need to pay NewGlobe forever (hopefully, I am sure, from the company's perspective) is baked into the model because lesson plans are tweaked and are downloaded each week. Old lesson plans simply disappear from the tablets so they cannot be used again next year – like the Snapchat of education.[57] And since there is no overall lesson plan, but rather a series of screens that the teacher navigates through, there's nothing that could easily be printed out and kept and learned from and reproduced.[58] There is no actual record that can be archived as to what the corporation had the teachers teach their students, beyond the national curriculum documents that the government will have to give to the company in order to design (in an office in the United States) the e-reader-based lesson plans. The Kenyan government had tussles with NewGlobe over this issue in the past.

The company's website describes how they build a quality assurance system in the government agencies that they partner with – this from a company that failed to build systems to address child abuse happening in schools while cataloguing at least seventy allegations of this.[59] But other than some of the monitoring and support techniques for quality assurance staff and classroom management techniques for teachers, it is hard to see how their systems and ways of working could hope to have a lasting effect beyond the end of a contract between government and company. The service government is paying for is to 'teacher-proof' the classroom process, and so if teachers are simply reading from a script, take that script away and they will be nearly back where they started, albeit with some more concrete knowledge of how to teach. And take away the ability to pay the recurrent fees to the company, and I am quite certain that ultimately those scripts will indeed be taken away. Bridge (private) schools had parents sign an undertaking that they would always send children to school properly fed and with all the materials they needed.[60] Teachers were hand-picked and trained from the general public (although they were largely unqualified) who have no civil service expectations of job security.[61] Knowing that the conditions will be very different with regard to NewGlobe as a government school support service provider, any failures to raise learning outcomes could easily be blamed on government schools for their failures to provide materials and motivated staff, and on households for not sending appropriately supported students to school.

The company's current website shows only the rebranded NewGlobe, entirely separate from the sites for Bridge International Academies or Bridge Schools as they are known in the countries where they run as fully private schools. NewGlobe states that it was founded in 2007 and that Bridge was just its initial education programme, its experiment or 'proof of concept', and the website is clearly orientated towards attracting governments as potential clients. When you land on NewGlobe's homepage, you are welcomed by 'Leaders in Learning' who are 'supporting visionary governments' which 'invest in the transformation of public education'. These governments apparently 'know that to do so unlocks enormous potential, empowering populations to create economic growth, deliver security and drive development. NewGlobe supports national and state governments by creating powerful technology-enabled education systems'.[62] They are here peddling the myth that education does all these things that there is no evidence whatsoever that it does, and bizarrely: 'NewGlobe has unequalled experience in dramatically transforming educational outcomes at speed and at scale. Education is a science.'

There is no evidence that I am aware of that the company has dramatically transformed anything at speed or at scale, but then scale is one of those words that is not so easy to pin down – as is 'transformed', for that matter. 'Scale' is an obsession in the education and development worlds despite its self-defeating nature. Nothing that is good when small ever grows to what most people think of as 'scale' – that is, a national-level solution to a given problem, or at least one that would cover a large area of a country – while maintaining the qualities and aspects that made the small programme special. The lack of 'scalability' of so many of these initiatives is explained through various flaws in the original design, and the commentators who write about this simply fail to see or accept the message that is shouting straight at them: when a small initiative that is run by a small local organization succeeds, its small size and local touch will be two of the most significant reasons why the initiative succeeded. The obsession with scale continues despite the fact that the only system that has ever scaled is often widely perceived as failing, this being government school systems the world over, and some of these haven't even managed to reach all of the children they should be reaching (leading to the necessity for private schools). Scale also continues to be a word used and abused as spin for particular axes that are being ground – the World Bank referred to Omega Schools as having 'scaled rapidly', while they had only reached around 30 schools in total at the time. 'Scale' is used as a propaganda tool for this type of corporation, or as a stick to beat or dismiss small, high-quality or localized initiatives. Lastly, in none of the evaluation reports I have read concerning Bridge or NewGlobe have I read evidence of a 'dramatic transformation', no matter what the scale. The true picture tends to show improvement but with no proof that they are on some linear upward trajectory (recalling the drop-off in years 2 and 3 in Liberia). I have been told that teachers in Nigeria have indeed learned some applicable teaching skills through the PPPs, but this is anecdotal evidence.

Oversight of what is happening in schools in dispersed, difficult-to-access locations is a key challenge that was meant to be addressed through tech and the occasional in-person visit in the Bridge model. Yet one report, for which Kenyan Bridge teachers were interviewed, tells of staff refusing to use the core tool, the lesson scripts on the e-reader, because of its effects on their autonomy. They told of skipping pages in the script randomly and thereby sending back nonsense data to the back-end system – data that Bridge said it used to improve lesson quality – because if the e-readers showed that the lesson was never opened, this would trigger intervention from headquarters.[63] Failure of the tech-enabled oversight system is also demonstrated through the International

Finance Corporation's investigation of many instances of child sexual abuse by teachers in Bridge schools over the years. This is not to say that tech-enabled remote monitoring does nothing, but that it is not the accountability silver bullet that some might have hoped for. Nor is this to say that there is any form of education management under the sun that can stop a determined rogue teacher from abusing a child – with NewGlobe, it is how they and their funders dealt with it after it was discovered that is so problematic.

This PPP model seems to be the most sensible and profit maximizing for the company – if governments can manage to scrape together the money to pay them, or if donors are interested enough to provide the funding instead. So far, NewGlobe's continuation has been based entirely on venture philanthropy, investors and international development donors, and considering their target clients, it seems like it will continue to be reliant on these funds for a long time to come. To put this in context, NewGlobe has existed for 18 years, while it took Amazon a decade to reach profitability. NewGlobe states repeatedly on their website that 'education is a science', as though a method to get a child to fluent reading and sums is the same for every single child. Just pour in the ingredients, stir, and hey, presto. But this is not how things worked out in Liberia, where it seems they reaped only the very lowest-hanging fruit. Arguably, the scripted approach might make some sense as an interim measure, but to try to pass it off as anything but a set of crutches for a near-crippled patient is entirely disingenuous. The crutches may enable the patient to move around a bit, but getting the patient out in the world living normally, they will not. Underlining this point, the Michael Kremer-underpinned evaluation study that NewGlobe has trumpeted found that Bridge had a positive effect on children's learning when comparing socioeconomically similar children, but the effect was much stronger at the pre-primary and primary 1 levels. This again points to 'low-hanging fruit', and the school day for pre-primary children at Bridge is much longer and more intensive than at other schools.[64]

While this might be NewGlobe's final destination/model within education itself (EdisonLearning also found the end of the road here), this is far from the end of the line for the company's branching out. Indeed, as Graham Brown-Martin wrote years ago, they harvest enormous amounts of data (something they themselves boast about), which they plan to monetize. It is unlikely that parents know or understand what they are doing in that area, even if it is explicitly stated in some small print somewhere. And while every type of enterprise under the sun is monetizing data, including text-based suicide helplines for young people in the United States,[65] why on earth would data around primary schooling be any more sacred? This was the play years ago when they were as yet mostly a company targeting fee-paying parents directly – people actively choosing their schools. Now they are engaging with children and teachers on a larger scale through their work with governments, meaning they are engaging with people who have no real choice and are not opting into their world. Now they have captive markets whose data they will be able to splice and repackage to be sold off for profit, with the excuse that if names have been removed from records, it is no longer personal data.[66] Their website notes the millions of datapoints it accumulates every day. This means the company aims to be paid twice: firstly and directly by their clients, government or individuals, and then they may likely be paid in valuable data, a la Big Tech.[67] So, while I suspect they are still far from the land of profit, I could be wrong. The data play is something they might not want to shout too much about.

***

The jury is very much out on the end results of such partnerships. Companies seek to profit from poor countries in all manner of ways, and there is no reason they would treat education any differently. International teacher union movements, while playing an important role in promoting the recognition of teaching as a profession on the one hand, on the other are forever fighting any initiative to get teachers to act responsibly and to feel accountable for whether their schools are actually working for the poor children enrolled.[68] If they justifiably want Northern corporate actors out, then what will they offer to the children of the poor instead? One way to look at all this is that if governments seem to have tried everything to improve education and nothing else has worked, including more of the same-old, same-old donor projects and programmes, then why shouldn't they try this PPP thing? Donors like the World Bank are highly likely to be involved here, and donor funding for such a model fits into the long-established way of working that means that a large share of aid spending comes in a boomerang-shaped package, returning to where it came from after being virtue-laundered through development aid-funded technical assistance. Money flows from North to South to North again.

Failed policies from the North are suggested for more-corrupt countries in the South that lack the strength of government (in terms of funding, people and resolve to fight corruption) that even the still-often-corrupt Northern countries tend to have.[69] The 'context matters' argument, which I am such a fan of, could be trotted out to justify trying these policies in ever more locations to see if they will work. The logic: charter schools failing spectacularly in Ohio doesn't mean they won't work in Liberia, with the floor as low as it was. But with Northern companies benefitting from contracts and Northern donors benefiting from reputation-laundering through 'aid' spending, I have the hunch that it is not a sincere belief that partnership policies might finally have found their proper home that motivates them. I have a vivid picture in my mind of the over-confidence blended with dilettantism that leads people like Patrinos and colleagues to dream up policy prescriptions that will not work as prescribed. Ultimately, allowing any private entity to have too much sway and importance in any area of public life has been shown by history to be a mistake. In India, allowing the East India Company to operate was a mistake of inestimable proportions.

11

Searching for Solutions That Don't Exist

All the fuss and propaganda could stop right now. If we stopped spinning stories about what education does for national development, we could see clearly that the cart has been put before the horse. If we stopped thinking that there is even *a solution*, or even *a few solutions* for different situations, we could relax a little bit about the range of states of being that exist in schooling in different places today, and we could turn our attention to far greater emergencies in this world. To unpack: the idea is that the right to education is a human right that enables all sorts of societal and economic development. If we help poor countries get this right, they will become more open and democratic (and read also *less traditional* and therefore more subsumed into an increasingly generic Western/Northern culture of consumerism); the right sets of skills will become common enough that industries will be able to develop and prosper; people will get richer and feel less insecure, so they will have fewer children, and fewer people will seek to migrate to richer countries in search of opportunities. According to UNESCO, education has a major role to play in mitigating climate change and environmental breakdown.[1] The naïve view that was espoused when I still worked there in 2015 that more educated people would be more inclined to take positive action for the climate has by 2024 been downplayed, I assume in recognition of the glaring fact that the best-educated, richest populations on the planet are also the most polluting.

The rider to all the good news about the fruits of education is that we must find a solution to the global learning crisis. It is, however, somewhat problematic to describe something as a crisis, using this purposefully emotive language, when it has been brewing for decades and those labelling it a crisis helped to create it. The dominant model of education that has been brought in and imposed from outside in places where it never belonged is one that is alien and assumes the desirability of this model, imposing new norms from a vastly different culture. But now there is indisputably large-scale demand for this form of education, which justifies all efforts; indeed, there is a clamouring in places, with people truly believing that education is the only way out of circumstances of poverty. While I experience daily evidence of how this rigid form of education clashes with local cultures and values in rural India, still I know the genie will not be put back in the bottle.

If education is the key to progress and development, it seems evident we must get children into schools, and in a very rudimentary way, this has been achieved for a great many in the Global South. Still, we lament that not all children are in school yet, at the same time that we document ever more clearly that shocking proportions of children in poor countries do not learn at school. Nadia Naviwala writes about the astonishing mix of languages with which the poor children of Sindh, Pakistan, are meant to cope, and she, like me, questions the point of mass school enrolment if it doesn't help children become literate and numerate in a language that they understand.[2]

If getting children into school is not the solution – then what next? Researchers have gone into schools and documented the myriad problems that I have catalogued earlier in the book: problems of over-crowding or lack of sufficient space and materials; too few teachers; teachers with too little subject knowledge and skills, and motivation and morale that have evaporated into the ether – if they ever existed, and no support or supervision. So we have to train the teachers, send in textbooks and make sure that there is sufficient infrastructure, or not (depending on your view, you might think it is okay and perfectly reasonable for poor children to learn under a tree). We have to feed children who are too hungry to concentrate and learn; we have to give them free books and materials and sometimes even free uniforms. We have to provide incentives for them to even make it to school. Yet still, the children do not learn, and still many children stay away from or cannot access school – and still inexplicably, the promoters of the Right to Education do not question the model, as Naviwala and I have done, backed by what seems to us to be rather overwhelming evidence.

Researchers and commentators document that none of these things have worked, leading many to argue that we need more and more of the same (expecting a different outcome – the definition of insanity?), while others call for something else: school choice. If those rotten public systems won't work, citizens should be encouraged to just abandon them. This will solve things in the here-and-now for the children let down by failing schools, but it also has the added benefit of making the government school teachers get their act together and start teaching. Faced with the threat of losing all their students to the private sector, which is inherently better just for being private, government schools will start working because they will recognize the need to compete to ensure their own survival. School choice has been brought in through government policies in rich countries, but has been more unplanned and 'organic' in poor ones. Yet still, public systems remain terrible and private schools for the less-well-off are marginally less terrible. This is now pretty well-documented, even by the pro-school-choice people. However, the relaxed, idle government school teachers whom I visited in my 2005 doctoral research villages a couple of winters ago, where there were nearly no students present and no lessons going on, seemed entirely unfazed by their pupil numbers being so low as a result of wholesale abandonment by parents.

So, where do we go next? Getting children into school – government school – hasn't worked. Children not infrequently come out illiterate and innumerate. Getting children into private schools has hardly worked any better when all of a country's children are taken into account. The children of the most motivated and slightly better-resourced are corralled together into schools serving like-minded people, and so we see the predictable outcome that those siloed children seem to achieve higher levels of learning, relative to the parlous situation for poor children in government schools in poor countries. While my own research focus has always been the poorer countries of the Global South, I have also kept track of developments in rich countries with large degrees of social and economic inequality, like my own home of the United Kingdom. It seems that pinning hopes on school choice has been about as successful in the home of school choice, the United States, as in poor countries. So, where do we turn next? Perhaps to cajole the 'education market' to work better as a UK-funded project tried to do in Lagos. Alas, meaningfully tweaking markets requires much more of a budget than donors will ever give.

When the purported promise of education does not materialize, it is perhaps easy to explain away because of the documented lack of learning that results – so we can comfort ourselves that, like communism, if it had ever been done properly, *then* it would have worked. There is the perennial call for the training of ever more teachers. But giving some teachers a bit of teacher training isn't going to do very much when the teachers have gone through the same terrible schooling system that they are now teaching in, and even worse, so have the teacher-trainers. If today's students aren't learning anything, how likely is it that recent crops of new teachers learned much during their own school days? Many education systems have old teachers who are clinging on until retirement, who became teachers back in the day when you could get some training straight out of primary school and then be given a job for life based on a short education that might or might not have been any good. There are even teachers who have gone through fewer years in school than the children they are teaching. What about private school teachers? These schools have to draw on the same populations to find teachers as the government schools, except that they often get totally untrained individuals (which won't really mean anything if the training that 'trained teachers' are getting is worthless). They get lower pay and much more pressure and are more accountable but have only the same type of education, broadly speaking, to draw on as any other teacher.

The truth is, however, that no matter what you do to these teachers – squish them into a mould, put them through the wringer, apply the thumbscrews – they will still be the same teachers even if their behaviour changes a bit. They won't be able to do any more than impart a level of curriculum material that they themselves can handle, and likely they will be missing the pedagogical knowledge – knowledge of the nuts and bolts of actually *how to teach*, to impart even that much. Added to this: while countries are going through demographic transitions at different rates and will ultimately be able to contract their education systems at some point, for the time being, taking the poorer countries of the Global South as a whole, they need ever more proper teachers and the funding to hire and deploy them, just to stand still, never mind getting ahead of the problem and progressing. Philip Coombs was writing about this problem back in the 1960s and then again in the 1980s and no one has yet invented a way to come up with large numbers of qualified teachers to fill the gaping and widening breaches. Sub-Saharan African countries need untold numbers of brilliant teachers to make a dent in the education goals that governments, the international system and local communities are expecting them to achieve. *But where are the motivated and effective teacher trainers to come from?* I remember finding it quite surprising to learn that teachers often are not trained in the use of textbooks or any other materials (other than a blackboard); they are not trained in how to probe for children's level of understanding of material, and they are not equipped with various strategies for explaining and re-explaining (differently) various concepts when children fail to understand.

What then to do? The next step has been to look towards EdTech, enabling *standardization* for brown children in the Global South, passed off as great-quality education. Rising Academies show groups of African children parked in front of devices with headphones clamped over their ears, and they seem to be proud of this. But, counterintuitively, EdTech is meant to provide *individualization* for any and all poor children in the Global North. For poor children in the United States attending on-line charter schools, virtual teaching is done largely through sending supposedly individually tailored material to children based on their ability or inability to solve problems sent their way, as determined by an algorithm.[3] In Kenya and Nigeria, if teachers read scripts beamed to their devices originating with lesson plan developers a continent and a vast ocean away, does this do the trick? Does the claimed 'world-class education' or even just passable education result? NewGlobe's long-awaited evaluation by none other than Nobel-laureate Michael Kremer finds that their original model, Bridge International Academy-branded schools, did indeed show greater learning in absolute terms than other schools, especially compared to government schools. Yet they studiously avoid stating whether or not the children at the schools were actually learning consistently at grade level (meaning, were they able to show a grasp of the subject matter that they were learning, at the level set by the national curriculum for their age and grade). They report on a greater likelihood of timely grade progression, but this does not quite answer my question. I suggest that if this degree of research and development leading to an incredibly expensive form of scaffolding of student knowledge is not enough to get children just basically learning at grade level, then nothing will (in the short-to-medium-term, I mean).

What is implicitly denied here – meaning in the UN-backed push to get children into any old school as well as the EdTech claims of good quality resulting from a bit of IT kit and some algorithms – is the fact that teaching is an incredibly complex task, requiring people with a specific aptitude, skill and drive to get it right through continual learning and adaptation based on experience. We would never be so naïve or flippant as to expect this in regard to teaching similar children in rich countries, so the fact that we expect this to work in the most challenging of circumstances is astonishing. Scripted lesson plans and 360-degree wrap-around support for 'teachers' who are completely and utterly out of their depth – and I do not say that lightly or with blame (their own education is certainly not their fault) – can do very little. The Kremer study of Bridge found that the impacts were greatest at the very earliest stages, that is, pre-primary level and primary grade 1, and got smaller as the levels (and therefore the difficulty of the material) increased.[4] It's just not a credible way of getting children in all their complexity and individuality to learn ever more difficult subject matter, while it might be useful for under-skilled teachers to cope with teaching at the most basic levels.

***

So then, we are looking in vain to various ideas and reform agendas to make schooling better, but is the education sector silo even the right place to be looking? I remember well from my doctoral studies days, the graph comparing educational investment and expansion data from Ghana and South Korea, overlaid with national wealth (probably per capita) plotted over time from the 1960s to the 2000s, showing a growing contrast between the two countries. The point was that Korea was, after colonial subjugation and a horrific civil war, poorer than Ghana back then. I return to the Cambridge University economist of a previous chapter, with personal experience of growing up in Korea in the 1960s, Ha-Joon Chang. He writes that in 1961, 'South Korea's yearly income stood at $82 per person. The average Korean earned *less than half* the average Ghanaian citizen ($179)' (emphasis in the original).[5] Chang explains that the war had killed four million people, also wiping out half of the existing manufacturing base and three-quarters of the railways. They had by 1961 managed to raise the literacy rate to 71 per cent from the low 22 per cent at the time that the Japanese colonial masters left in 1945. But like so many poor African countries today, Korea's main exports were primary commodities that had undergone no 'value addition': tungsten and fish significant among them. In the 1950s, USAID regarded the country as a no-hoper, dubbing it a 'bottomless pit'.[6]

While Ghana's independence day in 1957 came later than South Korea's, the country had a comparable literacy rate of somewhere approaching 20 per cent on independence. The fable goes that these two countries strongly diverged, much as hare and tortoise, at least to a good extent because in the 1960s Korea poured money and effort into education and expanding participation at the secondary level, allowing the economy to boom over time despite such bumps in the road as the 1997 financial disaster. At university the phrase 'correlation is not causation' is drummed into you. To illustrate this point, the joke is made that when heatwaves occur in more northern countries, both ice cream consumption and violent assaults increase; the two are correlated, but we're pretty sure it is not eating ice cream that causes outbreaks of violence. It's unlikely, had Korea allowed its education sector to languish in a similar state as Ghana's, that the country would have boomed the way it did over the last half century or so. However, Korea's success had an enormous amount to do with a vast array of other enabling factors, not just because it made sure young people were completing high school.

Let there be no doubt that to read about the educational transformation of Korea is astonishing, particularly when told from the first person in Chang's writing. Chang describes starting his primary education in 1970 at, similarly to so many of the schools that I have written about, 'a second-rate private school' with sixty-five children in his class – an improvement on the government school competitor's ninety children per class. He describes that the best schools had around forty pupils per class, and that in some burgeoning urban areas the schools were 'stretched to the limit, with up to 100 pupils per class and teachers running double, sometimes triple, shifts. Given the conditions, it was little wonder that education involved beating the children liberally and teaching everything by rote'. Chang states that it was only by these means that the government managed to ensure that virtually every child received at least six years of education since the 1960s.[7]

But what is crucial is that it is not just in education that the government began to show some resolve to get things moving. In 1973, a state-owned steel mill came into operation for which the government was turned down for financing by the World Bank for reasons of non-viability. Japanese financiers felt differently, and the state-owned enterprise became one of the most efficient steel producers and is now one of the largest in the world.[8] The Samsung corporation decided to get into electronics and had to subsidize operations in that area with profits from its textiles and sugar refining businesses before they became profitable a decade later. Hyundai, a world leading car maker now, started life as a backyard auto repair shop in the 1940s and certainly did not become a successful manufacturer overnight. The picture of Korea's transformation is made whole through Chang's description of the old saying about 'Korean time', meaning that people were lax with timing and didn't bother to turn up at an appointed hour – the same term is applied in many different countries now but has been forgotten in Korea. But back then, as Chang describes, Korean time meant 'the widespread practice whereby people could be an hour or two later for an appointment and not even feel sorry about it'.[9] Lastly and perhaps most surprisingly, the government, in its modernization efforts, used to send bureaucrats to Pakistan and the Philippines for training, such was the state of things. It is nearly unimaginable today that things were at one time more organized and advanced in Pakistan than in South Korea, and I've heard countless times about 'Indian time' or 'Nigerian time', but would never have thought the same would ever have applied to Korea.

What Chang describes when he writes about countries like South Korea and Finland too, countries that emerged poor and backward from terrible wars to become rich and technologically advanced, is a clear direction for the country chosen by leaders who then pursued policy angles to develop both the economy and society. With the right protections and encouragement of fledgling industries, these were allowed to flourish, with now well-known results. In Finland, state-owned enterprises were at the forefront of technological modernization in forestry, mining, steel, transportation equipment, paper-making machinery and chemical industries.[10] It is hard to imagine now that Nokia, despite its mobile phone heyday having decidedly passed, started out producing rubber boots, while Samsung started as a fish, vegetable and fruit exporter in 1938, moving into sugar refining and textiles from the 1950s to the 1970s. Both companies were part of a movement in their respective countries to go all-in on investing in technological and industrial advancement, and neither found success quickly.

At the same time that the Korean and Finnish governments were engaging in policies to support infant industries and even starting state-owned enterprises, efforts were put into education systems and other aspects of societal development. As these economies picked up and policies began to gain traction, culture-change came along with it, and education took off. In my own Finnish family, I have had uncles who trained as veterinarians and aunts who trained as nurses, and almost all of their education took place in other Nordic countries – Sweden and Norway gave them their start. It would be entirely unnecessary today for Finns to go abroad to study these demanding subjects; so much has changed in the country since they were young in the 1950s and 1960s. My family members and so many others returned with the skills needed to build expertise at home.

What Chang does not describe is a process whereby governments invest in education and then there is a time lag of a generation or more, allowing for good governance to develop, and then results are seen in economic and social advancement, as the greater level of education of the new adult generation comes into the workforce. The historical record describes nothing of the kind, entirely unsurprisingly if Chang's memories of learning by rote are a fair reflection of the general situation in Korea's schools. No matter what UNESCO or any pro-education groups say, it is not education that brings about the kind of change witnessed in the post-war period in Korea and Finland. Education is just one factor, and it was clearly seen as beneficial for Koreans and Finns to go abroad to learn and bring the skills back. Education is a vital piece of the puzzle but it's not the cause of the puzzle's coming together.

Good governance is another education-development-project hobbyhorse that is confusingly required to bring about change in education systems, while a well-educated population is also necessary for well-governed institutions to develop. The vital ingredients include democracy, an effective and honest bureaucracy and legal system, property rights protection (including intellectual property), good corporate governance including rules governing bankruptcy, and thriving financial institutions, buoyed by strong contract enforcement.[11] So which feeds which? Does education lead to strong and honest governance, or does the latter enable education systems to be properly run so that children become educated?

How culture-change takes place is a key question here – I suggest that when governmental and societal determination kicks in, it will feed through into most sectors in something like an organic way, creating positive feedback loops.

A striking example of a country that confounds the mistakenly expected education-to-development pathway is Cuba. The country provides full wrap-around early childhood services to ensure that young children and their mothers thrive from pregnancy into the child's early years and beyond. Universal medical care of a very high standard is particularly important at this vulnerable stage of life. The country's education system is the best in Latin America, built up over decades starting with a concerted adult literacy campaign in 1961, which created the necessary foundation for the building of a learning society. It was through intentional policy formation and implementation that they created a committed, highly skilled and respected teaching cadre as the foundation and the most important element of the education system, with the best teachers deployed to the most challenging roles and locations. The latter does not happen in most countries; quite the contrary. Martin Carnoy describes with care the virtuous circle that has developed, whereby good secondary schools produce great graduates who then enter the highly respected profession of teaching, to pass on their knowledge to the next generation.[12]

Yet despite this highly successful Cuban manifestation of school education, the country has not been allowed to thrive economically, largely because of severe and enduring sanctions imposed by the United States acting in its adopted role as global bully. Similar positive things could be said about Iraq's education and health systems pre-2003, and perhaps Cuba should count its blessings that it hasn't been utterly destroyed by the United States as Iraq has been. The point is this: education and the state of a country's schools (along with the healthcare system) is a reflection of the wider society and its values. Cuba has got it right, and yet education has not led to the miraculous outcomes for society that are claimed by UNESCO and others[13] because the United States is far more powerful than a great education system. But if a country wants to solve this problem for themselves, they can and they will, even with the boot of the United States on their neck.[14] If they don't prize education and health for all highly enough, and they don't care enough about great inequality, then these problems won't be solved by anyone, and certainly not by outsiders.

***

But getting back to economic development, there is a myth now, a re-writing of history, that says countries get rich through free trade policies. The key rich countries today promote free trade through the World Trade Organisation (never mind all of the agricultural subsidies in Europe and North America), and because they are pro-free trade, it must mean that this is the way for today's poor countries to get rich. But this too is no better than a legend. Britain and then the young United States became rich through protectionism and fostering, protecting and encouraging infant industries. I continue to draw in this part of the chapter on the brilliant work of Ha-Joon Chang, who masterfully sets out the evidence for how England transformed itself in the Tudor period from a mere supplier of a primary commodity, sheep's wool, to the advanced value-adding industry of woollen cloth production in the Low Countries, world leaders at that time. If Henry VII and his descendants had taken their cue from the market on Ricardian comparative advantage terms, the English would have stuck to sending unprocessed wool over the channel, leaving the really lucrative skilled work to their continental counterparts. Instead, over the course of nearly a century, various policies were implemented and then adjusted, stopping any out-flow of skill; poaching skill from abroad; subsidizing the development of weaving capacity; and ultimately stopping completely the outflow of the raw material the Dutch needed to keep their own industry going at all. Without English wool, the Dutch industry was ground down to nothing, and England gained the upper hand.

Politicians in London understood how this had gone very well, and, fearing the potential of the American colonies, the government did its best to confine the latter to the fate of primary commodity producers. This strategy only worked for so long and, of course, after independence, the United States was able to go all-in on industrial development, once again using protection and encouragement of fledgling industries. Chang writes about the vast menu of policies used by today's rich countries in order to get rich, stating that it was certainly not done by tariffs alone; they were not even necessarily the most important policies used. Countries also used export subsidies, tariff rebates on inputs used for export manufacturing, conferring monopoly rights, cartel arrangements, directed credits, investment planning, manpower planning, support for research and development, and the promotion of institutions that allow public-private cooperation (early PPPs!). Chang stressed that 'there was a considerable degree of diversity among the now-developed countries in terms of their policy mix, depending on their objectives and the conditions they faced. For example, the United States used tariff protection more actively than Germany, but the German state played a much more extensive and direct role in infant industry promotion than its US counterpart. As another example, Sweden relied upon public-private joint activity schemes far more than, say, Britain did.'[15] There was far from a 'one-size-fits-all' approach to developing industry and the national economy.

At the same time, for the earliest developers like Britain and then Germany and others, mass education systems were not a major factor in any of this. There was also massive corruption in the British parliament, particularly in the era of the East India Company, when an enormous share of parliamentarians were company stock owners. Good governance was not really 'a thing' back then, the exact time that corporate bailout by government was pioneered.[16] And all of the other ingredients that today's major international organizations state are essential for development? Probably there, or partially there to varying extents in various countries, but not uniformly so. Even without mass education and with massive corruption, today's rich countries became rich. They pursued goals using various approaches, common among which were protectionist and infant industry promoting policies of varying types.

So what is the point of all this discussion? The international education and development community work furiously to figure out solutions to the global learning crisis, and while it is quite easy to spot all the things that have gone wrong, it is not so easy to find the solutions. And the proof has been in the pudding – whatever piecemeal development projects and suggested policies (including PPP experiments) have been tried, have not worked well. From the example of the rich countries we can see that culture changes and education systems develop and skills are imported as part of the process of a country developing its industrial sector, turning away from the role of primary commodity providers. But as with the British and their American colonies, today's rich countries keep poor countries in their Ricardian comparatively 'advantageous' roles of providing coffee beans, cocoa beans, rubber and the like. The IMF pushes off-the-rack, standardized policies onto developing countries.[17] The individuality of countries is effectively denied and the mantra that one hears so often in the development sector, 'context matters', is ignored, despite Chang's careful documenting of the different policy combinations and the tailored choices made historically by governments in the countries that are rich today.

Education and the development of skill for various approaches to economic development are important parts of a country's development journey, but education alone does not *lead to* development. Further, looking to development projects or government policies without budgetary backing, or just packing children into under-resourced classrooms while the country remains poor and hobbled by WTO rules, IMF policies and the growing burden of climate disaster, is farcical. The only thing that can really work is if countries have more freedom and leeway to pursue their own paths, preferably on something approaching a level playing field, and it is only policies arrived at from within that can ever work. When countries can lift themselves out of poverty, they will have the wherewithal to support their own policies to support their population's wellbeing, including health systems, education, and other types of development. Recent discussions with an old research collaborator of mine in Nigeria have reinforced this message for me – over a distinguished career in education and government, she has grown downright disdainful of donor-funded education projects. She said decisively that only Nigerians can devise solutions for Nigeria – and until that time comes, individuals have come together in support of their community private school as the way forward, for now.

Vietnam illustrates perfectly what my friend and collaborator was getting at with regard to Nigeria and solutions from within. Vietnam has forged its own path towards soaring education system results, beating out many European nations in international assessments such as the OECD's PISA.[18] In 2020, I was writing about Vietnam as a prime example, along with Cuba and Finland, of policy and practice directed and fired from within and being part of a society-wide approach to national development.[19] I wrote about how, during the 1990s, the economy (and tax collection) expanded at the same time as government policy came to focus on educational development. Sensible education policies were formulated and sustained over time with significant spending to underpin them – economy and education system strengthening in tandem. Teachers were set up for success through extensive preparation for the role and through strong support and accountability from highly engaged school leadership. Teachers were also deployed across the country with importance placed on serving remote and marginalized communities, and school infrastructure and materials were invested in, country-wide. The curriculum is relatively modest in the number of subjects and its level of ambition in the early years of primary school, proving achievable for students and their teachers.

There is an officially mandated role for Parents Boards which fosters school-community partnerships, with parents feeling empowered to speak up and be involved in their local school. The revenue sharing model is arguably a key factor in parents' feelings of investment and rights in the education system, leading them to be highly involved in their community schools. Through what is officially an informal system of in-kind or financial contributions to schools, two-fifths of the budget for public education comes from parents' pockets in a move that would, in most cases, have been highly criticized by the human rights and Education For All crowd. The policy was instituted at a time of serious government budget constraints in the late 1980s and has persisted ever since. It has not played out perfectly, with some poorer families perceiving that payment was compulsory while contributions were meant to come only from those who could comfortably afford to pay or provide a service or resources. In the end, notwithstanding various imperfections, education policies are discussed and debated in the media and teachers and parents have stood up to and rejected policies or unsuitable aspects of policies suggested from outside.

One researcher has observed that Vietnam's education system 'is deeply embedded in its social context' and that 'many features of [its] education system and its performance around learning can be traced to specific features of the country's political settlement and an extraordinary and sustained societal commitment to promoting education'.[20] This last point must be understood – Vietnam is not a rich country, but has developed a strong and successful education system that is an integral part of local communities and also of overall national development and virtually all of this has come from within. The country has bucked the trend of bowing to the totem of free primary education that has done schools in other countries no favours. A case in point was the story told in Chapter 3 of the Liberian parent–teacher association, which was eviscerated through being prevented from making financial and in-kind contributions to the school to which it was attached, in the name of the Right to (free) Education. As I indicated earlier, I am sure the pupils and their families were heartened in the crumbling of their school by the knowledge that this took place in service of the protection of their human rights.

***

To bring together the threads of this chapter, the various stories told are meant to illustrate some crucial points from history, recent and not-so-recent, related to education and development. First, all the talk of expansion and development of education systems does not necessarily lead to other positive developments. It certainly does not lead to industrialization and economic growth as there does not seem to be any historical example where such a trajectory can be traced. Rather, education systems tend to develop (or not) in tandem with other developments in a given society – when the conditions are right for one type of development, they tend to be right for the other as well. But the case of Cuba shows starkly that a country can get everything right and yet education doesn't lead to all sorts of development and growth when the most powerful country in the world is determined to keep them contained and isolated. Indeed, however, the very notion of education leading to growth and Western-style industrial development is highly problematic as this will only hasten the destruction of the planet's ability to sustain humans at their current rapaciousness. On the other hand, to try to deny poorer countries their chance for everything rich countries have enjoyed while the latter refuse to change the way they live, is unconscionable. So, as a species, we gallop headlong towards the cliff edge with no nation willing to be the one to apply the brakes first, fearing to be left behind.

Secondly, schools are manifestations of the wider society; they are shaped by the governmental and societal approaches of the country, and if these are unequal and corrupt, so schools will appear as visible symptoms of the diseased situation in the country. Schools do not, and cannot, shape society and mould youths when young people have no other positive influences in their lives. The United States is a case in point: that highly unequal society has a highly unequal education system, with ghettoized schools serving poor, marginalized neighbourhoods and well-equipped, successful schools serving rich suburbs like the one I grew up in. Finland provides nearly a perfect counterpoint, while all is nowhere near perfect even there. Liberia, facing an array of challenges with nearly no domestically generated government revenues to fund systems, will not be fostering great schools in the foreseeable future – until the entire country arrives at a more conducive situation, a sort of societal agreement that things must change. Sadly, for so many countries in the Global South, departing colonial powers have much to answer for in cobbling together various groups of people into artificial countries that did not truly start out as nation-states, and having deployed the strategy of divide and conquer, exacerbating tribal divisions during the colonial administration. These newly independent countries started the race to develop far behind and carrying an enormous weight, while the retreating colonial powers were able to streak ahead, relatively unburdened.

Thirdly, positive change can only come from within. No intervention from outside will be significantly impactful, and alien policies applied to a given context, particularly when pushed through some 'development project' will never take hold and gain the traction needed. The cases of countries that have succeeded, such as Korea, Cuba, Vietnam and others, have done so as a result of arriving at policies from within, backed by a truly domestic drive to change and improve. Finland provides an interesting case, because the country did actually look outside of itself to find a policy model. After a period of recovery from the Second World War, they looked west to neighbouring Sweden, which had been applying social democratic welfare state policies for years. Finland brought similar policies home and made them their own, but what was key to the success of this 'policy borrowing' was that no one pushed these policies from outside, and the government and society developed a Finnish model which was not always plain sailing but ultimately succeeded. In the education sphere, a commitment to common schooling for all was fostered, and a fee-paying education sector was not allowed to develop. The relatively equal schooling system with a commitment to doing things right is a reflection of a relatively equal society with a similar commitment. Yet nothing is perfect, and the education policy tinkering that has happened in recent years there seems to have been undermining the education system rather than improving it further.[21] The case of Tudor England's development of a woollen textile industry out of nowhere, overtaking and sinking the world leaders in the Low Countries, is an example of how long-term, sustained policy application must be in order to reap the intended rewards. The later example of Korea's development is a more recent example.

Lastly, context matters supremely, and Chang's work shows that in the past, the rich countries of today came up with their own policy cocktails to foster their own economic development. In the education world, there is a large interest in looking to countries that have succeeded in developing good school systems, to see how they can be copied in another context. Scotland has had ambitions to copy Finland, but with a quarter of Edinburgh's children attending private schools, the base conditions are so very different that there would be no way to meaningfully apply the Finnish model here, with things already so vastly unequal. The Cuban model would be impossible to apply to Liberia for similar reasons; the base conditions are just too different. As my Nigerian collaborator said, solutions for Nigeria can only come from Nigerians. But this should be taken as a positive message for the utterly countless failed education and development programmes and projects that recent history is littered with – they never had a serious chance of success. Nothing positive can come from these initiatives on a sustained, large scale, but what would be helpful is if international systems did not actively hinder and penalize the countries of the Global South. In the education sphere in particular, countries should be left alone to get on with things, with international aid spending serving only to distort national activities. To any reader bridling at the idea that we in rich countries help nothing by meddling in education in the Global South, I ask to be pointed to any solid and enduring successes from such efforts to date. I contend that we've been searching in vain for education solutions that do not exist – we need to look to the soil and the environment in which Gandhi's beautiful tree needs to grow, not to the tree alone.

12

Thousands of Tiny Lights in the Darkness: In Defence of Small Endeavours

In the early morning mist that hangs over Makoko in Lagos, Nigeria, people are already up and starting their day. Children are getting dressed and being fed by their mothers, their bags readied and their shoes or sandals put on. People are on their way to work, selling in the market or hawking on the streets, going out fishing or working at the sawmill. This community won't win any accolades for its architecture, and its narrow streets and alleyways are neither picturesque nor charming. Children leave their homes and pick their way along often muddy and sometimes flooded arteries through the community to get to school. Flooding is sometimes present within as well as without, and some places are reached only via wooden catwalks over foetid, dark water. There are further communities that stretch out onto the lagoon itself, with houses, businesses, schools and even a *Médecins Sans Frontières* clinic, all built on stilts, where the only way to get around is by canoe.

In Makoko, schools are often housed in flimsy constructions and lack the facilities one would hope for when thinking about what schools should be like. The rooms are small and sometimes dark, and there isn't enough air circulation. What they have is a teacher at the blackboard, and benches and rudimentary shared desks to write at. With space at a premium out on the water, classrooms there are often utterly packed with children so that there is no space to move. Depending on the school, the people working there, and how well the owner keeps tabs on things, the teacher might be doing a good job, teaching as actively as possible given the confinement of the space. There are probably at least a few textbooks in the room. The children who spend their day in such schools usually walk a short distance from their homes, and depending on how young the children are, parents might feel comfortable with them finding their way to school alone. Nothing about any of it is remarkable to them; this is their daily reality.

Across the community on Makoko Road, leading out to the somewhat more organized and developed world of the rest of Lagos Mainland, there is a large compound with imposing multi-storey school buildings. These buildings are a bit more like what you would envisage as a school, and in fact, in this compound, there are three separate government primary schools. The facilities are not too bad. The classrooms are large and have windows that allow air-flow, although many of the glass louvres are broken or missing. There's not much in the classrooms except for the usual blackboards and some desks, very few textbooks or materials, and the teachers look jaded and demotivated. There's almost nothing here in the school that you'd think was necessary to ignite the imagination and facilitate true learning. The compound has a fair amount of space to play, much more than any of the schools deep inside Makoko, but there is also flooding here when the rains come, as on the day I first visited. Luckily for everyone involved, there are many fewer students present in the large classrooms than there are at many other Lagos government school compounds.

What's going on in this community is that most of the parents have opted to pay to have their children attend tiny private schools tucked away in so many of the corners and crevices of the community. They have dismissed the much more impressive government schools' compound and for some it's because the government schools are just too far across the community to be convenient or safe for small children to get to. But for more of these parents, it is because, as they tell it, the teachers there don't do anything, and when they come to complain, they are just dismissed, the idea of complaining about a government service being nearly anathema. Writing these words at quite some remove of time, about fifteen years, I've just reminded myself of what Makoko is like by looking back at photos I took in 2009 – rubbish everywhere, cramped and overcrowded without proper plumbing, sewage and refuse collection. The 'feeling' of my memory is that the community is vibrant, noisy and lively, and the welcome I got during my research was usually warm and open. My memories are positive towards the community and my time there, but when I look at the photos, it is a depressing sight, and many people I spoke to talked about their desire to move out, somewhere else.

Part of people's plan for their own betterment was to get an education for their children; to make sure that they really learned something through going to school. It's the quality of what went on in classrooms that was the key draw to the myriad little cheap private schools – they felt that they were just doing better than government schools, added to the issue of traversing the entire community that government school attendance would have entailed for some families. This poor-looking community is at the heart of Nigeria's commercial capital, neither out of sight nor out of mind, and yet people live this way, and their government schools are shunned because they are not good enough. With how terrible and dark and dank some of the small private schools were that I found, documented and photographed, it's a damning indictment on the public system that people would choose to pay for them instead of going to a free-of-cost government school, and yet choose this, they did.

But in other places, other not-well-off places in Nigeria and in many other countries, the private schools were equally small and lacking in space, but were bright, cheerful and clean. The teachers were fun with their youngest charges and taught to the extent of their ability with their older pupils. These cheap private schools come in all shapes, sizes, locations, circumstances and hopefulness, and because people are choosing them, they do something to serve their students in return. Any community where these schools are common is being failed by the public systems that are exhorted to serve them and provide a good quality, fee-free education. The people have come up with their own solution from within their own community; they are not relying on anyone else or waiting for hand-outs; they are not in receipt of support and they are not waiting for anyone's permission. The result is a slightly chaotic market, with parents enrolling children and promising to pay, but then having to be chased and cajoled by schools to get the money out of them to pay the teachers. Sometimes parents cut and run and the school must absorb the loss. This is just how it is, and if a free-of-cost public service was available and seemed to be working okay, then parents would choose that, and save themselves some money – money they can ill afford to waste.

But in today's circumstances, there is simply no question which of these options any parent would choose, who was even remotely in a position to make choices (a position that presupposes some spending power as well as a local private school offering). And so, these tiny private schools have 'mushroomed', and I characterize them as a *crisis response* to utterly failing government education, which seems fitting in light of the UNESCO-dubbed 'global learning crisis'. While poor countries continue to be stifled and held back by dictates handed down through international financial institutions (replacing formal political colonialism), a fire for education has truly been lit, but the wherewithal to feed the flames is missing. This book has documented how, in this situation, a million tiny lights of small, individual endeavours have also been sparked –

although the light they shed might be very dim indeed – to help people cope with the care and education needs of their children.

***

Outsiders of all stripes have swooped in on this phenomenon from the full range of possible motivations. The extreme human rights end of the spectrum, for whom principle trumps just plain coping strategies for a difficult reality, would like to see cheap private schools banned or regulated to death. They feel that the schools violate children's human right to education by operating behind a pay wall; they exploit parents by making them pay from meagre incomes for this service that should be free; and they exploit teachers who work for meagre wages. The human rights perspective dictates that no one should profit from the provision of education, but they fail to address satisfactorily that for the person who establishes and runs the school, they will usually just be making a living (or at least trying to) by performing the work of running the school (a job for which government school head teachers also draw a salary). Secondly, they do not provide any rationale as to why education is special – more so than other basic essentials of life that are more fundamental by far than education, such as food, water and shelter. Thirdly, they do not address the fact that many people profit from the provision of education and education services in their own countries – right across the world. The decision by outsiders that people in poor countries must be prevented from paying for education smacks of Carnegie and his *Gospel of Wealth*, in which he determined how money for the benefit of poor people should be spent. The poor couldn't be trusted to make their own choice, for their own good – a paternalistic approach indeed. No one is swooping in to solve the problems of these people's difficult lives, and yet commentators and pundits see fit to pass judgement on how these people work things out for themselves. No one is helping these communities, making sure they have proper services that would make their communities, and therefore their lives, more pleasant.

At the other end of the spectrum are those who observe the parental drive for education, demonstrated through the existence of cheap private schools, and want to capitalize on this in some way. Call it following the trends and encouraging 'what works' or whatever else. If there is a more benign form of this to be had, it can only be with regard to those involved in development aid who feel that if winds of parental demand are blowing this way, then these schools should be incorporated into development plans. If the schools are also not so great, then development programmes should aim to incorporate them into the education system and work to improve their quality alongside government school quality. The fact that improving government schools, which are usually many times fewer in number, hasn't worked yet is somehow beside the point. There's profit to be made for consultants and service-providers through development programmes telling people in poor countries what to do, no matter whether the ideas work or not.

But the most malign form of outsiders' interest in poor countries with many cheap private schools is from those seeking to profit directly from this grass-roots self-help crisis response – sucking money out of these poor communities and siphoning it to their rich home countries in the form of corporate profit. Bridge International Academies was the first to come along as the better-organized version of cheap private schooling, backed and funded by foreigners providing a possibly-better-quality service, with the idea of profiting off the actual provision of schooling. It appears impossible to earn profits this way, although a few other for-profit, foreign-backed and designed chains entered the arena anyway. I could never quite see how this could work because education is such a labour-intensive enterprise, so there is very limited potential to take advantage of economies of scale. With regard to Omega Schools in Ghana, James Tooley explained to me via email that materials could be printed abroad and uniforms could be stitched in India to save money (presumably once some minimum critical mass was reached), but I took a dim view of this because one of the wonderful aspects of cheap private schools is that all the money that flows around and through them stays local, in the community. Teaching itself requires a person present for each class (ideally), until things develop (or rather, degenerate) to the point where virtual charter schools are introduced, but the American evidence on those is certainly not encouraging, and it's not possible to think of those yet for very young children or for remote rural areas.

The profit-seeking from non-state involvement in education has moved on from the idea of branded chains of schools, although these still exist as the original form of NewGlobe's and Rising Academies' businesses. It's now all about education support services, much of which is now revolving around apps. NewGlobe's model has always focused on tech solutions to solve the problem of low teacher knowledge levels and low managerial capacity for school head teachers. Teachers and managers are monitored and held accountable through their engagement with the tech that they must use. Rising Academies now seems to be moving towards tech too, with apps for school and class management, and now a chatbot for students to use outside of school hours, and photos proudly displayed showing children wearing headphones plugged into a screen that they are staring at, in company in body but isolated through tech. The language is eerily similar to that used to describe the charms of virtual learning at charter schools in the United States – individualized tech-based learning. Other supposed 'innovations' are coming in to prod and cajole educational improvement to happen, like 'paying for results' through the involvement of impact investors. Experiences from governments of rich countries contracting out for various services show that quality or delivery of results has no bearing on getting ever more contracts, as the example of Fujitsu's utter failure of an accounting software for the UK Post Office shows. Despite a debacle of monumental proportions, the company continues to win more contracts.[1] This must surely be encouraging for Western companies seeking contracts with poorer country governments, but seeking to profit off the backs of those in the Global South appears particularly venal and grasping.

One way or the other, things always seem to find their way around to the issue of scale. Nothing is ever good enough if it is small and rooted in its context. All of these corporate and donor responses come from this deep drive to organize and standardize things because we have to get *all children into school* as quickly as possible, and we need to make sure schools are providing uniformly acceptable levels of quality. There seems to be discomfort with the idea of a community served by a few small schools, one of which might be really fairly bad while the other two might be better. There might also be communities not served by any decent school – but there might not be anyone who is even educated enough in that community to be worthy of the title 'teacher'. There is this deep discomfort with the idea that these might be things that we can't do anything about, especially in light of the usual expectation of improvement across the board, now, now, now, with a standardized, universalized approach. This, while maintaining the dream of producing the critically thinking, environmentally conscious individuals of tomorrow. But here I have tried to set out things as they are in the real world, not often ventured into for extended periods by consultants and World Bank and UNESCO staff. To date, there has been nothing that donors, governments, companies and charities have been able to do about the situation, but there is ample unwillingness to accept this.

I close this book not by summarizing all of the various aspects of education in the Global South that I have written about in the preceding chapters, but by reminding anyone who reads this that many communities have come up with their own interim solutions to their drive for education that relies on no one else's support and waits for no one's approval. It's not perfect by any stretch of the imagination – for the most basic reason that these schools have to draw on the same ill-educated populations that governments have to draw teachers from.

But the school owners have 'skin in the game' – they live in the communities they serve, and are unlikely to get away from it and the families of the children they teach. If they do wrong, they will have to face these parents, who live all around them. They pay teachers out of the fee income from local people, and those teachers receive and spend that pay as local people themselves. They pay to live, eat, sleep and buy clothing in that same local community, although all of these people have bought an idea of education sold very much from outside. Well, at least this form of schooling is not sucking away any of the wealth from these communities, while the extreme penny-pinching people must do to afford to pay fees is far from anyone's notion of an ideal situation. Indeed, it is desperately sad, considering how much is spent on government education in countries like India.

In a way these schools *have* actually 'scaled', or at least the phenomenon has. In places like Lagos and Kampala, the coverage of the cheap private schooling movement is remarkable. But it is hard to think of any standardized pilot projects of school provision that have scaled up to a national or even regional level, because usually what drove the small version of the project to succeed – often the extreme interest and enormous time and effort given by the organizer, is just not something that can be replicated or mass-produced and distributed far and wide. Where the individual responsibility and stake in the success of the enterprise disappear, then the fraying at the edges starts – a painful truth that does no one any good to ignore. In poor countries there just aren't the monitoring and accountability mechanisms and transparent, corruption-free systems necessary to ensure that standards are maintained 'at scale' without this individual stake in each school's success. These are sad observations that I make, not being in any way a fan of privatization as a notion – I am quite the opposite, in fact – realizing fully the immense capacity for corruption in the private sector. As Thomas Sowell astutely observed, 'there are no solutions; there are only trade-offs. You try to get the best trade-off you can get, that's all you can hope for.'[2]

So, I end this text shouting out in defence of the thousands of tiny lights in the educational darkness that twinkle across the landscapes of so many countries where public services are just not working. As E.F. Schumacher wrote in 1973, *Small Is Beautiful*, and, at the present time, the best that anyone has been able to manage, and almost the only thing many people have to rely upon. What commentators and interested parties from rich countries need to accept is that they do not have all the answers, far from it. Indeed, the imperative is to pause before repeating the economic and social crimes of the British in eighteenth- and nineteenth-century India, who stamped out what people were doing for themselves. They destroyed, and failed to replace what they destroyed with anything good, sucking unimaginable wealth from a place replete with learning, spirituality, high culture and material wealth to enrich themselves back home. Thinking about education the way Starbucks thinks about coffee is the modern-day, neo-colonialist equivalent – and if we can do no better than this horrific idea, or failed development project after failed development project, we'd best just *leave these countries alone.*

Notes

Chapter 1

1. Benson (2023).
2. I worked for Nobel Laureate Kailash Satyarthi's organization, Global March Against Child Labour. There I learned what courage in direct action is, when members of the team would come back from factory raids to free child labourers, bloodied and injured.
3. *The Guardian* (2023).
4. See again the editorial in the previous note, as well as most of the writing of the economist Ha-Joon Chang and the anthropologist Jason Hickel.
5. I am using this as a shorthand for all of the challenges that I write about in Chapter 4.
6. I hold the British version of 'middle class' in my mind rather than that used in the United States, which tends to overlap more with the British working class, particularly those working in skilled trades.
7. I do not like this word as it sounds negative, however I will sometimes use it in preference to 'informal settlements' or 'low-income neighbourhoods' as the latter terms are rather cumbersome. I mean to imply nothing negative when I use 'slum' as short hand, and have enormous sympathy and solidarity with all the people I have spoken to and visited in low-income neighbourhoods as part of my research.
8. Tooley (2015).
9. Mwesigwa (2022). See also Mwesigwa (2021) and *The Guardian* (2022).
10. Baleegh (2022).
11. Ravitch (2013).
12. Wording borrowed here from Dickens' Ghost of Christmas Present in *A Christmas Carol*.
13. Dharampal (1983).

Chapter 2

1. *The National*, 8 August (Scotonomics, 2023).
2. World Bank (2019), cited in Gatti et al. (2021, p. 54).

3   Härmä, J. (2015).
4   Lewin (2007). This report may be old, but it describes why children drop out using the author's model of 'zones of exclusion', all of which continues to be valid today, and I have never read a better summing up of the ways that children end up excluded from education.
5   These include Uwezo and Twaweza '*Are Our Children Learning? Annual Learning Assessment Reports*' carried out in East African countries, and India and Pakistan's Annual Status of Education Reports.
6   One criticism has been levelled at the way the community volunteers approach a particular habitation – if they start on one edge and simply work their way in from that edge, stopping when they have done the requisite number of tests, it means that they might take samples from only a particularly poor or well-off part of the community, rather than getting a cross-section of it. However, with the enormous numbers of communities visited, any skewing in a particular community is probably balanced out by opposite skewing in another.
7   Wadhwa (2014, p. 19).
8   Wadhwa (2014).
9   ASER (2015).
10 Uwezo Uganda (2019).
11 Uwezo Uganda (2021, p. 12).
12 Uwezo Uganda (2021, p. 22).
13 Uwezo Kenya (2021). Key facts from pp. 15 and 16.
14 Uwezo Tanzania (2019) key fact, p. 9.
15 Härmä (2016a).
16 The countries and latest year of Social Development Indicator (SDI) surveys conducted are: Kenya (2012), Madagascar (2016), Morocco (2016), Mozambique (2014), Niger (2015), Nigeria (2013), Tanzania (2016), Togo (2013) and Uganda (2013). The SDI survey initiatives have now expanded far beyond sub-Saharan Africa.
17 Gatti et al. (2021), p. 56.
18 Gatti et al. (2021), pp. 58–60.
19 Wane and Martin (2016), p. 25.
20 Uwezo Uganda (2021), literacy facts p. 8 and numeracy, p. 10.
21 Wane and Martin (2016), p. 25.
22 Martin and Pimhidzai (2013), p. 23.
23 Ngware et al. (2013).
24 World Bank (2014), p. 37.
25 Härmä (2016a), my study found nearly no private schools above the pre-primary level.
26 World Bank (2014), p. 16.
27 Härmä (2016b).

28 Molina and Martin (2015), p. 31.
29 Molina and Martin (2015), p. 20.
30 World Bank (2015), p. 20.
31 Härmä (2011); EDOREN (2015).
32 EDOREN (2018), p. 12.
33 EDOREN (2015), p. 1.
34 Based on my own analysis of the Government of Ghana's National Educational Assessment data, 2018, presented in the official 'Report of Findings' by Ghana's Ministry of Education, the Ghana Education Service and the National Education Assessment Unit; discussed in my own work, Härmä and Moscoviz (2019).
35 This is elaborated in the various sources in this chapter.
36 Härmä and Moscoviz (2019).
37 OECD (2018), p. 6.
38 OECD (2018), p. 6.
39 PROBE Team (1999).
40 Assessments are run by The Southern and Eastern Africa Consortium for Monitoring Educational Quality (SACMEQ); Program on the Analysis of Education Systems (PASEC) and the Annual Status of Education Report, Pakistan. There is also the Early Grades Reading Assessment and Early Grades Mathematics Assessments that are conducted in a wide range of countries. UNESCO also supports the LLECE-ERCE, large-scale student assessment programmes in Latin America and the Caribbean.
41 Coombs (1967).
42 I conducted a desk-based study on this topic, providing background to an education project there.

Chapter 3

1 This goes back even further in time than the writing of Philip Coombs (1967).
2 Fredriksen (2009b).
3 This is made very clear in Ha-Joon Chang's (2002) book, *Kicking Away the Ladder*.
4 Lee (2021).
5 Fredriksen (2009b), p. 4.
6 See Winkler and Sondergaard (2008).
7 See UNESCO's *Global Monitoring Report* series from 2002 onwards, rebranded the *Global Education Monitoring Report* in 2016.
8 I worked on education data with Nigerian government colleagues in three states. Per-capita funding to schools incentivizes the reporting of inflated enrolment numbers.

9   Morgan et al. (2014).
10 Fredriksen (2009a), p. 24.
11 Fredriksen (2009b).
12 UNESCO (2024b).
13 The short supply is documented as being particularly acute in sub-Saharan Africa, where an estimated 15 million more teachers are needed, and where the poorest, most remote countries and parts of countries remain an enormous challenge to deploy teachers to. UNESCO (2024b).
14 Angbulu (2022) *We'll sack more underqualified teachers, says El-Rufai*, this is a news article in the popular Punch newspaper in Nigeria. The article addresses the issue of secondary school teachers with only a primary school education.
15 This conversation took place in confidence in December 2023.
16 Fredriksen (2009a), p. 16.
17 At the same time, Ministry of Education inspectorate staff lacked the person-power, vehicles and funding necessary to get out to schools to monitor what was going on there; this is discussed in more detail in Chapter 10.
18 Akyeampong et al. (2011).
19 There is, of course, great variation in situations, especially between urban and rural areas. Some urban Indian teachers do what they can with large numbers of students.
20 This fact was shared with me in confidence by a retired government official.
21 These sums, divided per head, still prove insufficient.
22 UNESCO (2024b).
23 I have direct experience of this situation, in my own family. Gaurav's niece has received a teaching qualification from a single room on a small plot of land where no teacher training actually happens. Her qualification is useless.
24 UNESCO (2024b).
25 Hansen (1965); Indire and Hanson (1971).
26 UNESCO (2024b).
27 Mayengo et al. (2015).
28 Bhatta (2014); Phillipson (2008).
29 Naviwala (2016, 2019). Naviwala's work sets out in painful detail the travails facing children whose mother tongue is a less-common language, and one in which there are no books and in which teaching is not done.

Chapter 4

1   Carnoy (2016), p. 68.
2   Mani et al. (2013).

3 Graham and Forstadt (2011).
4 Brockmeyer and D'Angiulli (2016), p. 24.
5 UNICEF (2018).
6 Hertz Picciotto et al. (2018), p. 2.
7 Nelson (2018).
8 Rauh et al. (2011).
9 Liu and Schelar (2012).
10 Brockmeyer and D'Angiulli (2016).
11 Brockmeyer and D'Angiulli (2016).
12 Rees (2017), p. 6.
13 Brito and Noble (2014), p. 1.
14 Dryden-Peterson (2010).
15 A number of research studies arrive at this conclusion, including Alcott and Rose (2016); Baum and Riley (2019); Bold et al. (2013); Gruijters and Behrman (2020); Ravitch (2013); Shores et al. (2016); Tulloch et al. (2014); UNESCO (2010). Most of these sources focus on poorer countries but Ravitch writes about the United States.
16 Here I draw on the personal experience of Gaurav, in teaching children in our school.
17 Cheadle (2008), Sirin (2005).
18 UNESCO (2024b).
19 Wadhwa (2014), p. 19. It is unclear what proportion of the 70 per cent is down to the household and how much is due to the child's innate qualities.
20 Pritchett (2015). I read this paper with great difficulty as it was required reading for the Liberia programme I found myself a part of. This could only have been written in an office far, far away from a real-world situation; it was an exercise in expressing a simple (but unrealistic, out-of-touch) idea in needlessly complicated language.
21 There are serious criminal, physical assaults too, most of which remain firmly hidden. In running a school for girls in Uttar Pradesh, we have known of many children who have been the victims of all degrees of sexual assault, often incestuous. While I can attest that these horrors are far from uncommon, some might dismiss what I personally know about as anecdotal stories, but in the end I do not even feel equipped to write about this painful subject.

Chapter 5

1 Instances of this from one school alone, the one started by Gaurav and me in 2004, could fill a complete book without any other topic addressed.
2 Romero and Sandefur (2022). Interestingly, this source that I draw in later, in Chapter 10, also found that in Liberia, better quality might not lead to greater demand at a school.

3   This was the phrase used by many parents during my doctoral study fieldwork.
4   See the references in Chapter 2: the World Bank's Service Delivery Indicators survey reports provide details of assessments of teachers' knowledge and skills for teaching. Another source from Chapter 2, Ngware and colleagues' work in multiple locations in Kenya also documents the poor subject content knowledge and pedagogical knowledge of the teachers involved, at both government and private schools. My first run-in with poor teacher knowledge was during my first job in Nigeria after my doctorate: of 19,125 government school teachers in Kwara State, only seventy-five (i.e. 0.4 per cent) were able to pass an exam of primary 4 level material (David Johnson, Baines, and Williams, 2008, p. 2).
5   Most of this section on ragged schools draws on the following source, and the direct quotation is from p. 173: Schupf (1972).
6   Professor Keith Lewin, an old colleague and professor at Sussex, where I did my doctoral work, has been working on education financing for decades. Very recently, he was on the FreshEd podcast talking about the daunting and growing size of the challenge. FreshEd podcast episode number 138, 9 October 2023.
7   UNESCO (2024b).

Chapter 6

1   Carnoy (1974), p. 15.
2   Carnoy (1974), p. 16.
3   Gaurav's family are closely associated with people who worked with Dharampal and knew him well. As he died in 2006, I could easily have met him and I regret very much that I was too young and uninformed back then to have known of him.
4   I too am a St Andrews graduate, in Modern History, but I completed my degree some 225 years later.
5   Dharampal (1983) *The Beautiful Tree: Indigenous Indian Education in the Eighteenth Century*, Collected Writings Volume III. Freely available online here: https://www.dharampal.net/sites/default/files/2021-02/beautifultree1.pdf, p. 21. In another relevant passage of Dharampal's own commentary in his long introduction: 'it is suggested here – and there is voluminous data scattered in the British records themselves which confirm the view – that in terms of the basic expenses, both education and medical care, like the expenses of the local police, and the maintenance of irrigation facilities, had primary claims on revenue. It was primarily this revenue which not only maintained higher education, but also – as was sometimes admitted in the British records – the system of elementary education. It is quite probable that, in addition to this basic provision, the parents and guardians of the scholars also contributed a little according to their varying

capacities by way of presents, occasional feeding of the unprovided scholars, etc., towards the maintenance of the system. But to suppose that such a deep rooted and extensive system which really catered to all sections of society could be maintained on the basis of tuition fees, or through not only gratuitous teaching but also feeding of the pupils by the teachers, is to be grossly ignorant of the actual functioning of the Indian social arrangements of the time' (p. 75).

6   This refers to Bell and Lancaster.
7   Dharampal (1983), pp. 261–62.
8   Dharampal (1983), p. 262.
9   Dharampal (1983), p. 263.
10 Dalrymple (2002) *White Mughals: Love and Betrayal in Eighteenth-Century India.*
11 Dharampal (1983), p. 17.
12 Dharampal (1983), p. 18.
13 Dharampal (1983), p. 30.
14 Dharampal (1983), p. 20.
15 McGilvary (2019).
16 Dharampal (1983), p. 79.
17 Dharampal (1983), p. 79.
18 Dharampal (1983) p. 192.
19 It is the British who introduced child labour in India as a crisis coping mechanism.
20 Again, just such was I until 2019.
21 This whole discussion takes place over pp. 252–5 of Dharampal (1983).
22 Tooley (2009).
23 See note 5 above where Dharampal makes this point.

Chapter 7

1   My old team at UNESCO used to love this sort of thing and probably still does.
2   Chang (2008) and Chang (2002).
3   Lipcan, Härmä et al. (2018).
4   I know people who have received contracts from the World Bank and been paid for no work simply because the contracting person had a budget to spend and did not want to send the funds back unspent. I presume this was to justify another similarly sized budget the next year. Worst case scenario was him treating his friend with a work-free contract.
5   Lipcan, Härmä et al. (2018).
6   Kim et al. (2022).
7   These quotes were taken from the website of Development Alternatives Incorporated (DAI) for the programme they implement, Partnership for Learning

for All in Nigeria, funded by the UK government: the site was accessed 26 October 2023, but the website has since changed.
8 Stiglitz (2002).

Chapter 8

1 The cheap private school model revolves around the low fees charged: this means little to spend on teacher salaries and on infrastructure, furniture, teaching aids and inputs, and maintenance. A generalization that holds is that the vast majority of school budgets (government and private) in the Global South is spent on the recurrent cost of staffing, with little left over for capital investment.
2 Härmä (2019).
3 UNESCO (2022).
4 I have been told that with improvements made to public schools in Edo State, Nigeria, has come a move away from private schools, as I have for years said would happen. Few parents are wedded enough to the status element of private schooling to want to keep on paying fees.
5 This number was estimated to have reached 18,000 many years ago. I have no information on what the figure is in 2024.
6 There was considerable media coverage of the 2012 Makoko demolitions, including this from the BBC (2012), https://www.bbc.co.uk/news/world-africa-18870511.

Chapter 9

1 The words of Jay Kimmelman, Bridge International Academies co-founder, Gray-Lobe et al. (2022), p. 1.
2 Tooley (2007).
3 I have gathered the costs related to attending Bridge schools (through friends) in the same place where I have conducted studies at cheap private schools such as in Kampala.
4 Grim and Wadekar (2023).
5 Wadekar and Grim (2023).
6 Åstrand (2016).
7 I think this says rather a lot. Gaurav begged his brother to send his son and daughter, our niece and nephew, to our school in the village in western Uttar Pradesh, because we felt that it was honestly better than the expensive upper-middle-class school they attend in up-scale Gurgaon. The parents refused,

presumably because of how it might appear in society to send children from such a place as Gurgaon to such a place as Chakarsi village, a tiny rural hamlet.

I heard second-hand that when asked why their children did not attend a Bridge school in Nairobi, May and Kimmelman explained that their international children required an international school (as well, presumably, as a helicopter to get to the beach house more easily, saving time for homework?). Perhaps there is a level above 'world class' and above the type of 'international' that is in their own schools' name, required by their children but not the children of Kenya. This information came from a teacher at the elite Nairobi school where May and Kimmelman educated their children. I guess I understand part of their position, I too would not have suggested my niece and nephew attend a school made of wooden planks and chicken wire.

8   Härmä (2021).
9   Tooley (2007); Riep (2014). This is also as described to me by Jay Kimmelman, Bridge International Academies founder, in-person in Nairobi, 2011.
10 Härmä (2017).
11 Singh (2017); Ravitch (2013).
12 Education International (2016).
13 EDOREN (2018).
14 Härmä (2021). I discuss the evaluation on p. 135. I was provided with the results by a key informant but the report is not published and I was never sent a copy.
15 Johnson and Hsieh (2019), pp. 47–8.
16 Härmä (2018).
17 Ngware et al. (2013).
18 Gates and Gates (2018); Hess (2018). Regarding Zuckerberg's activities, an evaluation found that there was significant progress in English as a result of closing and replacing bad schools, but no progress in mathematics. Chin et al. (2017).
19 I am a proponent of this sort of instinct only in cases as extreme and clearcut as this.
20 Their tech-enabled systems track and direct their employees at all times, as is well-known about their model.
21 There are also glowing reviews on Glassdoor.com – but also reviews stating that staff are cajoled into going onto the site and writing positive reports about what it is like to be a NewGlobe employee.
22 Tyre (2017).
23 www.newglobe.education/home-page/ (accessed 1 November 2023).
24 The story is elaborated in detail in the exemplary articles in The Intercept by Neha Wadekar and Ryan Grim, one dated 23 March 2023 (Wadekar and Grim 2023), and the second even more explosive article on 17 October 2023 (Grim and Wadekar 2023). These articles are open access and set out the whole sorry tale in detail, and

since then, there has been much media coverage. I was able to get access to the key pieces of core source material that they used, a leaked investigation report into the International Finance Corporation's failure to do anything about reports of child sexual abuse at schools they were funding – NewGlobe's Bridge International Academies in Kenya. This report and other materials are now available publicly at the Compliance Advisor Ombudsman website: https://www.cao-ombudsman.org/cases/kenya-bridge-international-academies-04learn-capital-01-04. For a very useful quick summary, see Sandefur (2024) *A Timeline of the World Bank Child Sexual Abuse Scandal.*

25 Tunza Child Safeguarding (2020).
26 Grim and Wadekar (2023).
27 Bridge/NewGlobe already had an ostensibly limited playbook in this regard – they would file an ethics complaint about him, claiming he had impersonated Bridge staff in order to gain access to schools, something they had already done to the Canadian researcher, Curtis Riep, earning a tarnished reputation in the process. The lack of variation here is as puzzling as it is comical.
28 IFC (2024); see also Sandefur (2024), and Saldinger (2023).
29 Sandefur (2024), and IFC (2024).
30 Jay Kimmelman explained to me, in person, in 2011, that the aim of the company is profit, and they chose Kenya as their first country of operation because market research pointed them there. It is his partner, Shannon May, who puts on the emotive performances about 'doing it for the kids'. My favourite such performance can be found here: Dr. Shannon May of Bridge Intl Academies, WISE 2015. https://www.youtube.com/watch?v=vELjzJXgzqk&t=411s; in particular from minute 6:49. It appears that Kimmelman is not often allowed out, probably because he tells the truth about the company's pure profit motive and May's theatrics go down better with the smug, self-satisfied/gullible audiences that listen to her.
31 Leaked text of Banga's email to World Bank staff available on X (formerly Twitter) via Ryan Grim's feed: '@NehaWadekar Here is the email from Ajay Banga to World Bank staff. If I were petty I'd say he ought to have apologized to The Intercept too. Why he fought against doing/saying this for so long and so hard is mystifying, because he wasn't even in charge amid all the wrongdoing. In any event', / X, https://twitter.com/ryangrim/status/1768120083841245192.
32 World Bank (2024). This press release was the final instalment in this sorry saga before this manuscript was finalized and no more additions could be made.
33 Education International (2016).
34 I want it to make it clear that what I am describing here is the situation in reality, not as I think it should be, where all child abusers would be duly prosecuted, punished and prevented from ever working with children again.
35 Grim and Wadekar (2023).
36 Compliance Advisor Ombudsman (2023).

37 Banga's email (see note 31) states that the IFC should have rallied other important investors to take the company to task.
38 The IFC broke its own rules in ignoring the fact that they were investing in a company that intentionally broke Kenyan law, as made clear in the Compliance Advisor Ombudsman Compliance Investigation Report.
39 Education International (2016).
40 IFC (2016).
41 Formerly the Commonwealth Development Corporation, formerly the Colonial Development Corporation.
42 Novastar website: https://www.novastarventures.com/portfolio/newglobe/ (accessed 3 December 2023).
43 House of Commons International Development Committee (2023), p. 44.

Chapter 10

1 Ravitch (2013); Burris and Bryant (2019); Green et al. (2018). For an extremely good but quick and light-hearted overview of these issues, one could not do better than watch Charter Schools: Last Week Tonight with John Oliver (HBO) – YouTube, https://www.youtube.com/watch?v=l_htSPGAY7I.
2 Patrinos et al. (2009).
3 I encountered this in Enugu State, Nigeria, where my civil service colleague had a sheaf of receipts for office supplies and the like that he kept in the hope that one day he might be reimbursed. I know this to happen in many government employment settings in Nigeria, India and elsewhere.
4 When I say 'corporate entities', I refer first and foremost to the leader in this area, NewGlobe. Kimmelman (2014), co-founder of Bridge International Academies speaking at an event for Khosla Ventures, where he discusses how they have a legal department aimed at running circles around government officials.
5 Post Office Horizon scandal explained: Everything you need to know, https://www.computerweekly.com/feature/Post-Office-Horizon-scandal-explained-everything-you-need-to-know; What is the UK's Post Office IT scandal about and who is involved? *The Guardian*, https://www.theguardian.com/uk-news/2024/jan/11/what-is-uk-post-office-horizon-it-scandal-about-who-involved.
6 Education Partnerships Group, whose raison d'être was forming PPPs in education, was a spin-off of Absolute Returns for Kids operating in London, that runs academy (charter-like) schools in the UK. It was basically just another consultancy outfit, but a specialist one. In the process of fact-checking in June 2024, I discovered that the company was dissolved in November 2020, according to Companies House.

7 Donnelly et al. (2019). This report is nearly pure propaganda.
8 Patrinos et al. (2009).
9 As described to me by someone high up in the Delhi Police.
10 Bano (2008).
11 *The Economist* (2015).
12 Ansari (2020).
13 I personally met several of their early hires in senior positions, in 2008.
14 Pegg (2021).
15 O'Donoghue et al. (2018).
16 Reinikka and Svensson (2004).
17 Afridi (2018).
18 This is my summing up of the situation, based on Afridi's work (2018).
19 E-Pact (2021).
20 Marginalization brings additional barriers that require more effort and therefore more resources to overcome. See OECD (2012).
21 E-Pact (2021).
22 Afridi (2018).
23 Afridi (2018), p. 5.
24 Andrabi et al. (2018).
25 Afridi (2018), p. 36.
26 See Diane Ravitch's vast body of work on similar policies in the United States.
27 Naviwala (2019).
28 Naviwala (2019); Naviwala (2016).
29 I came to know this story of how the PPP plan for Bridge to take over the entire public primary schooling system through various discussions with people involved, and from David Archer, head of education at ActionAid, during 2016. I learned that Katie Meyler was involved from this early stage through the reporting of ProPublica, *Unprotected* (propublica.org), which led to the downfall of her charity in 2019 due to child rape that was taking place at her school, the More Than Me Academy and even before its establishment when the charity was running a scholarship programme.
30 See the large catalogue of work done by the international teachers' union, Education International, on Bridge International Academies. They and Civil Society groups were instrumental in fighting Bridge.
31 Front Page Africa (2016).
32 Romero et al. (2017). This is the source for all of the first-year evaluation information in this section.
33 Romero and Sandefur (2022). After the 2017 elections, the new administration stated that it would stop prioritizing the schools being studied by the international evaluation team with regard to deployment of newly (ostensibly better) qualified teachers.

34 Romero and Sandefur (2022).
35 In my hotel in Monrovia, I was told this by a foreign consultant working on this very issue for the country.
36 All of my information on More Than Me comes from Finlay Young's 2018 and 2019 reporting at ProPublica.
37 Wingard (2013) – this is a leaked document (also referred to in the next paragraph) that was submitted by the charity's country head who only lasted a few months due to the chaotic and unprofessional way things were run, available online at https://www.documentcloud.org/documents/5000434-MTM-Risk-Management.html. One parent whose child was taken out of the neighbourhood without consent, hunted Meyler down and threatened to kill her, leaving little room for ambiguity as to whether Meyler's attitude to children was considered acceptable.
38 See the source in the previous note.
39 Romero and Sandefur (2022).
40 This latter point is highlighted in the leaked ombudsman's report for the IFC Compliance Advisor Ombudsman (2023).
41 Sandefur (2024).
42 Abrams (2016).
43 Compliance Advisor Ombudsman (2023). Regarding a CAO Vice Presidential Triggered Investigation of IFC's Investment in Bridge International Academies (Bridge 04).
44 Brown-Martin (2016). Brown-Martin cites page 10 of the 'pitch deck' specifically.
45 See their website where they call their private school model 'community schools', developed as 'proof of concept'. The term 'community school' has been wrongly appropriated by their corporate fee-paying model. 'Community school' is a term to denote a school started and usually run by members of the community in a joint effort, not schools owned by individuals or corporations, started as commercial enterprises, www.newglobe.education/home-page/ (accessed 1 November 2023).
46 They have been working state by state in the federal countries Nigeria and India.
47 IFC (2016).
48 According to this website How NewGlobe is transforming education systems in Nigeria – https://tosse.ng/how-new-globe-is-transforming-education-systems-in-nigeria/ (accessed 7 June 2024).
49 See Glassdoor.com and also https://newglobe.education/abou/careers/ (accessed 7 June 2024).
50 Compliance Advisor Ombudsman (2023).
51 One can only speculate at this stage that this will be the case also for Benin and the Central African Republic.

52 Countless newspaper articles can be found online, with several to be found at AllAfrica's website. *Bridge Academies Under Fire in Uganda and Kenya* available at https://allafrica.com/view/group/main/main/id/00057084.html (accessed 5 June 2024). See also Education International's website section dedicated to Bridge and associated coverage.
53 Gray-Lobe et al. (2022), p. 55.
54 Wadekar and Grim (2023).
55 I learned from a friend in Nigeria that at least one of the state partnerships came with an increase in teacher numbers to facilitate the working of the model.
56 The socioeconomic differences between public school parents (usually fairly poor or otherwise disadvantaged) and private school parents are widely documented, and I have done this myself from Uttar Pradesh, India, as part of my doctorate (Härmä 2009) and in Nigeria (Härmä and Siddhu 2017), and in my last-ever research study in rural Ghana (Härmä and Moscoviz 2019).
57 Because repeated requests for interview over a span of years were ignored, I have only the original Bridge model to go off in writing this. If there is a significant difference here between the PPP model and the private school model, I was unable to get the company to tell me.
58 This would likely be explicitly covered by contract rules.
59 Compliance Advisor Ombudsman (2023).
60 I found this out through friends in Uganda whom I asked to visit a Bridge school to ask about the fees and costs, in summer 2016.
61 Gray-Lobe et al. (2022).
62 NewGlobe's website home page: https://newglobe.education/home-page/ (accessed 27 October 2023).
63 Education International (2016).
64 Gray-Lobe et al. (2022), p. 36.
65 Levine (2022).
66 This is not a unique situation – consider the recent news of the massive contract between the UK's National Health Service and the Palantir corporation: Campbell (2023).
67 Brown-Martin (2016). Again, the company's refusal to engage in an interview means I have to use hedging language here.
68 I put it this way, rather than 'whether their students are actually learning', because of everything I write in Chapter 4 – the vast numbers of reasons that poor children face an uphill battle in trying to learn.
69 See my first footnote in this chapter on the astonishing amount of corruption in charter schools in the supposedly developed, strong-governance country of the United States.

Chapter 11

1. UNESCO (2024a).
2. Naviwala (2019).
3. Ravitch (2013). Industry proponents, of course, dress it up to be something very positive; see Evanick (2023).
4. Gray-Lobe et al. (2022).
5. Chang (2008), p. 3.
6. Chang (2008), p. 3.
7. Chang (2008), p. 6.
8. Chang (2008), p. 109.
9. Chang (2008), p. 196.
10. Chang (2008), p. 110.
11. Chang (2002), pp. 69–70.
12. Carnoy (2016).
13. When I was working on the 2015 Global Monitoring Report at UNESCO, I was not allowed by the report director to highlight Cuba as a shining example of support to young children in my chapter on early childhood care and education, perhaps down to Americans' ideological views about the country.
14. Providing, that is, that they have not been bombed 'back to the Stone Age'.
15. Chang (2002), p. 65.
16. Dalrymple (2019).
17. Stiglitz (2002).
18. OECD (2022).
19. Härmä (2021).
20. London (2021) and London (2019).
21. Discussions with family during a summer 2024 trip to Finland revealed that poorly thought-out changes to the education system have been having negative impacts and rarely a day goes by when some education-related problem is not hitting the headlines. However, Finland's results are still towards the top of the pile – for now.

Chapter 12

1. Sweney (2024).
2. Sowell (1987).

References

Abrams, S. (2016). *Education and the Commercial Mindset*. Cambridge: Harvard University Press.

Afridi, M. (2018). *Equity and Quality in an Education Public-Private Partnership: A Study of the World Bank-supported PPP in Punjab, Pakistan* (August), 1–64. Retrieved from www.oxfam.org

Akyeampong, K., Pryor, J., Westbrook, J., and Lussier, K. (2011). *Teacher Preparation and Continuing Professional Development in Africa* (July). Retrieved from https://app.box.com/sierraleoneeducationdocs/1/187375169/1412848487/1

Alcott, B., and Rose, P. (2016). Does Private Schooling Narrow Wealth Inequalities in Learning Outcomes? Evidence from East Africa. *Oxford Review of Education*, 42(5), 495–510. https://doi.org/10.1080/03054985.2016.1215611

Andrabi, T., Das, J., Khwaja, A. I., Ozyurt, S., and Singh, N. (2018). Upping the Ante: The Equilibrium Effects of Unconditional Grants to Private Schools. *American Economic Review*, 110(10), 3315–49.

Angbulu, S. (2022). We'll Sack More Unqualified Teachers, Says El-Rufai. *Punch*. Retrieved from https://punchng.com/well-sack-more-underqualified-teachers-says-el-rufai/?msclkid=b5f8274fb26d11ec895ac5be85198653

Ansari, A. H. (2020). Cream Skimming? Evaluating the Access to Punjab's Public-Private Partnership Programs in Education. *International Journal of Educational Development*, 72(October 2019), 1–12. https://doi.org/10.1016/j.ijedudev.2019.102126

ASER (2015). *Trends Over Time 2006–2014*, 143. Retrieved from http://img.asercentre.org/docs/Publications/ASERReports/ASERTOT/fullasertrendsovertimereport.pdf

Åstrand, B. (2016). From Citizens into Consumers: The Transformation of Democratic Ideals into School Markets in Sweden. In F. Adamson, B. Åstrand and L. Darling-Hammond (Eds.), *Global Education Reform: How Privatization and Public Investment Influence Education Outcomes* (pp. 73–109). London: Routledge.

Baleegh, M. (2022). Over 400 Private Schools Close in Afghanistan: Report. *The Siasat Daily*. Retrieved from https://www.siasat.com/over-400-private-schools-close-in-afghanistan-report-2387844/

Bano, M. (2008). *Public Private Partnerships (PPPs) as 'Anchor' of Educational Reforms: Lessons from Pakistan*. Paris: UNESCO.

Baum, D. R., and Riley, I. (2019). The Relative Effectiveness of Private and Public Schools: Evidence from Kenya. *School Effectiveness and School Improvement*, 30(2), 104–30. https://doi.org/10.1080/09243453.2018.1520132

BBC (2012). Lagos Makoko Slums Knocked down in Nigeria. Retrieved 4 June 2024, from BBC News website: https://www.bbc.co.uk/news/world-africa-18870511

Benson, C. (2023). Child Poverty Rates Still Higher than for Older Populations but Declining. Retrieved 4 June 2024, from United States Census Bureau website: https://www.census.gov/library/stories/2023/12/poverty-rate-varies-by-age-groups.html

Bhatta, P. (2014). Public Desire for Private Schooling in Nepal. In I. Macpherson, S. Robertson and G. Walford (Eds.), *Education, Privatisation and Social Justice: Case Studies from Africa, South Asia and South East Asia* (pp. 67–88). Didcot: Symposium Books.

Bold, T., Kimenyi, M., Mwabu, G., and Sandefur, J. (2013). The High Return to Low-Cost Private Schooling in a Developing Country. *Africa Growth Initiative Working Papers*, 5 (February). Retrieved from http://www.cgdev.org/files/1425807%7B_%7Dfile%7B_%7DSandefur%7B_%7Det%7B_%7Dal%7B_%7DHigh%7B_%7Dreturn%7B_%7DFINAL.pdf

Brito, N., and Noble, K. (2014). Socioeconomic Status and Structural Brain Development. *Frontiers in Neuroscience*, 8, 276. https://doi.org/10.3389/fnins.2014.00276

Brockmeyer, S., and D'Angiulli, A. (2016). How Air Pollution Alters Brain Development: The Role of Neuroinflammation. *Translational Neuroscience*, 7(1), 24–30. https://doi.org/10.1515/tnsci-2016-0005

Brown-Martin, G. (2016). Power, Corruption and Lies. Retrieved 23 January 2020, from Medium website: https://medium.com/friction-burns/power-corruption-and-lies-53b2fd2ed558#.7npuqipif%0D

Burris, C., and Bryant, J. (2019). *Asleep at the Wheel*. New York: Network for Public Education.

Campbell, D. (2023). Patient Privacy Fears as US Spy Tech Firm Palantir Wins £330m NHS Contract. *The Guardian*. Retrieved from https://www.theguardian.com/society/2023/nov/21/patient-privacy-fears-us-spy-tech-firm-palantir-wins-nhs-contract

Carnoy, M. (1974). *Education as Cultural Imperialism*. Boston: Addison-Wesley Longman.

Carnoy, M. (2016). Four Keys to Cuba's Provision of High Quality Public Education. In B. Astrand Frank Adamson and L. Darling-Hammond (Eds.), *Global Education Reform: How Privatization and Public Investment Influence Education Outcomes* (pp. 50–72). London: Routledge.

Chang, H.-J. (2002). *Kicking Away the Ladder: Development Strategy in Historical Perspective*. New York: Anthem Press.

Chang, H.-J. (2008). *Bad Samaritans: The Guilty Secrets of Rich Nations and the Threat to Global Prosperity*. London: Random House Business.

Cheadle, J. (2008). Educational Investment, Family Context, and Children's Math and Reading Growth from Kindergarten through the Third Grade. *Sociology of Education*, 81(1), 1–31.

Chin, M., Kane, T., Kozakowski, W., Schueler, B., and Staiger, D. (2017). *School District Reform in Newark: Within- and between-School Changes in Achievement Growth* (No. 23922). Retrieved from https://cepr.harvard.edu/files/cepr/files/newark_ed_reform_nber_w23922_suggested_changes.pdf

Compliance Advisor Ombudsman (2023). *Compliance Investigation Report: CAO Initiated Investigation of IFC's Investment in Bridge International Academies (Bridge-04)*. Washington, DC: Compliance Advisor Ombudsman.

Coombs, P. (1967). *The World Educational Crisis: A Systems Analysis*. New York: Oxford University Press.

Coombs, P. (1985). *The World Crisis in Education: The View from the Eighties*. New York: Oxford University Press.

Dalrymple, W. (2002). *White Mughals: Love and Betrayal in Eighteenth-Century India*. New York: Harper Collins.

Dalrymple, W. (2019). *The Anarchy*. London: Bloomsbury.

Dharampal (1983). *The Beautiful Tree*. Mussoorie: Society for Integrated Development of Himalayas (SIDH).

Donnelly, K., Nagarajan, A., and Lipstein, R. L. (2019). *Beyond the Mirage: How Pragmatic Stewardship Could Transform Learning Outcomes in International Education Systems*. Unpublished Report.

Dryden-Peterson, S. (2010). Barriers to Accessing Primary Education in Conflict-Affected Fragile States. *Toolkit.Ineesite.Org*. Retrieved from https://resourcecentre.savethechildren.net/node/2942/pdf/2942.pdf%0Ahttps://toolkit.ineesite.org/resources/ineecms/uploads/1150/R2_Dryden-Peterson.pdf

e-Pact (2021). *Performance Evaluation of the Punjab Education Sector Programme (PESP2)*. Retrieved from https://www.opml.co.uk/files/Publications/a2107-punjab-education-sector-project/a2107-final-report.pdf?noredirect=1

EDOREN (2015). *What Are Children in Private Schools Learning?* Abuja: Oxford Policy Management and UKAID.

EDOREN (2018). *Learning in Lagos: Comparing Student Achievement in Bridge, Public, and Private Schools*. https://doi.org/10.1017/CBO9781107415324.004

Education International, and Kenya National Union of Teachers (2016). *Bridge vs. Reality: A Study of Bridge International Academies' for-profit schooling in Kenya* (p. 82). Brussels: Education International.

Evanick, J. (2023). From One-size-fits-all to Tailored Online Education: The Advantages of Personalized Learning. Retrieved 27 October 2023, from eLearning Industry website: https://elearningindustry.com/from-one-size-fits-all-to-tailored-online-education-advantages-of-personalized-learning

Fredriksen, B. (2009a). *Abolishing School Fees in Africa: Lessons from Ethiopia, Ghana, Kenya, Malawi, and Mozambique*. Washington, DC: World Bank. https://doi.org/10.1596/978-0-8213-7540-2

Fredriksen, B. (2009b). Rationale, Issues and Conditions for Sustaining the Abolition of School Fees. In Birger Fredriksen and D. Craissati (Eds.), *Abolishing School Fees in Africa* (pp. 1–41). Washington, DC: World Bank. https://doi.org/10.1596/978-0-8213-7540-2

Front Page Africa (2016). Is Bridge Bullying Liberia into Submission? Liberia's Education Outsource Plan Dilemma. *Front Page Africa*. Retrieved from https://frontpageafricaonline.com/politics/is-bridge-bullying-liberia-into-submission-liberia-s-education-outsource-plan-dilemma/

Gates, B., and Gates, M. (2018). Our 2018 Annual Letter: 10 Tough Questions We Get Asked. Retrieved 26 October 2023, from Gates Notes: The Blog of Bill Gates website: https://www.gatesnotes.com/2018-Annual-Letter?WT.mc_id=02_13_2018_02_AnnualLetter2018_BG-media_&WT.tsrc=BGmedia

Gatti, R., Andrews, K., Avitabile, C., Conner, R., Sharma, J., and Yi Chang, A. (2021). *The Quality of Health and Education Systems across Africa*. Washington, DC: World Bank. https://doi.org/10.1596/978-1-4648-1675-8

Graham, J., and Forstadt, L. (2011). Children and Brain Development: What We Know about How Children Learn. Retrieved 18 October 2023, from University of Maine Cooperative Extension Publications website: https://extension.umaine.edu/publications/4356e/#:~:text=At birth%2C the number of,normal part of brain development.

Gray-Lobe, G., Keats, A., Kremer, M., Mbiti, I., and Ozier, O. (2022). *Can Education Be Standardized? Evidence from Kenya*. Retrieved from https://bfi.uchicago.edu/working-paper/2022-68/

Green, P., Baker, B., and Oluwole, J. (2018). Are Charter Schools the Second Coming of Enron? An Examination of the Gatekeepers That Protect against Dangerous Related-Party Transactions in the Charter School Sectors. *Indiana Law Journal*, 93(4), 1121–60.

Grim, R., and Wadekar, N. (2023). 'Neutralize Adler' – Whistleblower: The World Bank Helped Cover Up Child Sex Abuse at a Chain of For-Profit Schools It Funded. *The Intercept*. Retrieved from https://theintercept.com/2023/10/17/world-bank-whistleblower-bridge-international/

Gruijters, R., and Behrman, J. (2020). Learning Inequality in Francophone Africa: School Quality and the Educational Achievement of Rich and Poor Children. *Sociology*, 93(3), 256–76.

Hansen, W. L. (1965). Human Capital Requirements for Educational Expansion: Teacher Shortages and Teacher Supply. In C. A. Anderson and M. Bowman (Eds.), *Education and Economic Development* (pp. 63–87). London: Frank Cass and Co. Ltd.

Härmä, J. (2009). Can Choice Promote Education for All? Evidence from Growth in Private Primary Schooling in India. *Compare*, 39(2), 151–65. https://doi.org/10.1080/03057920902750400

Härmä, J. (2011). *Lagos Private School Census 2010–2011 Report*. Abuja: DFID Education Sector Support Programme in Nigeria.

Härmä, J. (2015). *A Preliminary Investigation of the Potential for Private School Chains in Lagos*. Lagos: UK-DFID DEEPEN.

Härmä, J. (2016a). *Study of Low-Fee Private Schools in the Slums of Dar es Salaam, Tanzania*. Chicago: CapitalPlus Exchange.

Härmä, J. (2016b). *Study of Non-State Provision of Education in Maputo*. Maputo: DFID Mozambique.

Härmä, J. (2017). *Whose Children Go to Bridge International Academies? A School Choice for the Middle Class in Ijegun, Lagos*. London: ActionAid.

Härmä, J. (2019). Ensuring Quality Education? Low-Fee Private Schools and Government Regulation in Three sub-Saharan African Capitals. *International Journal of Educational Development*, 66, 139–46. https://doi.org/10.1016/j.ijedudev.2018.10.007

Härmä, J. (2021). *Low-Fee Private Schooling and Poverty in Developing Countries*. London: Bloomsbury Academic.

Härmä, J., and Economic Policy Research Centre (2018). *Evaluation of the PEAS Network under the Uganda Universal Secondary Education (USE) Programme: Endline Evaluation Survey Report*. Kampala: Economic Policy Research Centre.

Härmä, J., and Moscoviz, L. (2019). *Learning in Ghana: Exploring the Challenges Faced by Pupils and Teachers at Government and Private Schools in Central Region*. Chicago: IDP Foundation.

Härmä, J., and Siddhu, G. (2017). *Why Do Parents Default? Parental School Choice and Affordability in a Time of Recession*. Lagos: DFID Developing Effective Private Education Nigeria.

Hertz-Picciotto, I., Sass, J. B., Engel, S., Bennett, D. H., Bradman, A., Eskenazi, B., Lanphear, B., Whyatt, R. (2018). Organophosphate Exposures during Pregnancy and Child Neurodevelopment: Recommendations for Essential Policy Reforms. *PLOS Medicine*, 15(10), e1002671. Retrieved from https://doi.org/10.1371/journal.pmed.1002671

Hess, A. (2018). Bill and Melinda Gates Have Spent Billions on US Education, but Haven't Seen As Much Progress As They'd Like. Retrieved 26 October 2023, from CNBC website: https://www.cnbc.com/2018/02/13/bill-and-melinda-gates-have-spent-billions-on-us-education-initiatives.html

House of Commons International Development Committee (2023). *Investment for Development: The UK's Strategy towards Development Finance Institutions*. Retrieved from https://committees.parliament.uk/publications/41461/documents/203966/default/

IFC (2016). *Bridge International Academies – IFC Inclusive Business Case Study*. Retrieved from https://documents1.worldbank.org/curated/ru/878261506582798912/pdf/119876-BRI-PUBLIC-Bridge-Builtforchangereport.pdf

IFC (2024). *Management Report and Management Action Plan in Relation to the CAO Compliance Investigation Report on Bridge International Academies (04)*. Washington, DC: IFC (International Finance Corporation).

Indire, F., and Hanson, J. (1971). *Secondary Level Teachers: Supply and Demand in Kenya*. East Lansing: Michigan State University.

Johnson, D., and Hsieh, J. (2019). *A Longitudinal Study of Learning, Progression, and Personal Growth in Sierra Leone: Final Report*. Oxford: University of Oxford.

Johnson, D., Baines, S., and Williams, E. (2008). *Education Sector Support Programme in Nigeria (ESSPIN) An Assessment of the Development Needs of Teachers in Nigeria Kwara State Case Study December, 2008*. Abuja: Education Sector Support Programme in Nigeria.

Kim, J., Robinson, N., Härmä, J., Jeffery, D., Rose, P., and Woldehanna, T. (2022). Misalignment of Policy Priorities and Financing for Early Childhood Education: Evidence from Ethiopia, Liberia, and Mainland Tanzania. *International Journal of Educational Research*, 111, 101891. https://doi.org/10.1016/j.ijer.2021.101891

Kimmelman, J. (2014). New Solutions – Jay Kimmelman Co-Founder and CEO of Bridge International Academies. Retrieved 26 October 2023, from Khosla Ventures Youtube Channel website: https://www.youtube.com/watch?v=QZdVysvowEU

Lee, D. (2021). South Korea's Infamous 8-hour Suneung College Exam Faces Growing Protests amid Fears over Students' Mental Health. *South China Morning Post*. Retrieved from https://www.scmp.com/week-asia/people/article/3156412/south-koreas-infamous-8-hour-suneung-college-exam-faces-growing

Levine, A. (2022). Suicide Hotline Shares Data with for-profit Spinoff, Raising Ethical Questions. Retrieved 27 October 2023, from Politico website: https://www.politico.com/news/2022/01/28/suicide-hotline-silicon-valley-privacy-debates-00002617

Lewin, K. (2007). *Improving Access, Equity and Transitions in Education: Creating a Research Agenda*. Brighton: Consortium for Research on Educational Access, Transitions and Equity.

Lipcan, A., Härmä, J., Majeed, Z., Law, B., Tesfay, N., Aghajanian, A., Taylor, A., Grover, V., and Bordewieck, C. (2018). *Early Learning Partnership Systems Research: Liberia Diagnostic Report*. Oxford: Oxford Policy Management.

Liu, J., and Schelar, E. (2012). Pesticide Exposure and Child Neurodevelopment. *Workplace Health & Safety*, 60(5), 235–42. https://doi.org/10.1177/216507991206000507

London, J. (2019). *Vietnam: Exploring the Deep Determinants of Learning*. Retrieved from https://assets.publishing.service.gov.uk/media/5ed0ee72e90e0754d8fb3a02/2019719_London_Deep_Determinants_of_Learning_VN_Insight.pdf

London, J. (2021). *Outlier Vietnam and the Problem of Embeddedness: Contributions to the Political Economy of Learning*. Retrieved from https://riseprogramme.org/sites/default/files/2021-02/RISE_WP-062_London.pdf

Mani, A., Mullainathan, S., Shafir, E., and Zhao, J. (2013). Poverty Impedes Cognitive Function. *Science*, 341(6149), 976–80.

Martin, G., and Pimhidzai, O. (2013). *Service Delivery Indicators: Kenya* (March), 1–88. Retrieved from https://www.sdindicators.org/sites/sdi/files/SDI-Report-Kenya.pdf

Mayengo, N., Namusoke, J., and Dennis, B. (2015). The Testimony of Neoliberal Contradiction in Education Choice and Privatisation in a Poor Country: The Case of a Private, Undocumented Rural Primary School in Uganda. *Ethnography and Education*, 10(3), 293–309. https://doi.org/10.1080/17457823.2015.1050687

McGilvary, G. (2019). The Benefits to Edinburgh and Leith from East India Company Connections: c. 1725–c. 1834. In R. Jeffery (Ed.), *India in Edinburgh: 1750s to the Present* (pp. 22–46). New Delhi: Social Science Press.

Molina, E., and Martin, G. (2015). *Education Service Delivery in Mozambique*. Washington, DC: World Bank.

Morgan, C., Petrosino, A., and Fronius, T. (2014). Eliminating School Fees in Low-Income Countries: A Systematic Review. *Journal of MultiDisciplinary Evaluation*, 10(23), 26–43.

Mwesigwa, A. (2021). 'I'll Never Go Back': Uganda's Schools at Risk as Teachers Find New Work during Covid. *The Guardian*. Retrieved from https://www.theguardian.com/global-development/2021/sep/30/ill-never-go-back-ugandas-schools-at-risk-as-teachers-find-new-work-during-covid

Mwesigwa, A. (2022). Term Starts in Uganda – But World's Longest Shutdown Has Left Schools in Crisis. *The Guardian*. Retrieved from https://www.theguardian.com/global-development/2022/jan/14/term-starts-in-uganda-but-worlds-longest-shutdown-has-left-schools-in-crisis

Naviwala, N. (2016). *Pakistan's Education Crisis: The Real Story*. Washington, DC: Wilson Center.

Naviwala, N. (2019). *Why Can't Pakistani Children Read?* Washington, DC: Wilson Center.

Nelson, A. (2018). Ban Entire Pesticide Class to Protect Children's Health, Experts Say. *The Guardian*. Retrieved from https://www.theguardian.com/environment/2018/oct/24/entire-pesticide-class-should-be-banned-for-effect-on-childrens-health#:~:text=Ban entire pesticide class to protect children%27s health%2C experts say,-This article is&text=Evidence that an entire class

Ngware, M., Abuya, B., Admassur, K., Mutisya, M., Musyoka, P., and Oketch, M. (2013). *Quality and Access to Education in Urban Informal Settlements in Kenya* (October). Retrieved from http://aphrc.org/wp-content/uploads/2013/11/ERP-III-Report.pdf

O'Donoghue, J., Crawfurd, L., Makaaru, J., Otieno, P., and Perakis, R. (2018). *A Review of Uganda's Universal Secondary Education Public Private Partnership Programme*. London: Ark Education Partnerships Group.

OECD (2012). *Equity and Quality in Education: Supporting Disadvantaged Students and Schools*. Paris: OECD.

OECD (2018). *PISA for Development: Results in Focus*. Paris: OECD.

OECD (2022). *PISA 2022 Results*. Retrieved from https://www.oecd.org/publication/pisa-2022-results/

Patrinos, H., Barrera-Osorio, F., and Guaqueta, J. (2009). *The Role and Impact of Public-Private Partnerships in Education*. Washington, DC: World Bank.

Pegg, D. (2021). Fifth of UK Covid Contracts 'Raised Red Flags for Possible Corruption'. *The Guardian*. Retrieved from https://www.theguardian.com/world/2021/apr/22/fifth-of-uk-covid-contracts-raised-red-flags-for-possible-corruption

Phillipson, B. (2008). *Low-Cost Private Education: Impacts on Achieving Universal Primary Education*. London: Commonwealth Secretariat.

Pritchett, L. (2015). *Creating Education Systems Coherent for Learning Outcomes: Making the Transition from Schooling to Learning*. Retrieved from https://riseprogramme.org/sites/default/files/2020-11/RISE_WP-005_Pritchett.pdf

PROBE Team (1999). *Public Report on Basic Education in India*. New Delhi: Centre for Development Economics.

Rauh, V., Arunajadai, S., Horton, M., Perera, F., Hoepner, L., Barr, D. B., and Whyatt, R. (2011). Seven-Year Neurodevelopmental Scores and Prenatal Exposure to Chlorpyrifos, a Common Agricultural Pesticide. *Environmental Health Perspectives*, 119(8), 1196–201. https://doi.org/10.1289/ehp.1003160.

Ravitch, D. (2013). *Reign of Error: The Hoax of the Privatization Movement and the Danger to America's Public Schools*. New York: Vintage Books.

Rees, N. (2017). *Danger in the Air: How Air Pollution Can Affect Brain Development in Young Children*. New York: UNICEF.

Reinikka, R., and Svensson, J. (2004). Local Capture: Evidence from a Central Government Transfer Program in Uganda. *Quarterly Journal of Economics*, 119(2), 679–706.

Riep, C. (2014). Omega Schools Franchise in Ghana: 'Affordable' Private Education for the Poor or For-Profiteering? In I. Macpherson, S. Robertson and G. Walford (Eds.), *Education, Privatisation and Social Justice: Case Studies from Africa, South Asia and South East Asia* (pp. 259–79). Didcot: Symposium Books.

Romero, M., and Sandefur, J. (2022). Beyond Short-Term Learning Gains: The Impact of Outsourcing Schools in Liberia after Three Years. *The Economic Journal*, 132(644), 1600–19.

Romero, M., Sandefur, J., and Sandholtz, W. A. (2017). Can Outsourcing Improve Liberia's Schools? Preliminary Results from Year One of a Three-Year Randomized Evaluation of Partnership Schools for Liberia. *SSRN Electronic Journal* (September 2017). https://doi.org/10.2139/ssrn.3062941

Saldinger, A. (2023). IFC Policy for When Projects Cause Harm Lambasted as 'Letdown'. *Devex*. Retrieved from https://www.devex.com/news/ifc-policy-for-when-projects-cause-harm-lambasted-as-letdown-105007

Sandefur, J. (2024). A Timeline of the World Bank Child Sexual Abuse Scandal. Retrieved 9 June 2024, from Center for Global Development website: https://www.cgdev.org/blog/timeline-world-bank-child-sexual-abuse-scandal

Schupf, H. (1972). Education for the Neglected: Ragged Schools in Nineteenth-Century England. *History of Education Quarterly*, 12(2), 162–83.

Scotonomics (2023). Why Do One in Four Edinburgh Students Attend Private School? *The National*. Retrieved from https://www.thenational.scot/news/23709036.private-schools-one-four-edinburgh-students-attend/#

Shores, K., Reardon, S., and Kalagrides, D. (2016). CEPA Working Paper No. 16-10. The Geography of Racial / Ethnic Test Score Gaps. *CEPA Working Paper* (16). Standord: Standford Center for Education Policy Analysis.

Singh, S. (2017). Confessions from a Charter School Teacher – Part One. Retrieved 26 October 2023, from Medium website: https://medium.com/@sukisingh/confessions-from-a-charter-school-teacher-part-one-45376bb92858#id_token=eyJhbGciOiJSUzI1NiIsImtpZCI6ImEwNmFmM GI2 OGEyMTE5ZDY5MmNhYzRhYmY0MTVmZjM3ODgxMzZmNjUiLC J0eXAiOiJKV1QifQ.eyJpc3MiOiJodHRwczovL2FjY291bnRzLmdvb2dsZS5jb20iL

Sirin, S. (2005). Socioeconomic Status and Academic Achievement: A Meta-Analytic Review of Research. *Review of Educational Research*, 75(3), 417–53.

Sowell, T. (1987). *A Conflict of Visions: Ideological Origins of Political Struggles.* New York: William Morrow & Co.

Stiglitz, J. (2002). *Globalization and Its Discontents.* New York: W.W. Norton & Co.

Sweney, M. (2024). UK Government Urged to Review £2bn in Fujitsu Contracts amid Horizon Scandal. *The Guardian*. Retrieved from https://www.theguardian.com/business/2024/jan/10/uk-government-urged-review-fujitsu-contracts-horizon-scandal#:~:text=The Japanese company%2C which continues,since the landmark legal ruling.

The Economist (2015). Learning Unleashed. *The Economist*. Retrieved from https://www.economist.com/briefing/2015/08/01/learning-unleashed

The Guardian (2022). Uganda's Pupils back to School after Record 83-week Covid Shutdown. *The Guardian*. Retrieved from https://www.theguardian.com/world/2022/jan/10/ugandas-pupils-back-to-school-after-record-83-week-covid-shutdown

The Guardian (2023). The Guardian View on Germany's Economic Miracle: It Was Built on Debt Relief. *The Guardian*. Retrieved from https://www.theguardian.com/commentisfree/2023/feb/26/the-guardian-view-on-germanys-economic-miracle-it-was-built-on-debt-relief?CMP=Share_iOSApp_Other

Tooley, J. (2007). Educating Amartech: Private Schools for the Poor and the New Frontier for Investors. *Economic Affairs*, 27(2), 37–43.

Tooley, J. (2009). *The Beautiful Tree.* Washington, DC: The Cato Institute.

Tooley, J. (2015). Malala Attended a Low-Cost Private School – As do Thousands of the World's Poorest Children. Retrieved 20 October 2023, from Institute of Economic Affairs website website: https://iea.org.uk/blog/malala-attended-a-low-cost-private-school-as-do-thousands-of-the-worlds-poorest-children

Tulloch, J., Krämer, A., and Overbey, L. (2014). *Private Schools for the Poor: Educating Millions in the Developing World.* Berlin: Endeva.

Tunza Child Safeguarding (2020). *Keeping Pupils Safe in Kenya: A Review and Assessment of Child Safeguarding in Kenya*. Nairobi: Tunza Safeguarding.

Tyre, P. (2017). Can a Tech Start-Up Successfully Educate Children in the Developing World? *New York Times*.

UNESCO (2010). *EFA Global Monitoring Report: Reaching the Marginalized*. Paris: UNESCO.

UNESCO (2022). *Non-state Actors in Education: Who choses? Who loses?* Paris: UNESCO.

UNESCO (2024a). *Education and Climate Change: Learning to Act for People and Planet*. Retrieved from https://www.unesco.org/gem-report/en/2024ccec

UNESCO (2024b). *Global Report on Teachers: Addressing Teacher Shortages and Transforming the Profession*. Paris: UNESCO.

UNICEF (2018). *Understanding the Impacts of Pesticides on Children*. New York: UNICEF.

Uwezo (2019). *Are Our Children Learning? Uwezo Tanzania Learning Assessment Report*. Dar es Salaam: Uwezo Tanzania.

Uwezo (2021). *Are All Our Children Learning? Uwezo 7th Learning Assessment Report*. Nairobi: Uwezo Kenya.

Uwezo Uganda (2019). *Learning Outcomes in Literacy and Numeracy Have Remained Low, with Little, if Any, Signs of Improvement* (Vol. 1). Retrieved from https://twaweza.org/wp-content/uploads/2021/05/UweUG-PressRelease-8th-learning-assessment-report-launch_Final-1.pdf

Uwezo Uganda (2021). *Are Our Children Learning? Illuminating the Covid-19 Learning Losses and Gains in Uganda. Uwezo National Learning Assessment Report, 2021*. Kamala: Uwezo Uganda.

Wadekar, N., and Grim, R. (2023). A Is for Abuse: Two Harvard Grads Saw Big Profits in African Education. Children Paid the Price. *The Intercept*. Retrieved from https://theintercept.com/2023/03/23/bridge-schools-africa-kenya-education/

Wadhwa, W. (2014). *Government vs Private Schools: Have Things Changed?* 19–21. Retrieved from https://neqmap.bangkok.unesco.org/wp-content/uploads/2019/08/Government-vs-Private-schools-Dr-Wilima-Wadhwa.pdf.

Wane, W., and Martin, G. (2016). *Education Service Delivery in Uganda*. Washington, DC: World Bank.

Wingard, M. (2013). *MTM Risk Management*. Retrieved from https://www.documentcloud.org/documents/5000434-MTM-Risk-Management.html

Winkler, D., and Sondergaard, L. (2008). *The Efficiency of Public Education in Uganda*. Washington, DC: World Bank.

Wolf, K., Kalinich, M. K., and DeJarnatt, S. (2016). Chartering School Discipline. *The Urban Lawyer*, 48(1), 1–46.

World Bank (2014). *Education Service Delivery in Tanzania*. Washington, DC: World Bank.

World Bank (2015). *Education Service Delivery in Nigeria.* Washington, DC: World Bank.

World Bank (2024). External Review to Probe CAO Investigation into IFC Investment in Bridge International Academies. Retrieved 9 June 2024, from Press Release website: https://www.worldbank.org/en/news/press-release/2024/05/16/external-review-to-probe-cao-investigation-into-ifc-investment-in-bridge-international-academies

Young, F. (2018). Unprotected. *ProPublica.* Retrieved from https://features.propublica.org/liberia/unprotected-more-than-me-katie-meyler-liberia-sexual-exploitation/

Index

Absolute Return for Kids (ARK) 141
academic success 51
Adler, D. 134
adult literacy campaign 171
advise, education planning 89
    fee-free education 96
    national governments 101
    poor countries 90, 92, 97–8
    well-thought-out budget 98
Africa 15, 121
    cheap private schools in 71
    fee abolition 28
    poor countries 168
    pre-primary classes 71
Afridi, M. 148, 198 n.18
air pollution problem 46, 48–50, 56
allure of schooling 76
American charter school movement 128
Angbulu, S., *We'll sack more underqualified teachers, says El-Rufai* 190 n.14
Archer, D. 198 n.29
Ashley, Lord 72
assessments (tests) 12–14, 189 n.40
    Calcutta School-Book Society 85
    chain schools 132
    citizen-led assessments 14–15
    high-stakes examinations 13, 132
    international 174
    language assessment 16, 18
    no-stakes system-monitoring 20
    of teachers' knowledge and skills 192 n.4
Atkeson, S. 134

background of children 20, 45–6, 50, 55, 57
Banga, A. 135, 196 n.31, 197 n.37
Barber, M. 142
Basu, B. D. 84
Bell, A. 78, 81
Big Tech 160
black box process 140
Blair, T. 142
Bono 3, 27
brain development, child 47–8, 50, 58
Bridge International Academies (Bridge)/NewGlobe 119–21, 134, 137, 139, 142, 150–1, 153, 155, 157, 167, 183, 194 n.3, 195 n.21, 196 n.27
    Academy Manager 136
    child-energy-channelling techniques 127
    child sexual abuse scandal 126, 134–5, 153–4, 159, 196 n.24
    classroom management 124, 127–8
    crafting with paper, lesson 125
    dramatic transformation 158
    with Edo State Government 153
    e-reader 128, 156, 158
    expansion plans in Rwanda 134
    final destination/model 159
    formalization 128
    knowledge for all 122
    learning outcomes 138
    lower-middle-class 122
    operational theory 124
    parent-paid opportunity 154
    point of sale ordering system 120
    PPP plan for 198 n.29, 200 n.57
    proof of concept 133
    teachers at 136–7
Brown-Martin, G. 159, 199 n.44, 200 n.67

Calcutta School-Book Society 85–6
Campbell, A. D. 83
capital investment 106, 194 n.1
capitation grant 31–2, 143
Carnegie, A., *Gospel of Wealth* 182
Carnoy, M. 76, 171
Centre for International Education 26
chain school model 131–2
chalk-talk methods 70
Chang, H.-J. 92, 168–70, 172–3, 177, 187 n.4

cheap private schools xi, xiii, 1, 3, 5–7, 17–18, 20–1, 26, 37, 39, 61–3, 66, 74, 87–8, 103, 111, 139, 180, 182, 194 n.1
   Africa 71
   Global South 63, 121
   human rights of children 104
   illegal 72
   Kampala (Uganda) 5, 120, 185
   Lagos (Nigeria) 72, 185
   regulations 103–10
   teaching at 136
child labour 2, 88, 187 n.2, 193 n.19
child's development 1, 6, 46
   brain development 47–8, 50, 58
   healthy diet 56
child sexual abuse scandal 119, 126, 133–5, 138, 152, 155, 159, 196 n.24
Chin, M. 195 n.18
Christian mission schools 7
classroom environment 35, 41–2, 45
classroom management 124, 127–8, 156–7
climate catastrophe 69
colonial destruction 87–8
colonial school model 53
colonization 75–7
communities 7, 41, 46, 61–3, 68–9, 72, 78, 109, 115–16, 153, 175, 179–85
community schools 174, 199 n.45
community volunteers approach 188 n.6
Compliance Advisor Ombudsman 134–5, 196 n.24, 199 n.43
   Investigation Report 197 n.38
Coombs, P. 166, 189 n.1
   social demand for education 76
   world educational crisis 22
corporal punishment 52, 153
corporate entities 140, 197 n.4
corruption 2, 23, 32, 38, 67, 108, 113, 141, 144, 173, 185
   in charter schools 200 n.69
   leakage of funds 101
   single mention of corruption 146
cost-sharing model 85
COVID-19 pandemic 15, 33, 144
   school closures 5
Cuba 174, 177, 201 n.13
   education-to-development pathway 171

culture changes 171, 173
curriculum material 124, 130, 147, 149, 166

Dalrymple, W. 81
   The Anarchy 75, 121
dame schools 63, 72
Dar es Salaam, study 18, 52
Della Valle, P. 80
demolition 8, 85, 115, 194 n.6
demonstration effect 26, 61–2, 76
Development Alternatives Incorporated (DAI) 193 n.7
development assistance 85, 88
development professional 84, 100
Dharampal 78–83, 87, 192 n.3
   The Beautiful Tree 87, 192 n.5
Dickens, C. 71, 73
   A Christmas Carol 73
   Our Mutual Friend 71
dominant model of education 163
donors and advisors counsel 29, 41, 89, 91, 98, 101, 142–3, 153, 155, 159–60
   demands on implementing agencies 98
   DFID 99
   governments and 154
   international donors 93–4, 142, 150, 159
   for pilot 151
   reputation-laundering 161
double-shift schools 18

early childhood development 47–8
early childhood education 93, 201 n.13
East India Company 8, 75, 78, 81, 83, 121, 161, 173
The Economist 142
economy and education system 168–9, 174
   economic development 163, 171, 173, 177
   economic/social theory 27
   Korea 27
Edinburgh Enlightenment 81
EdisonLearning 154, 159
Edison Schools 154
EdTech 120, 123, 166
   good quality 167
   individualization 166

education (educational) 1, 9, 46, 69, 92, 163, 170, 182
  budget 31, 95–6, 165, 174, 194 n.1
  challenges xiv, 1
  entrepreneurs 122
  as human right and public good 5, 8, 163
  and industrial developments 27
  market 99, 105, 133, 142, 165
  memorization of material 17, 21
  and model of schooling xiv
  non-state actors in 116
  policies 174–5
  quality (*see* quality education)
  reform 11, 143, 146, 167
  social demand 76
  systems 1, 9, 40, 58–9, 75, 133, 135, 155, 157, 165–6, 170, 173, 175
Education for All (EFA) agenda 26–8, 37, 86, 116, 174
education management company 154
Education Management Information System 82, 100
Education Partnerships Group (EPG) 141, 142, 197 n.6
Education Voucher Scheme 143
elementary education 73, 79–80, 192 n.5
Elementary Education Act (1870) 71, 73–4
environmental and background factors 57
equal schooling system 177
e-reader-focused model 154
e-readers 124, 127–30, 137, 156, 158
Ethiopia
  Debt Crisis 27
  fee abolition 30
Eurocentric model of education 88
Europe, education in 80, 83

fact-checking process 197 n.6
fee abolition 5, 26, 28–30, 32, 37–8
fee-dependent schools 12, 88, 155
fee-free schooling 41, 93, 96, 116, 181
fee-paying schools 57, 156, 177, 199 n.45
  cheapest 110
  parents 160
  private 142, 147, 156
Finland 58, 169, 176, 201 n.21
  extra funding to support children 57
  government and society 177
  state-owned enterprises 169–70

first-generation learners 27, 30, 43, 54, 58, 147
flipped classroom, Khan Academy 123
food insecurity 1
foreign and far-too-costly model of education 8
formal education 26, 76, 90
Foundation Assisted Schools 143
free education 2, 5, 30, 93, 96, 104, 181
Friedman, M. 143
Fujitsu Horizon software scandal (UK Post Office) 141, 184
fully fee-dependent schools 12
functional national education systems 9
funding 57–8, 63, 68, 79, 83, 95, 98, 101–2, 122, 138, 143, 147, 153, 189 n.8, 196 n.24. *See also* donors and advisors counsel
  international 71
  municipal 87
  PPP 147–8, 159
  Series F 134

Galloway, S. 1, 4–5, 45
Gandhi, M. 85–6, 89, 177
Gates, B. 131, 195 n.18
Gates, M. 195 n.18
Geldoff, B. 27
Germany 172–3
Ghana 108, 168
  colonialism 27
  National Education Assessment survey (2018) xi, 13, 189 n.34
  Omega Schools in 142, 183
  PPPs 142
  school visit in 35–6
  study 20, 55, 107, 200 n.56
  teachers 52
ghettoization 40, 51
ghost schools 38
Glassdoor.com 132, 195 n.21
global learning crisis 163, 173, 181. *See also* solutions (global learning crisis)
Global March Against Child Labour 187 n.2
Global South 12, 21, 23, 119, 164–5, 176–7, 184
  cheap private schools 63, 121
  government schools/education 1, 5

school budgets 194 n.1
standardization 119, 166
good school management 145, 170, 177
government-private disparity 15-16, 19
government schools 1, 4, 14, 18-21, 29, 31, 39-40, 42, 55, 62, 107, 131, 139, 151, 158, 167, 180
　attendance 40, 42, 181
　determination on improving 111, 183
　fee-free 116, 181
　government education xiii, 2, 5-6, 11, 28, 116, 185
　lack of textbooks 70
　vs. private school children 15, 17, 19-20, 130
　quality 182-3
　shares 15
　stratification 51
　teachers 51, 131, 164-6, 192 n.4
Government School Support Program 143
Grim, R. 195 n.24, 196 n.31
group work and peer learning 78, 123

Härmä, J. 188 n.25, 195 n.14
Hess, A. 195 n.18
Hickel, J. 187 n.4
Holy Grail of economic growth 91
home-based learning surveys 14
homework 46-7, 52-3, 55-7, 123
Homo Economicus 9
human rights 5, 8, 72, 74, 104, 174-5, 182
　child rights and pro-education 68, 110
　right to education 163-4, 182, 175
　universal 111
Hyundai 169

illegal private schools 14, 72, 116
imperialism and colonialism 25, 27, 29, 76, 87
India/Indian education 8, 25, 35, 50, 57, 63, 77, 82, 86-7, 164, 185
　British in 185
　Charter Bill 82
　Delhi, air pollution problem 48-9, 56
　educational expansion 90
　fee abolition (primary school) 28
　free of cost, textbooks 34
　government school teachers 51
　impoverishment, Britain's 88
　locally managed education system 83
　Madras System 78
　non-school determinants, share 58
　Pratham 14-15
　private teacher training colleges 37
　PROBE 21
　Punjab, PPP 82, 143, 146, 149
industrialization 72, 92, 175-6
inequity and inequality, educational 58
informal settlements 5, 40, 106, 114, 136, 187 n.7
informal teaching 61, 105
innovations 122-4, 184
The Intercept 195 n.24, 196 n.31
international consultancy firms 93, 149, 151
International Development Committee 138
international donors 26, 93-4, 142, 150
international education-development industry x, 12, 86, 92, 173
International Finance Corporation (IFC) 133-5, 137-8, 155, 158-9, 196 n.24, 197 nn.37-8
International Monetary Fund (IMF) 173
Iraq, education and health systems 171

Johnson, M. 152

Kampala (Uganda), cheap private schools 5, 120, 185
Kenya 31, 129, 131, 195 n.7
　Bridge International Academies in 133-4, 138, 150, 152-6, 158, 196 n.24
　EACHRights 134
　fee abolition 29
　government-private school 15, 17
　schools 132, 155
　teachers 167
　UK-funded programme 91
　urban-rural score 15, 17
Kenya Certificate of Primary Education (KCPE) 13, 132
Khan Academy, flipped classroom 123
Kimmelman, J. 122, 128, 134-5, 138, 194 n.1, 195 n.7, 196 n.30, 197 n.4
Korea 27, 177
　educational transformation of 168-9
　second-rate private schooling 28
　state-owned enterprise 169-70
Kremer, M. 159, 167

Lagos (Nigeria) 30, 42, 64, 106, 115, 129, 138
    Association for Formidable
        Educational Development 72
    cheap private schools 72, 185
    DEEPEN programme 113
    DFID 99
    government schools 180
    Makoko, schools 179–80
    private school census xi
    terrible schools in 35
    UK-funded programme 19, 113, 130, 154, 165
language assessment 16, 18
Latin America, education system 171
learner-centred approaches 124
learning 12, 14, 16–17, 31, 45, 51, 80, 99, 140, 145, 147–8, 159
    home setting conducive to 56
    modest learning target 131
    peer learning 78, 123
    quality measurement tool 95
    virtual 125, 166–7, 169, 184
learning management system (LMS) integration 123
Lewin, K. 188 n.4, 192 n.6
Liberia 32–3, 93, 139, 142, 153–4
    catch-up programmes 93, 98
    Ebola epidemic 93
    fee-free schooling 41
    high-profile PPP 142, 152
    parent-teacher association 175
    partnership model 154
    Partnership Schools for Liberia project 98–9
    pre-primary/primary schooling 93–4, 96, 98, 150
literacy and numeracy 15, 29, 70, 79, 93, 130–1
    adult literacy campaign 171
    catch-up programme 93
    informal teaching of 61
    rate 168
London Ragged School Union 72
lower-middle-class family 4, 20, 68, 71, 122
low-income communities/neighbourhoods 4, 62, 121, 187 n.7

Malabar, instruction 80–1
Malawi 28, 30, 32
management theory 145

Maputo, study 18, 25, 35
Marley, J. 73
mass education systems 173
May, S. 122, 134–5, 138, 195 n.7, 196 n.30
McDonald's 119–20
Meyler, K. 150, 152, 198 n.29, 199 n.37
Millennium Development Goals (MDGs) 26–8
Ministries of education 30, 41, 95, 98, 101, 111–12, 139, 143, 189 n.34, 190 n.17
missionary schooling 7, 76
money problem (education) 3–4, 23, 71
More Than Me Academy 152–3, 198 n.29
Mozambique 18–19, 34
multi-storey school buildings 180
Munro, T. 82, 84–6

national curriculum 45, 70, 156, 167
national development 9, 27, 91, 163, 174–5
national education systems 9, 35, 131, 133
National Panel Survey (2012/13) 18
nation-states 25, 176
Naviwala, N. 43, 149, 164, 190 n.29
NewGlobe. *See* Bridge International Academies (Bridge)/NewGlobe
New School Program 143
Ngware, M. 192 n.4
Nigeria xi, 19, 33, 37, 42, 63, 129, 174, 181. *See also* Lagos (Nigeria)
    Federal Capital Territory 115
    government-private school split 19
    government school systems in 156
    irregularity 32
    Partnership for Learning for All in 193–4 n.7
    schooling participation 91
    shortage of teachers 31
    solutions (global learning crisis) for 174, 177
    teachers 158, 167
Nokia 170

OECD, PISA 11, 20–1, 174
often-hidden schools xi–xii
Omega Schools 120, 125–6, 131, 142, 158, 183
one-size-fits-all approach 173
online charter schools 125
over-age enrolment problem 93–6
Oxfam 147

Pakistan 149, 169
  poor children of 164
  teachers 71, 149
parents 1, 5, 28, 31, 41, 45, 49, 57, 61, 65–6, 68, 70, 108, 156–7, 165, 181–2, 200 n.56
  awareness-raising campaigns 98
  defending children from assaults 55–6
  effective communications strategy 144
  illiterate 51–2, 55
  middle class 15, 40, 47, 68, 71, 122
  Parents Boards 174
  parent-teacher association 41
  schools and 39
  spending on education 96
  teachers and 36
  and teachers, social distance 51, 53
Partnership Schools for Liberia project 98–9
Patrinos, H. 161
pauperization 40
pay-daily schools 68
PEAS 131
pollution 48
  air pollution 46, 48–50, 56
  industrial 109
  pollutants 50, 58
  vehicular pollution 50
  water and soil 48
poor countries 1, 3–4, 11, 14, 90, 97, 103, 160, 164, 166, 172–3, 181–3
  cheap private schools 183
  corporations 140
  crisis response 73
  educational expansion, advise 92, 97–8
  fee-free education 93
  governments 140
  markets and international investors 92
  ministries of education 140
  PISA 21
  regulatory regime 107
  schools 11, 40, 165
potential market opportunities 68
poverty 1, 4, 11, 18, 26, 28, 40, 42, 68–9, 103, 164, 174
  chronic 50
  deficits of 58
  hunger 45–6
  poor children 46, 51, 53, 55, 57–8, 113, 160, 165–6

Pratham (India), Annual Status of Education Report 14–15
pre-primary schooling 18, 71, 167
  education budget 95–6
  Liberia 93–4, 96, 98
pre-service teacher preparation 130–1
Pritchett, L. 191 n.20
private schools 4, 63, 99, 104, 110, 112–13, 124–5, 142–3, 152, 155, 165, 180. *See also* government schools
  cheap (*see* cheap private schools)
  community schools 199 n.45
  vs. government school children 15, 17, 19–20, 130
  low-income peripheral areas 111
  poor 70, 72–3, 114–15
  proof of concept 154
  second-rate 28
  stratification 51
  structure of 64–5
  teachers 66, 131, 192 n.4
  unregistered (illegal) 14, 18, 72, 112–13, 116
  website for 113
private tutoring 56–7
problems of education 9, 101
  money 3–4, 23, 71
  teacher deployment 36, 38
pro-child-rights 110
Programme for International Student Assessment (PISA) 11, 20–1, 174
proof of concept 133, 154, 156–7, 199 n.45
ProPublica, *Unprotected* 198 n.29
protection/protectionism 172, 175
  child protection 67, 121, 152–3
  industrialization 92
  right protections 169–70
public-private partnerships (PPPs) 9, 121, 132, 139, 141, 145–6, 154–5, 159, 172, 197 n.6
  Act (2020) 142
  effective communications strategy 144
  funding 147–8
  international businesses 149
  private management 150
  pro-PPP spin 142
  school teachers 148
  in Uganda 144

Public Report on Basic Education (PROBE) 21
Punjab Education Foundation (PEF) 142-3, 145

quality assurance system 147, 157
Quality Assurance Test (QAT) 145, 147
quality education 11, 13, 37, 63, 66-7, 119, 139
  good-quality education xiii, 22, 63, 71, 104, 108, 131, 167, 181
  at lower cost 139
  poor quality education 71, 116
  teaching quality, improving 105

ragged schools 63, 71-4, 114, 192 n.5
Ravitch, D. 6, 191 n.15
regulations 6, 8, 72-3, 103-6, 108-10, 116, 154
  private school operating 155
  regulatory regimes 105, 107-8
  rules-based systems 114
Rendel, J. 123
requirements, schooling 105-7
revenue sharing model 174
rich countries 4, 25, 48, 68, 86, 90, 92, 97-8, 102, 141, 150, 165, 167, 173, 177, 184-5
  aid programmes advise 103
  children of refugees 6
  corporations 139
  culture changes 173
  free trade 171-2
  industrialization 92
  schools in 6, 35
  teachers 11
Riep, C. 196 n.27
right to education 163-4, 175, 182
Rising Academies 123, 125-6, 131, 142, 151, 166, 183
Romero, M. 191 n.2, 198 nn.32-3

Sachs, J. 3
Samsung 169-70
Sandefur, J. 191 n.2, 198 n.33
scale, education 86, 137, 158
school(s) xi-xii, 13, 59, 132, 155. *See also* government schools; private schools
  choice 65, 164-5
  and families 39, 155
  fiscal measures 79
  improvement plan 113
  inspections 108, 112
  owners xii, 62-3, 66, 105, 107-9, 113, 116, 146, 148, 185
  per-capita funding to 189 n.8
  performance-focused schools and colleges 99
  schooling participation 85, 90-1
  slum 5, 120
Schumacher, E. F., *Small Is Beautiful* 185
Scotland 11, 53, 177
Skidmore, P. 126
Snapchat of education 156
social demand, education 76
Social Development Indicator (SDI) surveys 188 n.16
social enterprise 119
socioeconomic status of child 6, 45, 59, 130, 159
solutions (global learning crisis) 163, 173
  adult literacy campaign 171
  culture changes 171, 173
  educational transformation 168-9
  expansion and development, education 175-6
  good governance 170
  good quality education 166-7
  good school systems 177
  governmental and societal approaches 176
  for Nigeria 174, 177
  positive change 176-7
  school choice 164-5
Sonneborn, W. 134, 137
South Korea 27, 168-9
Sowell, T. 185
SPARK Schools, South Africa 123
special classes 54
standardization/standardized processes 119-20, 122, 124, 126, 166, 173
Starbucks 9, 119-21, 186
Starbucks-equivalent schooling model 119
state-owned enterprises 169-70
stratification 51
sub-Saharan Africa 1, 4, 11, 16-17, 74, 108, 166, 190 n.13
Sustainable Development Goal 4 26
Sweden 122, 170, 172-3, 176

Tanzania 15, 18, 52
  government-private disparity 16
teachers 1–2, 6, 11, 32, 35, 43, 66, 145, 148, 157–8, 167, 174, 183, 190 n.13
  continuous professional development 97
  crash-course training 156
  deployment 28, 36, 38, 171, 174
  employment market 67
  extra funding to hire 147
  ghost 38
  government school 51, 131, 164–6, 192 n.4
  parents and, social distance 51, 53
  pedagogical knowledge of 192 n.4
  poor quality of 132
  private schools 66, 131, 192 n.4
  real-world 37
  robots 37
  salaries 33, 69, 106, 185, 194 n.1
  and students 127
  Teacher Eligibility Test 14
  teacher-proofing 126, 157
  teaching qualifications 8, 34, 66, 105
  training 37–8, 66, 85, 97, 156, 165–6, 165–6
  travails 36
  unions and civil society groups 150
Teachers Service Commission 137
tech-based monitoring systems 137
technology-enabled education systems 157, 195 n.20
test-based accountability 148
tests. *See* assessments (tests)
textbooks 34, 38, 70, 130, 148, 156, 164, 166, 179–80
toilets issue 42–3
Tooley, J. 87, 120, 126, 183
Tyre, P. 132

Uganda 16, 39, 155
  case-by-case approach 113
  Certificate of Primary Education (CPE) 13
  COVID-related school closures 5
  fee abolition 28
  learning outcomes 15
  not-for-profit secondary schools 124
  PPP in 144

unequal education system 176
UNESCO 8, 29, 163, 170, 171, 181, 190 n.13
  Global Monitoring Report 201 n.13
  Institute for Statistics 12, 32
  LLECE-ERCE 189 n.40
  Task Force on Teachers 30, 37
UNICEF 50
United Kingdom (UK) 165
  aid agency 154
  British International Investment 138
  British tax revenues 82, 85
  education quality 11
  education reform 11, 85
  government schools, legislating 63
  impoverishment of India 88
  Indian pedagogical methods 83–4
  UK-funded programme 19, 34, 113, 130
United Nations (UN) 6, 102, 116
  Education for All (EFA) agenda 25–6
  fee-free schooling 41
The United States 13, 57, 76, 92–3, 132–3, 165, 172, 176, 191 n.15, 200 n.69
  aid agency 142
  charter schools 128, 166
  individualized tech-based learning 184
  tariff protection 172
  text-based suicide helplines 159
  virtual learning 184
universal primary education 5, 26–8, 34, 40, 63, 184
university-level education 77
urban informal settlements xi, 5
urban-rural disparity 15–16, 18
urban-rural gaps 18
USAID 168
Uwezo (citizen-led assessment) 15–16

vehicular pollution 50
Victorian/Carnegie-style paternalism 116
Vietnam 174–5
village schools 2, 5, 74, 79, 82–4, 87
  municipal funding 87
  system, British 8, 82
virtual teaching/learning 125, 166–7, 169, 184

Wadekar, N. 195 n.24
Wadhwa, W. 191 n.19
website for private schools 113
Werner, G. 150
white saviours 85, 152
Wingard, M., *MTM-Risk-Management* 199 n.37
World Bank 12, 17–19, 29, 93, 95–6, 137, 139, 146, 160, 184, 193 n.4, 196 n.32
   appropriate performance measures 144–5
   funding 155, 169
   and PPP theory 141–2, 145
   requirements for PPP success 143
   Service Delivery Indicator (SDI) surveys 16, 38, 192 n.4
world-class education 122, 125, 129, 132, 167, 195 n.7
World Trade Organisation (WTO) 172, 173

Young, F. 152, 199 n.36
Yousafzai, M. 4, 6

Zuckerberg, M. 131, 195 n.18